WHO RULES ISRAEL?

WHO
RULES
ISRAEL?

Yuval Elizur and Eliahu Salpeter

HARPER & ROW, PUBLISHERS

New York
Evanston
San Francisco
London

1817

FIRST EDITION

Designed by Sidney Feinberg

Library of Congress Cataloging in Publication Data

Salpeter, Eliahu.
    Who rules Israel?
    Translation of ha–Mimsad.
    1. Isreal—Politics and government.   2.   Elite
(Social Sciences)   I.   Elizur, Yuval, joint author.
II.   Title.
JQ1825.P3S2713   320.9'5694'05   73–5460
ISBN 0-06-011164-X

Contents

Preface

The idea of writing this book arose almost by itself in the course of a conversation between the authors about the nature of Israeli society. We came to the conclusion that it is enough to know one hundred, perhaps one hundred and fifty or at most two hundred, people in Israel in order to know who is responsible for decision making in the political and military spheres, who makes the wheels of the economy turn and who molds public opinion.

Despite immigration to Israel during its twenty-five years of existence, despite the fact that within that period its population grew almost fourfold—and perhaps because of these factors—the range wherein all political, economic and perhaps even cultural power is concentrated is extremely narrow.

Because of this, we decided to write about the people at the center of things in Israel, to describe the way in which they have attained their present positions and perhaps add something about the web of relations between them, since this group is in no way an amalgam or an oligarchy in the usual sense of the term.

We believe that the structure of the "control system" of Israel is unique and, therefore, that this book is also somewhat special. It is not an academic study, nor is it meant to be a "who's who." The people who are included were chosen in arbitrary fashion: if someone is not included, this is due entirely to our subjective judgment.

A minor consolation to us when faced with the difficulty of making up the list of Israel's power elite is that authors in other countries are faced with a similar dilemma. In fact, social scientists have not yet found precise or proven methods to study the base of power and control in any state or community.

In the last twenty years a number of attempts have been made to devise a scientific method for identifying those who control the sources of power in a country. The various schools of scientists who deal with this subject are divided into two main groups—the sociologists and the political scientists.

The sociologists are inclined to emphasize the factor of continuity in social life: they see social life as a complex fabric of human institutions and claim that this fabric has an existence of its own to the point where it is no longer dependent on its components. Human beings, as individuals, control these sources of power only by the fact that they are part of the general system and representatives of the social institutions of which society as a whole is comprised. The political scientists, on the other hand, tend to see control over society as a personal attribute. The complex of social relations in any society is therefore, according to this school of thought, a complex system based on the possession of power in the hands of individuals. In this system there are no permanent factors and there is constant change.

As opposed to the sociologists, who believe that the basis of power can be found in a number of institutions like the government, the army or even the business community, because of the very fact that there are such institutions and that those who head each institution have control as a result of the influence of the institution they represent, the political scientists believe that the importance of each institution varies as a result of the status of the people who head it.

Among the sociologists who have tried to formalize yardsticks for the identification of people who control their communities, two should be mentioned: Floyd Hunter, whose book *Community, Power, Structure: A Research on Decision-Makers* was published in 1953, and C.

Wright Mills, whose book *The Power Elite* was published in 1956. Hunter's method of identifying the power elite, called the "reputational theory of elitism," is based on research which he conducted in Atlanta, Georgia. Hunter gave a number of citizens of his town a list of the names of 175 personalities in the community and asked them to mark the forty most important ones, according to their order of importance. His basic assumption was that if in the community there is a prevailing feeling that attributes importance to a group of people within it, it can be concluded that this reputation is justified. The research method of C. Wright Mills, called the "positional theory of elitism," is based on his assumption that the real power in a society is concentrated in the hands of its institutions and therefore those who head those institutions are the sources of power.

A noted political scientist who developed a different method of research in this field is Robert A. Dahl, whose book *Who Governs* was published in 1961. Dahl's method, called the "pluralistic theory of elitism," is based on an attempt to ascertain—in each and every case—where a certain decision is made. It is no secret that not all the important decisions are made by the formal institutions whose prerogative it is to decide; very often the real decision is made on another level, before the issue is brought to the formal body. Dahl tries to identify the persons who take part in that initial decision and includes them in his elite group.

Each of these methods has evoked criticism. Questions are raised especially about the connection between the findings of each scientist and his research methods.

As much as one can classify our approach on the basis of the foregoing methods, it can be said that ours most closely resembles the reputational theory of elitism. We did not, however, prepare a sample nor did we distribute questionnaires. We were aided mainly by journalistic research methods, and also picked the brains of those who we felt were qualified in each field. The writing of this book involved considerable risk taking. We no doubt have antagonized many individuals who are convinced that their positions in Israeli society are more important than those of others whose names do appear in the book. We hope, however, that we have not made any permanent enemies.

We also must point out that our quick look at the Israeli reality and its power elite is not a historical survey but a description of the situation at one given moment. We deliberately did not focus on personalities like David Ben-Gurion, whose influence in the past was overwhelming, and who still have moral influence over those who have the power to make decisions today. There is no doubt that the present Israeli political and military leadership is imbued with deep admiration for David Ben-Gurion, Chaim Weizmann, Moshe Sharett, Levi Eshkol and other founding fathers of the Jewish national revival. It is obvious that those who hold the reins of power today consider themselves dwarfs sitting on the shoulders of giants. But we chose to concentrate only on those who influence decisions because of the formal and informal positions they occupy at the sources of power today, at the time of writing this book.

Our decision to limit ourselves to this "instant snapshot" and refrain from long-range analysis was not made unthinkingly. We believe there is room for such an approach in the same sense that there is room for a detailed study of the Israeli elite groups and the foundations upon which they developed. Just as we think that both methods are legitimate, we feel they should not be mixed, and we tried to avoid doing so.

We are grateful to many social and political scientists in Israel who were good enough to advise us and whose brains and time we exploited.

We have tried as much as possible to keep a mental distance from the personalities we describe, as if we were foreign correspondents arriving in Israel on a short visit. We do not know whether we have succeeded in our intention, because, as writers in Israeli daily newspapers, we are a part of the establishment which we have tried to analyze. Like the traveler who sees the scenery around him but not the outside of the car in which he is traveling, we know that proximity to the subject is not always an unqualified advantage.

1
The Dynamism
of a Young Establishment

WHEN Haim Bar-Lev, newly appointed Minister of Commerce and Industry and former Chief of Staff, tried to end a prolonged strike at the Elite chocolate factory in July, 1972, he told both sides that there was no room in Israel for class warfare because "we are an intimate society." This was an apt description of what is frequently observed on many levels of decision making in Israel, and in Israel's elite in general. It often seems that in Israel everyone still knows everyone else. People who have decision-making powers in many cases share a common background of service in the Palmach, the elite commando unit of the pre-independence Haganah defense organization, or were in the same brigade in the Army, still eat in the same restaurants and visit each other in their homes on Friday nights, when movies and theaters are closed in Israel.

However, this impression is only partially correct. In the wake of the mass immigration of the past twenty-five years, Israel's towns and cities have been settled by newcomers, some of them men of status in their countries of origin, others of newly-acquired status, who do not know each other on a national level and certainly do not belong to the intimate society of the top elite.

1

This does not mean that many of these people do not consider themselves part of the national elite. Indeed, at times one gains the impression that Israel is the most aristocratic country in the world: almost everybody is part of the establishment and almost everybody in the establishment believes that he is also part of the elite. Government officials, Army officers, bank directors, doctors, engineers and even bus drivers are all sure that they belong to the highest levels of Israeli society. Then there are more exclusive elites, like members of the Cabinet, friends of Finance Minister Sapir or the chauffeurs of Cabinet members and their families.

According to government statistics, 51.4 percent of all Israelis are employed in one type or another of public service. If we add those who are classified as managerial in the private sector, we reach the figure of 55 percent who work in jobs that make them feel very important. True, not everybody in this list is really important and certainly very few of them are genuine decision makers. What the statistics indicate is that in Israeli society two things coincide: the awe which immigrants from eastern Europe or from Near Eastern and North African countries, without any democratic traditions, have for anybody working for the State or in any public service; and the actual power acquired in modern society by individuals in services which can affect and even paralyze the daily life of a country. Consequently the concept of elites and "focal points of power" is still somewhat vague in the public mind in Israel.

The concept of elites in a more traditional sense—and the identity of those belonging to them—has undergone several changes in Israel since the beginning of the twentieth century. But it has always been closely related to ethnic origins.

During the pre-World War I Turkish rule, most of the established Jewish population was of "Oriental" origin, i.e., descendants of Jews who had immigrated from Near Eastern or North African countries. The elite were the leading Sephardi Jewish families, who traced their descent to the expulsion from Spain in 1492. Their patterns of life and behavior were similar to those of the Arab elite among whom they lived, and they too sent their sons to European universities, primarily to France. These families usually had branches in several Arab countries—in Syria (Damascus and Aleppo), Egypt (Cairo and Alexandria) or Iraq (Baghdad). The important families tended to indicate their status by writing the letters S.T. after their surnames—initials for "Sephardi Tahor" ("pure Spanish"), as distinguished from the "new immigrants" who had arrived in more recent generations from North Africa or from Turkey.

But the small Ashkenazi (i.e., of Central and East European origin) communities in Jerusalem, Safad and later in Tiberias and Jaffa, had their own elites composed of the families of important rabbis and sages. (Dynasties of famous rabbis were the only traditional inherited elite in European Diaspora Jewry.) As the number of Ashkenazi Jews in Palestine grew, more and more of them engaged not only in prayer and study but also in business and commerce; the elite of these were mostly scions of rabbinical families and thus, frequently, to the elite of education was added the elite of wealth.

For a long time there was no intermarriage between the important Sephardi families and their Ashkenazi neighbors. Therefore, when one Joseph Ben Nathan Meyouhas, scion of a family which traced its family tree in Palestine for nineteen generations, married the daughter of Yechiel Michael Pines, one of the notables of the Jerusalem Ashkenazi community, toward the end of the nineteenth century, it was a memorable historic occasion. This marked the beginning of a very slow merger process between the elites of the Sephardi and the old Ashkenazi families—a process which never gained overwhelming scope in Turkish times. More significantly, it marked the beginning of the slow decline in the importance of the Sephardi elite and the rapid growth of the Ashkenazi.

With the steadily growing numbers of immigrants from eastern Europe in the years immediately preceding World War I, a new cultural, economic and ideological elite crystallized, mostly among newcomers from Russia. This trend became dominant after the war, when the Russian immigrants provided the new elite of citrus growers and industrialists, on the one hand, and kibbutz pioneers on the other. At the same time the British authorities who ruled Palestine after the war gave preferred status to the less-numerous immigrants from English-speaking countries. Language played an important role in this, but more significant were their contrasting socio-political backgrounds: most other Ashkenazi immigrants came from countries with absolutist regimes and so did all who came from Near Eastern or North African lands; immigrants from English-speaking countries, on the other hand, came from democratic societies where there was an entirely different relationship between citizens and the authorities. This special relationship between the English-speaking immigrants and the Mandatory authorities, on the one hand, and the growing importance of the East European leadership among the rest of the population, on the other, created the first parallel elites in the Jewish population of the country.

Simultaneously, immigrants from Poland began to exceed considerably the number of those coming from Russia and some of them soon entered the settlement elite, especially in the collective sectors. Others joined the ranks of the industrialists. Thus began the pattern of socialist-capitalist dualism in the Jewish economy of Palestine. Among the East European immigrants there were also a number of doctors, who became the backbone of the medical elite, as well as two engineers who laid the foundations for Israel's first large industrial enterprises: Pinhas Ruttenberg, who laid the basis for Israel's power industry, and Moshe Novomeysky, who founded the Dead Sea Potash Works.

The large-scale influx of professionals began with the extensive immigration of German Jews after Hitler's rise to power in the 1930s. Since that time German Jews have assumed central roles in the country's academic and cultural life as well as in banking and the liberal professions. German Jews brought to Palestine's unsophisticated urban and rural middle class the cultural consumption patterns associated with upper-middle-class tastes: the piano, the gramophone with classical records, the camera to record family events, as well as the habit of devoting a relatively large share of the family budget to concert and theater tickets. Yet, despite their higher cultural standards, German immigrants took over relatively few key positions in the self-government institutions of the Jewish population, which established themselves even more firmly alongside the official British regime.

As a general rule one can say that the extent to which new immigrants entered the existing elites depended on a combination of two factors: the size of the newcomers' groups and the cultural and technological standards in their country of origin.

In every society ruled by a foreign power there emerges an elite which cooperates with the foreign rulers. It exists parallel to the native national elite. The line dividing these two elites at times becomes thin and even vague. Sometimes certain members of a family belong to one category while other members belong to the other. Frequently this is a question of generations—the older belonging to the "cooperating" and the younger to the "nationalistic" elite.

In the Jewish population of Palestine under the British Mandate, the division between the two groups was never clear-cut. There were several reasons for this: almost the entire Jewish population, and its elite members, were inspired by Zionist ideology; the high cultural and intellectual standards of the Jewish population in general, and in its elite, prevented the development of an inferiority complex toward the ruling foreign power; the predominance of European Jews, including West European Jews, in all levels of the local elite, made for a more equal status between them and the foreign power. Therefore, when the State of Israel was established there was no elimination of "collaborators" or transfer of power from the cooperating elite to the nationalistic elite, processes which have been characteristic of many other newly independent countries.

Since the establishment of the State, the elevation of Israeli-born figures into the elite has been accelerated. There also has been penetration of the elite by immigrants from the United States, who brought with them either financial means or technical and professional skill needed by Israel's rapidly developing economy. This demand for technological skills was among the factors aiding the entry of the Israeli-born into the elite, but the main impetus for their advancement came from the Israel defense forces, with their leading role in the nation's political and economic life and reputation for producing good executives.

The upper echelons of the Jewish elite, which became the top leadership of the country after independence, had already crystallized by the second half of the 1930's and early 1940's. It was this group which led the Jewish population's struggle against British rule in Palestine after World War II. This was a typically "multipurpose" elite: its members engaged in politics, cultural creativity, economic life, mass communications and trade-union affairs—frequently the same person was active in several of these fields. The parallel elites that developed did not divide along professional or economic lines but rather according to ideological allegiances, which became particularly significant in the last years before independence.

Two factors influenced mobility within the elites after the establishment of the State. One was the often dramatic change of status that occurred when an individual moved or was moved from one elite into another.

The other change occurred when there was a sudden shift in the importance of one elite in relation to another. For example, many people, during the British Mandate, held responsible posts both in the illegal immigration network and in the Haganah. If, with Statehood, the individual chose an Army career, he gained much more status than if he chose a post with the Ministry of Immigration.

The other change occurred when there was a sudden shift in the importance of one elite in relation to another. During the British Mandate, leaders of the Jewish Agency were the unofficial Jewish government and had considerable power, but after independence and the creation of a formal government apparatus, those who remained in the Jewish Agency became increasingly less important in the political life of the country, while their colleagues who moved to government service became much more influential. This, of course, was quite clear on the individual level as well: in the late 1940's a member of the Jewish Agency executive had almost the same status—and not only according to protocol—as a Cabinet member. Today it is standard practice for every political party to assign to the Jewish Agency executive its second-rank worthies, who are not quite up to Cabinet level.

Israel's present elites have four characteristics:

First of all, it is not a class elite. It includes sons of rich industrialists, orphans who came with Youth Aliyah (the program of rescuing Jewish children from Nazi-occupied Europe, whose parents were not permitted to enter Palestine), descendants of the founding fathers, as well as new immigrants and kibbutz members. The common denominator of all, with very few exceptions, is that three or four generations ago their grandfathers or great-grandfathers belonged to the poor Jewish masses of East Europe's ghettos or North Africa's mellahs, or at most were small tradesmen among the Christian population of large cities. Thus the Israel elite members or their parents achieved this status because of their personal qualities and the roles they took upon themselves in their new homeland. One can, nevertheless, discern numerous family ties among the members of the elite, interesting more among the labor and trade-union elite than in the capitalist group. Furthermore, a good name or an important father does not guarantee automatic belonging to the elite. There is a Ben-Gurion (the son of David Ben-Gurion) who is managing director of one of Israel's largest textile companies; but there was also a Ben-Gurion (brother of David) who had a soda-and-orange-juice stand on one of the street corners of Tel Aviv.

There are no exact statistics to show how many of Israel's elite are related to each other by family ties. But it is quite clear that family connections are far from being a dominant factor in establishing one's status. Moshe Dayan was the son of a well-known leader of the cooperative farm movement, but his rapid rise in the ranks of the Haganah (the Jewish underground army, before Independence) and especially later in the Israel defense establishment was due to his abilities and to David Ben-Gurion's recognition of them. Similarly it was a quick grasp of economics and financial talent, as well as the strong backing of Finance Minister Pinhas Sapir, that promoted an unknown new immigrant, Moshe Sandberg (who hebraized his name to Moshe Sanbar), to become governor of the Bank of Israel, in the space of twenty years.

Second, there is a high rate of absorption from the general population into the elite. In Israeli society an advancement in economic or political position can place an unknown newcomer firmly in the elite while in many other societies, if a man is not born to the upper class, he is not admitted to the elite no matter how important his job is. In many respects Israeli society demonstrates several precepts of the theory of social mobility: there has been no confrontation between the older and newer elites; the changes in the nation's economy and its rapid sophistication have opened up new avenues for entry into the elite by those with suitable professional qualifications and also created entirely new branches of the economy, with their own leadership. Thus the scientific elite developed around the expanding universities; the mushrooming construction industry gave rise to an elite of building contractors (the son of one of whom has become a university dean and one of the better-known Israeli television personalities); there are new elites composed of trade representatives of big foreign concerns and their colleagues among suppliers of the defense establishment.

Third, in Israel as in other democratic countries, there does not exist one single homogeneous elite, but several elites, each slightly different from the other. On the higher levels there are parallel national elites—political, economic, cultural, military. But each social grouping and subgrouping—development towns, immigrant groups, professional organizations—creates its own elite. Competition among the elites is part of the democratic game. Its formal expression comes once every four years: each subelite and each subgroup tries to assure that its representatives are given places on the ticket of one of the major parties in the national parliamentary elections. This effort is particularly evident in the behind-the-scenes jockeying for "safe spots" on the Labor party ticket. On a day-to-day basis the game involves a constant effort to make a representative of one's own subelite part of the national decision-making elite.

Fourth, there is a high degree of mobility within the top national elite. A leading general of yesterday can head a big business concern today or be a member of the Cabinet tomorrow. A distinguished commander in the Six-Day War can, in rapid sequence, become a university professor and one of the leading spokesmen of the "doves." Or vice versa, a retired officer who has been busy with the preservation of the country's parks and wild life can re-emerge as one of the country's most successful wartime generals. A judge of the Supreme Court decides to relinquish his life-term appointment to enter political life and become Knesset member for one of the opposition parties; one of the top officials of Israel's diplomatic service suddenly becomes a bank director; an important party leader with a distinguished "underground" record during the time of the British Mandate leaves party politics to become a major figure in world shipping.

Obviously, in his new role the elite member can utilize contacts and experience from his previous role; nor does he suddenly lose all his influence in the group to which he belonged earlier. A former head of Army Intelligence is now director-general of one of Israel's major industrial concerns but is still briefed quite regularly by his former subordinates, while another colleague in the Intelligence Branch is now a prominent lawyer and businessman, and he too is "kept informed." On occasion both act as semi-official commentators on defense matters for the official Israel Broadcasting Service. And, at the other extreme, a wealthy businessman finances a party paper for years, becomes a candidate of that party for a Cabinet job but at the last moment decides to stay with his business—and remains a power both in the party and in its contacts with the government.

Obviously, Israel is not the only country where mobility of this kind exists, but it seems that it is more prevalent there. Consequently the boundaries between elites become especially blurred at times.

Four qualities distinguish a member of the national elite but are not usually found among those who belong to one of the subelites:

- he has high status in his own profession or field of activity;
- his influence far exceeds his own specific area of activity;
- he can establish direct contact with the uppermost echelons of the national elite;
- he has access to "sources of information."

In Israel there are few arbiters of power who do not hold posts that make their inclusion in the top power elite inevitable. Nor are there figures who pull vital strings behind the scenes, unknown to the general public. Israel's "kingmakers," big and small, all hold some kind of public office, be it Finance Minister Pinhas Sapir, who is considered the country's most important "kingmaker," or Tel Aviv Mayor Yehoshua Rabinowitz, who probably pulls some of the most important strings in the Labor party machine.

This openness reinforces one of the more positive sides of Israel's power structure: the entry to it is secured by acquiring personal status derived from political or professional success. This is especially so in the Army and in the cultural field but also in politics and in economic life. The amount of influence exercised by a member of the power elite is often linked to his professional activity or official task. An editor of an important newspaper is influential because of the medium he controls; the chief of Army Intelligence exercises his influence not only by his recommendations but by the very choice he makes in selecting the information presented to the Chief of Staff or the Minister of Defense; the Prime Minister's political advisor is important not only because of his opinions but because of the access to his superior that he can provide for the opinions of others.

In other cases, influence stems more from tasks that are accessories to one's professional status. Hebrew University economics professor Dan Patinkin has acquired much of his importance through serving as chairman or member of important public-inquiry committees; Gad Ya'acobi is important not because he is Deputy

Minister of Transport but because he was a leading figure of the Rafi faction when it split from the Labor party and because he is believed to be close to General Dayan; Professor Amnon Rubinstein is welcome in homes of important people not because he is an expert in constitutional law, but because he is one of the leading columnists of the Tel Aviv daily *Ha'aretz* and appears frequently on television.

The Israeli power structure is an open one not only because entry into it is relatively easy, but also because of the openness of communications within it. Members of subelites have no difficulty communicating with the national elite and those belonging to the national elite can establish instant communication, if need be, with the very top national decision makers. The essentially egalitarian nature of Israel's society, even at the highest level, is the most important factor in this openness. An exceedingly large number of Israelis know each other from earlier service in the Army, from the Zionist movement, from organizing "illegal" immigration, or from youth movements. Today one man may be Minister of Agriculture, another a secretary of a kibbutz; one man may be a Deputy Chief of Staff, another a small manufacturer; but the functional distance that has emerged between them does not create any sense of superiority on the part of one or obsequiousness on the part of the other.

Changes in personal status in Israel are too rapid to permit the solidification of high walls or impermeable social frameworks between groups. In one town the former trade-union boss rose to national fame while his friend remained an unknown local councilman; in another town, the local councilman has risen to national prominence while his friend in the local union is still fighting his small-scale strikes.

Israel is a small country, and therefore the physical opportunities for contact and approach to the elite are relatively numerous. National figures often deal with purely local matters and, therefore, it is not surprising that the head of the Stevedores' Union in Haifa or in Ashdod knows the Minister of Finance very well or that a local party secretary can easily meet most Cabinet members in a Tel Aviv restaurant—and next day phone them at home "to arrange" some urgent business or personal matter for a constituent.

Access to inside information is an important attribute of any modern elite member. But in Israel, it seems, this is of particular importance. Centuries of persecution have led Jews to attach extraordinary weight to any bit of information emanating from a center of power that in the past could have had life-and-death implications for them. They brought this keen sense of the importance of information with them to Israel, and there the relative intimacy of the entire structure only adds to the value attached to "being in the know." With independence came the conviction that having inside information is part of a two-way communication system: those who know quickly what important people think or do can also influence decisions before they are made final. The small size of the country also accentuates the snob value of inside information: those who know what Moshe Dayan said yesterday can also create the impression, or at least try to create it, that they are part of the decision-making circle. Thus, information has become one of the most important coins of exchange at all levels of Israel's national and local elites.

Entry into the elite is possible through several paths. One of the more common ones is the "diagonal" ascent: a man moves from a lower rung in one elite to a somewhat higher rung in another. For example, a party functionary is rewarded by a diplomatic post in an unimportant foreign capital. If he is successful, he can become an important government official; this post can lead later to a "good spot" on his ticket in the next national election or to appointment as director-general of an important government-controlled enterprise.

This diagonal route is observable in a number of instances where people have reached the very highest political level. It is doubtful that outgoing Chief of Staff General Bar-Lev would have been appointed Minister of Commerce and Industry in 1972 unless General Dayan's opponents had believed that it would be good to have another top ex-officer in the Cabinet as a counterweight to Dayan's influence; nor is it certain that Ya'akov Shimshon Shapira would have become Minister of Justice if he had not rendered important services to the late Prime Minister Eshkol in the mid-1950's Lavon security flap, thereby earning Golda Meir's approbation.

A vertical rise to the top through party activities is the exception rather than the rule in Israel. It is very difficult to create a local power base which will propel a politician to the top. The national proportional representation system of election makes a local power base even less significant: a politician's "good" position on the party ticket, for example, is determined by the national party machine rather than by the extent of his support among local voters. Thus, one is elevated from above rather than pushed from below. The system means that party politicians are co-opted into the elite but do not reach it by competitive elimination of their opponents.

The Cabinet is the pinnacle of the power elite not only in politics but also in the country's economic life. But, again, not all Cabinet members are equal, and not all participate in important decisions. In a coalition Cabinet, members of the ruling party have more influence, not only because they form the majority of Cabinet members, but also because vital decisions are frequently thrashed out in a limited circle of Labor party Cabinet members , who consult top Labor functionaries. But not even Labor party Cabinet members are equally important. A select group of Cabinet members, close to Prime Minister Golda Meir, has great influence outside their specific fields of authority. For example, in foreign-policy matters: not only the Prime Minister and the Ministers of Defense and Foreign Affairs have an important say, but also Minister without Portfolio Israel Galili. In all domestic matters and in many external affairs, Justice Minister Ya'akov Shimshon Shapira's voice carries extraordinary weight. And, on all economic matters, Finance Minister Sapir's opinion is uncontested, outweighing by far any views held by the Minister of Commerce and Industry, Haim Bar-Lev, or the Minister of Agriculture, Haim Gvati.

Assignment to ministerial committees, through which most of the Cabinet's work is done, indicates a minister's position in the Cabinet pecking order. The most important, for years, has been the Committee on Security and Foreign Affairs, which, however, was of only secondary importance during most of Ben-Gurion's premiership: the "Old Man" made up his own mind, deciding alone on most vital issues, at times informing the ministerial committee, seldom consulting it and almost never accepting its opinion. But, under the premiership of Levi Eshkol and Golda Meir, this committee has become the most important one in the Cabinet.

Lately the tendency to expand the membership of the Ministerial Security and Foreign Affairs Committee (in response to pressure from the smaller parties in the government coalition which also wanted representation on the committee) reached its extreme; very frequently the Cabinet in toto declares itself its own Security and Foreign Affairs Committee, when it has to deal with a subject it wants to keep completely secret. Under existing legislation, military censorship can be applied to prevent the publication of anything that has been said or done in the Ministerial Security and Foreign Affairs Committee. And since the late Levi Eshkol as well as Mrs. Meir found it impossible to make Cabinet members keep silent about confidential discussions, they decided to impose obligatory silence concerning delicate deliberations by invoking the censorship rules.

Of course, it is no coincidence that it is so difficult to maintain secrecy concerning Cabinet deliberations. Since information is of such high value at every level of the elite, those who sit in top decision-making bodies use information obtained there as part of political payments to those just below them on the ladder, in order to ensure their support.

The importance of official committees in government and elsewhere depends not only on the level of their membership or the subject of their deliberations, but also on the extent of coordination between their approach and that of the government. The economic subcommittee of the Labor Alignment (the centrist Labor party plus left-of-center Mapam) has a dominant influence on the government's economic policy. This is due in no small measure to the participation of the secretary-general of the Histadrut (General Federation of Labor) Yitzhak Ben-Aharon: it can be taken for granted that any decision made by that committee will not only be approved by the Cabinet but will also hold up in practice without evoking a confrontation with the trade unions. On the other hand, the political committee of the Alignment is of very little importance. None of its members, not even all of them jointly, can exert influence on the Prime Minister, who makes her own decisions after consulting her confidants. Moreover, the committee's importance is weakened by the fact that most of its members are on the dovish side while Mrs. Meir and her close associates are of more hawkish inclination.

The "bloating" of governmental and party bodies is a common phenomenon in the Israeli establishment. Instead of fighting to keep them limited, despite constant pressures by interest groups who want to be admitted, the heads of government are ready to capitulate and then make them devoid of any real significance: the actual decision making is shifted to another, more limited body. This is what happened to the executive committee of the Labor party, which grew by some 300 percent within a few years but thereby became a mere rubber stamp, automatically approving (even if after some noisy debate) whatever had already been decided in some closed meeting of the top leadership.

Thus, several unofficial decision-making forums emerged within the Israeli establishment: "Golda Meir's Kitchen," "Yehoshua Rabinowitz's Tea Cabinet" for example. At the same time, some of the central elite bodies have been gradually emptied of whatever decision-making power they had. The most blatant example of this process is the stripping-away of the power and influence of the Knesset, Israel's parliament, whose members seldom take any independent stance against the will of their party. This is due in no small measure to the fact that each member feels himself dependent on the good will of the party machine that will decide, come next elections, whether he will be given a "safe" spot on the party ticket. Consequently most Knesset members believe that their loyalty belongs to the party and not to any independent opinions they may have on the merits of whatever subject is being debated.

Under these circumstances, Knesset membership is far from being synonymous with membership in the nation's decision-making elite. Nevertheless, there is keen competition for the privilege of becoming a Knesset member and remaining one. Besides the value of the title to those who have no other claim to membership in the national elite, the Knesset provides an important framework for instant contact and communication with those who really do constitute the power elite.

There are two bodies outside the political structure which provide high status in the national elite, as well as considerable real power. One is the Supreme Court, which in Israel does not have the authority to invalidate legislation but whose opinions carry overwhelming weight in public opinion and oblige even the most important Cabinet members to take them into consideration, not only in legal matters but also in the conduct of policy.

The second is the Office of the State Comptroller, who has established his position as general supervisor of all government branches, not only in the strict sense of proper management but also in the wider sphere of public accountability of government officials.

2

Protektzia and
Other Patterns of Contact

I f microphones were hidden under each table in the members' restaurant of the Knesset building in Jerusalem, they would probably record very few state secrets. Important decisions in Israel are made elsewhere. Yet these microphones would probably reveal secrets of a very different nature: they would expose the kind of communications which sociologists dub "patterns of contact" among Israel's power elite.

These patterns of contact between the various groups of the Israeli establishment are subject to predetermined rules of the game. This system of relationships is sometimes called *protektzia*, although one can discover minute differences between it and other forms of relationships called "nonbureaucratic contacts" by social scientists.

The Knesset members' restaurant is one of the most important meeting places for members of the parliament, party functionaries and others who are able to obtain entry permits to the building to "hunt" Cabinet ministers or their senior assistants. There they can try to convince them in short conversations to settle, or at least expedite, matters long under discussion in government departments. Senior government officials find the place convenient for meeting with Knesset members active in various parliamentary committees, mainly in order to remove hurdles which develop during the committee's work on draft laws, or to reach compromises on various issues in order to expedite the passing of a law.

In the old temporary quarters of the Knesset, the Froumin building in downtown Jerusalem, before the move to the present spacious building, with its long, wide corridors, office floor and accommodations for each parliamentary party grouping, there was much more intimacy in the Knesset restaurant. The chances of meeting personalities who controlled Israel's decision-making process were much greater than today. In those days the crowded restaurant was truly an exchange where appointments for jobs in the government and private sector were determined, where Cabinet ministers would decide on benefits to private enterprises in return for concessions on their part, and where officials would agree to reconsider decisions that proved unpleasant to those in power.

The restaurant in the new Knesset building, completed in 1966, is not so crowded and the atmosphere no longer so informal. Still, it serves as a most convenient arena for making contacts with those in power. Here VIP's are not protected by secretaries who refuse to transfer telephone calls to them; here nobody asks visitors to state their business in advance; here there is no danger that they will be politely told to go through channels.

The Knesset restaurant is, of course, not the only meeting place of Israel's power elite for the purpose of an exchange of favors. Inauguration ceremonies of new plants, meetings of political bodies, cocktail parties given by foreign diplomats in Tel Aviv's northern suburbs or even a casual meeting in the home of a mutual friend —all offer opportunities to settle complicated affairs. In Israel, unlike the United States, members of the power elite are seldom seen on the country's only golf course, nor do they frequent night clubs.

Friday-night social gatherings in Tel Aviv's residential suburbs of Zahala, Neve Magen, Herzliya Pituah and Savyon, and similar evenings in private apartments of Jerusalem's Rehavia and Beit Hakerem neighborhoods, have become an integral part of the Israeli scene. Even BBC television plays screened by Israeli television (such as *The Forsyte Saga*) have not interfered with the tradition of Friday-night gatherings, which start late and break up way after midnight.

Dress is informal, usually tieless, and, in the summer months, even without jackets. The food served at these evenings is not their strongest point. Often many of the guests are on diets and those who take sugar with their coffee are the minority. Participants look forward mainly to a relaxed atmosphere for talk. Unlike cocktail parties, often arranged for that purpose, it is not an atmosphere for doing business or settling affairs, nor is there any tendency to serious discussion of a crucial subject. On the contrary, those who are invited to these gatherings must obey an unwritten law not to bother the member of the power elite who is present with the day-to-day worries of his position. Even when a major topic, very much in the news at the time, is discussed, its lighter side and the anecdotes that accompany it are often emphasized. A new political joke, even malicious gossip which contains more than a hint of libel, is always welcome at these Friday-night social affairs. Yet the very fact that social contact is made there with members of the power elite often serves as an "entry permit" to the officials' office on weekdays.

Members of the ruling elite disperse among these gatherings: every week they can be found at a different place, almost as if they decide to do so in advance. Although a host never notifies his other guests who will be present on a particular evening, the chance to meet with the general, the senior civil servant or the deputy minister who is known to be among the friends of the host makes the parties particularly attractive.

Of course there is always the possibility of contacting a member of the power elite by picking up the telephone to his office or home whenever his help is needed. One can try to overcome the resistance of the secretary and simply drop in at his office. However, experience has shown that a casual, ostensibly unintentional meeting with the decision maker is usually more effective. Such an "accidental" meeting is less committing for the seeker as well as for the one whose help may be effective.

The Samuel Hotel, on Tel Aviv's seashore, where the Minister of Finance, Mr. Pinhas Sapir, used to lunch on Thursdays, served for a long time as the locus of attempts to contact him. At times it seemed as if the Minister himself sought opportunities to expose himself to chance meetings of this sort. When he would pass by the table of an industrialist or the manager of a large financial firm, Sapir himself occasionally was the one who seized the chance to make contact by asking a pointed question.

The brain trust which Mr. Sapir summons to his home once a month on a Thursday evening is an excellent opportunity to rub elbows with the influentials of the country. A middle-level civil servant is apt to remind a prominent businessman, "We met at Sapir's brain trust," in order to stress his importance. The custom of making this "pilgrimage" to Sapir's home in Kfar Saba by leaders of the economy also creates endless opportunities to make personal contact with the Minister for settling various matters.

Requests for assistance referred to in this connection are not one-sided, for the most part: here operates the delicate mechanism of give and take, known in Jewish tradition as "You help me, I'll help you." A member of the Knesset, a lawyer by profession, will not hesitate to ask the Minister for something on behalf of a client (in effect, for himself) even if he is a member of the opposition who misses no opportunity to attack the Minister and his party on the floor of the chamber or in committee. As for the Minister, he will not reject the request outright, for even if he does not expect to "buy" the opposition member, he knows that his consent to the request earns him credit, which is stored up in his favor.

This future credit will cause the Knesset member not to violate the rules of the game or exceed agreed limits. The storm which Uri Avneri, the editor of *Ha'olam Hazeh,* caused at the beginning of 1972 by asking for a loan from the goverment's Tefahot Bank, and the emotion which seized both the representative of the "Ha'olam Hazeh-Koah Hadash" faction in the Knesset and his opponents, arose out of the novelty of the case. Until then it had been accepted on all sides that Uri Avneri (like the Communist faction in the Knesset and the religious extremists outside it) was among the few who had no part in this game of give-and-take of "credits" in the country. The Tefahot Bank incident (and it makes no difference that in the end Avneri waived the loan) was an endless source of satisfaction to other participants in the game.

The argument over economic policy in Israel is, therefore, a game in which the benevolent father figure (represented by the Minister of Finance) encourages each participant to express himself. But in point of fact he can, with the aid of his assistants, terminate it any time he chooses.

The conflict between Pinhas Sapir and the head of the Histadrut, Yitzhak Ben-Aharon, over the notion of a "war economy" and the quarrel between them about wage policy, as well as the struggle with Moshe Dayan over the economic relationship between Israel and the occupied territories, go beyond the usual limitations of this game. But it is not by chance that the Finance Minister's opponents are not found in the opposition parties but are men from within his own party, each possessing his own power base.

Incidentally, this trade in "credits" is not based on the assumption that every appeal deserves a positive answer. On the contrary: in many cases, the appeal itself is enough to create a "credit account." An experienced Israel businessman explained this phenomenon to one of his assistants, saying, "I know the Minister will turn down my request. Still, I am submitting it because I know that the next time I make a similar appeal, he will consider it a double debt."

There is, of course, some connection between this "transaction game" among those who are in positions of power, and *"protektzia,"* the malaise of Israeli society, which has been condemned by politicians, studied by sociologists, and which serves as an unending source of jokes and anecdotes. In fact, in order to understand the patterns of contact in Israeli society, the real meaning of *"protektzia"* must be clarified.

In the Slavic languages from which this term is borrowed (it should not be confused with the English term "protection," which has a different meaning), *"protektzia"* has the double meaning of "bribery" and "exchange." In Israel, the first meaning has almost been forgotten. In most cases a *protektzia*-type preference is not associated with direct compensation, especially not with payments in cash. *Protektzia* in the Israeli sense usually means assistance given by a bureaucrat to a member of the public, not only because he deserves it but also because the bureaucrat may be his friend, come from the same hometown, be a member of his own community or have served with him in the Army.

Protektzia has two faces. One is of the simple, everyday variety and is found in relations between the public and the bureaucracy: in the waiting line for the doctor at the clinic, in making applications to universities (mainly medical schools), in the installation of a telephone or in the allocation of housing or a job. The other face is the delicate web of relationships that knits together the country's power elite.

The common denominator of the two forms of *protektzia* is the very narrow line that separates what is morally proper from what is improper. In fact, in a technocratic society it is most difficult to distinguish between bribery, corruption, preference and administrative efficiency. For example: is there a difference between a forged check and an auditor's signature on a financial statement which hides in various ways the basic fact that the company is insolvent?

Protektzia can be negative and destructive if its aim is to give someone preference he does not deserve, preference which goes beyond accepted norms and sometimes even is against the law. But *protektzia* can also be a way for the average citizen to overcome an inelastic bureaucracy, a way to "oil the wheels of bureaucracy." The "transaction game" which is conducted by the heads of the Israel establishment often consists of shortcuts and the removal of bureaucratic hurdles. Yet, in this context, some negative occurrences are also to be found.

Dr. Brenda Danet and Harriet Hartman of the Hebrew University and the Institute for Applied Social Research in Jerusalem published research on *protektzia* in Israel early in 1972. They diagnosed at least three factors that influence the exertion of personal influence in the Israeli bureaucracy: (a) the feeling of partnership and responsibility dating back to the experience of Jewish communities in the small towns of Eastern Europe; (b) the close personal relations typical in a small country, in which groups of residents have strong shared experiences as the result of belonging to the same collective settlement, or fighting in the same unit in one of Israel's many battles; (c) the need to give personal guidance, especially to immigrants from Oriental countries, who cannot find their way in the bureaucratic maze of the Western state.

The desire to help friends or relatives is often a leftover from Diaspora tradition that has lost its justification under Israeli circumstances. This system was exemplified in the attempt of a prominent Israeli who appealed to the Israeli Minister of Justice to allow Meir Lansky, the alleged U.S. crime czar, to settle in Israel. "Lansky hails from my hometown, Grodno," the Israeli explained, "and I cannot let him down." Although this tradition of mutual help is often based on positive motives, the research concludes, the results are often negative. In many cases it promotes the wrong persons and discriminates against those who have no "connections" ("Vitamin P" as the Israeli public jokingly calls *protektzia*).

There are countries in which a form of *protektzia* is exercised with the aim of exempting sons of friends from military service or of transferring them to safe assignments in the rear. In Israel, friends of senior officers often utilize their contacts for the opposite reason: they ask that their son or daughter be admitted to a crack fighting unit or a desired military course. They feel that in doing so they are not doing anything wrong, since they are not shielding their children, but, on the contrary, exposing them to even greater danger. It is obvious that even this form of preference is not desirable. It disrupts the procedure of selecting the most suitable candidates for the elite units of the Israel Defense Forces.

Preference based on sentiment in relations between the citizen and the bureaucracy is only one step away from preference based on money. Contacts that start as *protektzia* without remuneration may degenerate into contacts between a briber and bribee. The irregularities discovered early in 1972 in the distribution of apartments by Amidar Housing Company generated considerable excitement, since the impression was created that this was only the exposed tip of an iceberg, and that preferential treatment in return for money or another form of bribe had become a common phenomenon in Israel.

For the purpose of their research Brenda Danet and Harriet Hartman interviewed 1,885 adults, residents of four urban centers (Tel Aviv, Jerusalem, Haifa and Beersheba). Those interviewed were asked, among other things, whether in their opinion a citizen needs *protektzia* in order to obtain what is coming to him, whether acts of *protektzia* are common in Israel and whether they themselves had been aided by *protektzia* during the past year. The research concluded that the Israeli population, especially immigrants from Oriental countries, soon acquire bureaucratic norms, namely the norms of an organized regime, but at the same time nonbureaucratic behavior, based on the utilization of personal influence, also is engaged in. It can even be assumed that the latter phenomenon is gaining strength. Thus, there is a significant gap in Israel between the theory which negates *protektzia* and the practice, which compromises with it.

The research did not cover *protektzia* within the ruling elite, which, as mentioned, takes the form of a "transaction game" with the purpose of shortening the lines of communications, not between the private citizen and the bureaucracy, but among the most vital centers of Israeli society.

The need for the transaction game proves that, in its twenty-five years of existence, Israel has tied itself up with heavy ropes of bureaucracy which would put to shame a government with a tradition of hundreds of years of red tape. Apparently the inglorious heritage of red tape that marked the operations of the Jewish Agency and the Labor Federation in the pre-Statehood period contributed to the proliferation of the young Israeli bureaucracy. It seems that without the readiness of central figures of the establishment to act as "scissors" in order to cut some of this red tape Israeli society would have choked long ago.

When Pinhas Sapir was appointed Minister of Commerce and Industry toward the end of 1955, he proceeded to save his Ministry from total strangulation, which seemed to be inevitable as a result of control systems which had long since proved themselves unbearable. Sapir developed his own system of operations, which was based on direct intervention in almost every issue and the delegation of authority to a very small number of assistants, who helped him to "cut" in matters where decisions had been held up.

Sapir himself repeatedly denies that he "runs the country" with the help of a little black notebook (in which he jots down important data and matters that need his attention) as well as through little notes which he sends not only to his assistants but also to groups outside of government that are dependent on his good will. The Minister has even offered a prize amounting to a quarter of his salary to anyone who can produce one of these legendary notes.

It is, of course, of little importance if these notes actually exist or whether they are a "complete fabrication," as Sapir claims. It is a fact that he was forced to introduce shortcuts in bureaucratic procedure which bypassed existing administrative bodies. Direct intervention by Cabinet ministers, which was already practiced to some extent during the early years of the State (and even in the years that preceded it), became an organized system under Pinhas Sapir.

Dr. Zevi Dinstein, who for many years was Sapir's close assistant as well as Levi Eshkol's, has given the following definition of the way to overcome bureaucratic red tape: "We have to see to it that in our control of the economy we do not handle the small taps but the big faucets." He meant that the government should move away from intervention in day-to-day matters and exercise its power only over central issues. In reality, however, Pinhas Sapir, Levi Eshkol and even Zevi Dinstein have not acted this way: they often ignored the "little taps" altogether. It can thus be said that Zevi Dinstein and

others did not initiate an all-out fight against existing red tape or
overcome bureaucracy. They may have tried to establish objective
criteria for decision making but have not seriously attempted to
impose them.

Among examples of bureaucracy that are now history are the
following: the need for an exit permit from Israel, which has long
since been discontinued; the hundreds of inspectors who in the past
were empowered to prevent overcharging by retailers; foreign-
exchange controls which now are exercised through the banking
system. The private citizen today does not have to stand on line to
have his case considered in the corridors of the Ministry of Finance.
Even the internal-revenue authorities have, through the years, re-
duced their direct contacts with the individual taxpayer. Yet the
Israeli bureaucracy is still a many-headed monster. The citizen is in
the hands of the authorities when he wants to establish an enterprise, when he needs a loan, when he asks for a building permit or
when he wants to sell his products at a price that seems reasonable
to him. Those who are in positions of power would like to come to
the aid of the public, but since they are unable to do so by doing
away with red tape, they circumvent it.

These "outflanking" operations are sometimes a mixed blessing.
The *protektzia* practiced by the small group of Israel's power elite
does remove obstacles, but its negative implications also must not
be ignored. The fact that only a small group of the inner circle, a
group that numbers several hundred or several thousand at most,
benefits from this system is in itself a cause of serious distortion.
The remarkable growing concentration of power in the Israeli
economy—a concentration that is not always the result of efficiency
and which, in many cases, leads to the strangling of initiative in the
lower echelons—operates in favor of the big companies, those
whose heads are able to reach the few who are "worth knowing."
Their contacts are important in order to get quick decisions on
every topic, whether it be a loan from the Industrial Development
Bank of Israel or a permit from the Tel Aviv municipality to tear
down a fence.

One of the questions that puzzle students of Israel's power elite is whether the close ties among so many leading personalities are the result of a common past, country of origin, party, school, youth movement, the Haganah underground army, the Israeli Army or government service, or whether this *protektzia* among the elite is just a form of nepotism.

At first glance it would seem that the Israeli establishment is characterized by nepotism of the Bonapartist style, reminiscent of Napoleon, who made his brothers and brothers-in-law kings and princes of European states. Even a superficial review of the Israeli power elite reveals brothers, brothers-in-law, cousins, sons and sons-in-law in key positions in the government and in political parties. A foreign sociologist, unfamiliar with the formation of the Israeli establishment, might come to the oversimplified conclusion that Israel is ruled by clans and dynasties formed by its founding fathers.

Numerous examples can be found to illustrate this point. Even before the establishment of the State, three brothers-in-law, Moshe Sharett (later Foreign Minister and Prime Minister), Eliahu Golomb and Shaul Avigur, held key positions in the political and military leadership of the Jewish community of Palestine. Twenty years later two other brothers-in-law, Moshe Dayan (first, Chief of Staff in the Israeli armed forces, and subsequently Minister of Agriculture and Minister of Defense) and Ezer Weizman (Commander of the Air Force, then Chief of Operations in the General Staff and later Minister of Transport) sat next to each other in Army staff meetings and later at Cabinet sessions. Was this just a coincidence or was there a system behind it?

Moreover, Weizman did not get to the front ranks of Israeli Army officers from nowhere; his uncle, Dr. Chaim Weizmann, was the first President of the State of Israel. Dayan too does not exactly have an obscure past. His father, Shmuel Dayan, was one of the leaders of the moshav (cooperative villages) movement, one of the leaders of the Labor party and a member of the Knesset for many years before the world took notice of his son, "the one-eyed general."

And was it just an accident that the two sons of the late Chief

Rabbi, Dr. Yitzhak Halevi Herzog, both held senior positions in the government service? The older, Haim, is a former Army general and at one time was chief of Army Intelligence, and the younger, Ya'akov, before his untimely death, was Director-General of the Prime Minister's office and senior advisor to three Prime Ministers, David Ben-Gurion, Levi Eshkol and Golda Meir.

And how did it happen that when Rabbi Dr. Shlomo Ben-Meir, one of the leaders of the National Religious party, died suddenly in the spring of 1971, it was just the turn of his son, Dr. Yehuda Ben-Meir, to fill his father's Knesset seat?

And what about the Hacohen family? When David Hacohen, one-time director of Solel Boneh, the contracting company owned by the labor sector of the economy, and former Israel Minister to Burma, served as chairman of the Defense and Foreign Relations Committee of the Knesset, he was known as the "most related person in Israel." One of his daughters is married to Uzi Narkiss, at one time head of the Central Command of the Israeli Army and subsequently director of the immigration department of the Jewish Agency. His second daughter is married to Aharon Yadlin, secretary-general of the ruling Labor party and one-time Deputy Minister of Education. Hanna Ruppin, one of David Hacohen's sisters, is the widow of Dr. Arthur Ruppin, who headed the Jewish settlement movement in Palestine. One of Mrs. Ruppin's daughters is married to Professor Yigael Yadin, the noted archaeologist and one-time Chief of Staff of the Israeli Army. Her second daughter is married to Dr. Zevi Dinstein, the Deputy Minister of Finance. A further study of Hacohen family relatives would uncover many other persons holding senior positions in the Israeli establishment, including Yitzhak Rabin, Chief of Staff of the Israeli Army during the Six-Day War, and later Israel's Ambassador in Washington.

Asher Yadlin, the secretary of Hevrat Ha'ovdim, the Labor Federation's holding company, as well as the secretary-general of Kupat Holim, the Labor Federation sick fund, is to some extent the missing link between the Hacohen "tribe" and the "tribe" of Sharett-Golomb-Hoz. He is a cousin of Aharon Yadlin (married to David

Hacohen's daughter, as we have seen) and is himself married to Dalia, the daughter of the late Eliahu Golomb. Dalia's brother David ("Dodik") is one of the senior economists of Hevrat Ha'ovdim and heads a science-based industrial company which is part of the Labor Federation economy.

Yet the *protektzia* on which the positions of these members of the Israeli power elite is supposedly built proves most questionable and irrelevant following a study of each case. The fact that relatives have similar histories and are guided by similar values is to be expected. Nor is it atypical that people marry others who come from a similar background. It may therefore seem surprising, but it is a fact, that the "hundred families" who ostensibly rule Israel are not engaged in handing out preferential treatment to each other. Their close family ties are the result of the small dimensions of the population of pre-State Israel and not of the practice of *protektzia* by the ruling elite. The sons of the Chief Rabbi obtained their positions not because their father got them the jobs but because, as the result of the background in which they grew up, as well as their education and qualifications, they were found suitable for the positions to which they were assigned.

The Zionist roots of a family in many cases led to several sons' assuming central positions in the life of the State, yet not always being of similar mind. In the Katzneleson family, for example, the daughter Rachel (wife of the President of Israel, Zalman Shazar) and her brother Abraham joined the Labor movement, while their brother Reuben and his son Shmuel (Tamir) became active in more right-wing parties. Similarly, Menahem Bader was one of the founders of the leftist labor group Hashomer Hatzair and Kibbutz Mizra in the Valley of Jezreel, while his cousin, Dr. Yohanan Bader, is one of the leaders of the rightist party Herut, and has represented this party in the Knesset for many years.

The founding fathers of Israel did not choose a life of comfort for their sons nor did they send them to safe places of refuge in time of war. The sons of Israeli leaders were among the first to join the Haganah (the pre-State underground army), the British Army during World War II and the Palmach (the commando unit of the Haganah). They often volunteered for dangerous assignments and it is little wonder, therefore, that some of them reached positions of high responsibility in the army, in political parties and in government service.

In the psychological warfare conducted by the Egyptians by way of loud-speaker broadcasts from their side of the Suez Canal, they sometimes try to demoralize Israeli soldiers on the opposite bank by provocative questions such as: "Where is the son of Ben-Gurion? Where is the son of Moshe Dayan? Why are they not at the front with you?" These propaganda attempts are based on the reality of life in the Arab countries, not on that of Israel. *Protektzia*, as a form of transaction and creation of mutual "credits" in Israel's power elite, is related to issues that members of the elite are interested in promoting. There is very little proof that they include the promotion of their relatives among those issues.

3

The Queen and Her Heirs

THE famous "Golda's Kitchen," where Israel's important political decisions are supposedly cooked up, is actually a comfortable living room in the Prime Minister's house in Jerusalem's Rehavia quarter. Here she serves tea or coffee to a small circle of associates whom she consults, usually on Saturday nights, on current domestic and foreign-policy problems. Essentially, these meetings are intended to thrash out matters in advance of the weekly Cabinet meeting, held every Sunday morning, but very often the issues taken up do not concern any Cabinet question: appointments of various functionaries, a crisis in some important municipal coalition or any other issue high on the agenda of her Labor party.

The regulars at these gatherings include the Minister of Finance, Pinhas Sapir, the Minister of Justice, Ya'akov Shimshon Shapira, and the Minister without Portfolio, Israel Galili. Mrs. Meir listens to their views on practically all subjects, but each of them has his specialty. Sapir is the expert on finance and economics; he also advises on party affairs and personnel matters. Galili is the specialist on foreign policy, especially on phraseology of communiqués where verbal acrobatics are vital. Mrs. Meir also trusts Galili on questions which, in her opinon, require an "intellectual approach." Shapira, a lawyer, is, of course, the legal expert, but also gives counsel on other matters. He is the only one of the inner four who has other than honorary university degrees.

By his position as Deputy Prime Minister (a title he holds since his membership in the Cabinet of the late Levi Eshkol), Yigal Allon should belong to this inner circle. In fact, he is not one of the weekly regulars.

From time to time, when the "Kitchen" takes up matters in the official or unofficial purview of other officials, Mrs. Meir invites them to join the hard-core group. Occasionally Foreign Minister Abba Eban or Defense Minister Moshe Dayan is called in, while Tel Aviv Mayor Yehoshua Rabinowitz (the nearest local equivalent of a Tammany Hall boss) joins in when party affairs are discussed. Less often comes Yigal Allon (who is also Minister of Education and Culture), while Simha Dinitz, who used to be Mrs. Meir's trusted counsel–*cum* –political secretary and is now Ambassador to Washington, often would stay on after others left.

The four regulars—Mrs. Meir and Messrs. Sapir, Shapira and Galili—have three things in common: their East European origin, their advanced age (the youngest, Pinhas Sapir, was born in 1908) and their apparently genuine conviction that they know better than the public what is good for it. To the three men, their charter membership in the "Kitchen" gives a measure of status and prestige far above their own personal weight and influence—including the enormous influence of Mr. Sapir, who is the virtually unchallenged master of Israel's economic life.

But on the most important issue which such a group can decide, Mrs. Meir's "Kitchen" will probably have a rather limited influence: it is very doubtful that this forum will determine who will be Mrs. Meir's successor as Israel's next Prime Minister. It may be that Mrs. Meir (and her confidants) will choose the heir, but there is no certainty that on this matter her present enormous influence will carry the day within the party—even if the arrangements for succession are made while she is still in office. Mrs. Meir's power depends both on her being in office and on her threats to resign prematurely.

After she departs, there will be neither office nor threats of resignation to frighten her party caucus.

In early 1973, the list of potential successors still contained the same three names inscribed after the Six-Day War in 1967: Pinhas Sapir, Moshe Dayan and Yigal Allon, while on the sidelines emerged, surprisingly, the shadow of Foreign Minister Abba Eban's dark-horse candidacy, trailed by vague rumors about Galili. There are constant shifts in the relative strength of the three main contestants, yet one can discern what seem to be certain fundamental trends. The most significant may be the long-term improvement in Dayan's position. Mrs. Meir and Mr. Galili differ with him on practically every issue except the one that is most important in their order of priorities: they are all hawks when it comes to relations with the Arabs and the conditions of a peace settlement. Dayan's popularity with the public has not diminished to any significant extent with the end of the shooting along the Suez Canal, while his "original sin" of having joined David Ben-Gurion in the short-lived split of the Rafi faction from the Labor party is now receding into past history. It seems to weigh less and less in Mrs. Meir's and Mr. Galili's attitude toward Dayan. But the Minister of Defense apparently realizes now that nobody is going to offer him the premiership on a silver platter: he will have to fight for it.

Sapir's chances improved with the easing of tension along the Suez Canal: with most of the Soviet military out of Egypt, the threat of a new war has receded and so may some of the feeling that Moshe Dayan must lead the nation. Sapir personally may feel less reluctant now to take on the responsibilities of top leadership.

The slippage in Yigal Allon's political stock at the beginning of 1973 was quite evident, though he made several moves at that time possibly aimed at presenting himself as the candidate of the doves in the political establishment. More important, there is still reason to believe that, if and when the chips are down, Mr. Galili and the Achdut Ha'avodah faction in the Labor party, as well as many members of the party machine, will back Allon over Dayan, especially if Sapir will not run.

There can be no doubt that, when Mrs. Meir departs from the

Prime Minister's office, the last of the "old generation" will have left the forefront of Israel's national leadership. These were the veteran politicians from Eastern Europe who came to Palestine as pioneers before World War I and in the early twenties. With Mrs. Meir will probably disappear her extraordinary style of political action and rhetoric, based on the conviction that Israel's needs and deeds, as well as those who act on her behalf, should be judged by special criteria.

Indeed, the dominant quality of Mrs. Meir is her tendency to act as if she—and only she—is right. Her ability to transfer this sense of infallible righteousness from the personal to the political level has made Mrs. Meir Israel's most effective spokesman before world public opinion. First in her capacity as Foreign Minister and later as Prime Minister, this quality helped her to establish for herself an authority unmatched by any Israeli statesman since Ben-Gurion.

Her views and actions are, in fact, even less challenged than were Ben-Gurion's, not only because the "Old Man's" decisions were more original and daring, but also because Mrs. Meir so easily construes any substantive argument as personal criticism. Those who object to her views often are made to feel as if they were her personal enemies, and that such criticism reflects on their own character rather than on the quality of Mrs. Meir's opinions. This method of dealing with criticism is a reflection of her personality and of fifty years of experience in politics. In recent years, she has used it with increasing effectiveness in the context of the dread of a "war of succession" inside the Labor party. The term "the Queen," coined by the late Prime Minister Eshkol, has lost much of both the irony and the affection with which it was used by its originator.

There is, however, more than just self-righteousness behind Golda Meir's certainty of being right—a feeling, by the way, which is typical of many other politicians of the Second and Third Aliyahs.* First of all, she is sure that whatever Israel wants or needs is wanted or needed by the entire Jewish people, past, present and

*Waves of pre- and post-World War immigration to Palestine.

future. In addition, she is endowed with a capacity for hard work and grasp of essentials and with the ability to make quick—and often intuitively correct—decisions. She also has the charismatic qualities of a leader—though much less so than Ben-Gurion had. But, above all, her position as well as stature are buttressed by the fact that she usually voices the average Israeli's fears and hopes for security and national existence.

Golda Meir is never afraid to say things which sound like platitudes or threadbare clichés of Zionist rhetoric. When she says, "Now that the Jewish people has a State of its own in which it can defend itself, what else is there to ask for?" this does not sound like an outworn sentence. She is deeply convinced that every Jew must be a Zionist—out of the elementary necessity of Jewish self-protection. When, several years ago, an American Jewish lady remarked to her that "Not all Jews are Zionists," Mrs. Meir retorted: "Yes, and not all non-Jews are anti-Semites!"

The feeling that, deep in their hearts, most *goyim* do not like Jews has been embedded deeply in Golda Meir's picture of the external world, ever since the pogrom she witnessed as a child in her native Russia, which she still recalls as the event that made the deepest impact on her life.

Golda Meir was born Golda Mabovich in 1898 in Kiev, the capital of the Ukraine. Her father was a carpenter, five of whose eight children died in infancy. In 1906 the family emigrated to the United States, where they settled in Milwaukee, Wisconsin. Mr. Mabovich worked for the railroad and Mrs. Mabovich supplemented the family income by running a small grocery store.

At the age of fourteen, Golda ran away from home to Denver, Colorado, to her older sister Shaine (who died in Tel Aviv in 1972). There she met Morris Meyerson, a young immigrant from Russia, who later became her husband. After returning to Milwaukee, Golda went to a teachers' college and became active in Jewish organizations. First she worked to aid Russian Jews, and then Jewish education in America. Later, she joined the Poalei Zion movement, which in Palestine was the forerunner of Mapai, forerunner of the present ruling Labor party. Young Meyerson was an internationalist socialist and as such he rejected the Zionist solution of the "Jewish problem." But, when Golda made emigration to Palestine a condition of marrying him, he agreed and the young couple arrived in the country in 1921, settling in Kibbutz Merhavia.

"From him I received whatever love I have of things cultural," Golda Meir said later of her husband, "appreciation for poetry, music, books, ideas." His love of music was inherited by their son, Menahem, who is a cellist. Her inclination to live in a collective was passed on to their daughter Sarah, who lives with her husband and children in Kibbutz Revivim in the Negev (southern Israel).

It was a strange twist of fate that her husband's inability to adjust to kibbutz life—the epitome of Zionist fulfillment of those days—led Golda Meyerson back to the city and to her career in Labor-Zionist politics. Initially they moved to Tel Aviv, where Morris Meyerson got a job as cashier in Solel Boneh, the Histadrut (Labor Federation) construction company. Next they went to Jerusalem, where Golda got a job in the local trade-union offices and was elected secretary of the Working Women's Council. This was her last typically "woman's office." From then on she held men's jobs in a man's world in the Histadrut, first in charge of Mutual Aid and Kupat Holim (the unions' health insurance services), and later as head of the Labor Contracts Department.

Mrs. Meir does not like people to remind her too much about holding positions usually reserved for men. When a reporter asked her once, "How does it feel to be a woman Prime Minister?" she replied tartly: "I cannot make comparisons—I never was a male Prime Minister."

Golda Meyerson moved from trade-union matters to politics and diplomacy in 1940, when she was appointed head of Histadrut's political department. As such she represented the trade unions vis-à-vis the British Mandatory government. From the start she acted with the same tough single-mindedness which later became her trademark as one of Israel's top diplomats and statesmen. In World War II she represented the Histadrut on the joint Jewish-

Arab-British War Economy Council set up by the Mandatory government. When, on "Black Saturday" in 1946, the British arrested the first-rank leadership of the Jewish community in Palestine, Mrs. Meir took over as head of the Political Department of the Jewish Agency—and continued as de facto deputy head of the Department after the release from detention of Moshe Sharett, its permanent head, who later became Israel's first Foreign Minister.

On the eve of the 1949 UN resolution on the partition of Palestine into separate Jewish and Arab states, Mrs. Meir held the first of two meetings with King Abdullah of Transjordan. At that meeting, held in the villa of Pinhas Ruttenberg, pioneer of the power industry in Palestine, on the banks of the Jordan, the Arab ruler promised not to attack any territory allocated to the Jewish State under the partition resolution in exchange for acceptance of the annexation to his kingdom of those parts of Palestine allocated to the Arab State. But a few days before the proclamation of Israel's independence in May, 1948, a second meeting took place in the King's palace in Amman. Mrs. Meir, who crossed the border disguised as an Arab peasant woman, was told by Abdullah that the situation had changed and that he could not keep his promise. He urged that "the Jews not rush into proclaiming their Statehood." Mrs. Meir replied that "a nation which has waited two thousand years for Statehood can hardly be accused of rushing things too much."

Abdallah Tel, who was at that time commander of Jordanian forces in the Old City of Jerusalem and a close assistant of the King, recalls in his memoirs his ruler's remarks after that meeting. "With all due respect to Israel, where a woman can reach such a high position, one cannot expect me to take too seriously messages conveyed to me not by a man but by a woman. . . ."

Between the two meetings with the Transjordan ruler, Golda Meir traveled to the United States to raise money for the purchase of weapons. In a coast-to-coast tour she collected $50 million—an unheard-of sum in those days and circumstances. "It was Golda who got the money for the arms that brought the victory," Ben-Gurion used to remark after the war.

Her initial job after the war was that of Israel's first Ambassador to the Soviet Union. The woman who lacked any real diplomatic experience was suddenly faced with two difficult and interrelated problems: one, Moscow's disappointment that Israel, whose establishment it assisted both diplomatically and with arms (supplied by Czechoslovakia), chose to become a Western-type parliamentary democracy rather than a Soviet-type "people's democracy"; and the other—the Kremlin's fury over expressions of a widespread revival of national consciousness among its Jewish citizens as a result of the creation of the Jewish State. More than forty thousand Jews assembled around Moscow's Great Synagogue on the eve of Rosh Hashana (Jewish New Year) to welcome Israel's first Ambassador. Some observers believe that the sight of those forty thousand enthusiastic celebrants was one of the factors that launched Stalin on the anti-Semitic campaign which culminated in the murder of the cream of Russia's Jewish poets and writers and in the notorious "doctors' plot." For Golda Meir, those jubilant Jews were her second impression from Russia—a counterpoint to the pogrom she remembered from her childhood days.

In 1949, Mrs. Meir joined the Cabinet as Minister of Labor. In that post she had to create employment and build homes for hundreds of thousands of new immigrants who streamed into Israel from all parts of the world. At the same time, she laid the groundwork for the labor legislation of the new State. Mrs. Meir says that her seven years at the Ministry of Labor were the happiest period in her life.

A few months before the Sinai War of 1956, when David Ben-Gurion had his final split with Moshe Sharett over Israel's foreign policy, he picked Golda Meir to be the new Foreign Minister. He knew that Mrs. Meir would not only faithfully implement his will but the implementation would reflect the spirit of his decisions exactly. The first such policy decision which Mrs. Meir was called upon to translate into action was to yield to American and Soviet pressure in 1957 and evacuate the Sinai Peninsula and Gaza Strip, taken from the Egyptians. She was expected to obtain in exchange the best possible guarantees for Israel's security in the future. Mrs. Meir made a dramatic speech at the UN General Assembly announcing the withdrawal and proclaimed Israel's "hopes and expectation" that Sinai would remain demilitarized and that Israel would enjoy the right of passage through the reopened Suez Canal. It was a traumatic experience for her; there can be little doubt that her present firm stand against unilateral withdrawal from lands occupied in the Six-Day War of 1967 is due, to no small extent, to what she thought and felt standing on the UN rostrum in 1957.

In her first years as Foreign Minister, Israel's foreign-policy course was set by Ben-Gurion (who was also Minister of Defense) while Mrs. Meir's was the task of carrying it out. In fact, even implementation was not her prerogative in certain areas. The whole complex of Israel's relations with France, her main military supporter and unofficial ally, was under the control of the Ministry of Defense. This seems to be the root of Mrs. Meir's deep resentment of Shimon Peres, then Deputy Minister of Defense and Ben-Gurion's close collaborator.

In the relatively calm period of Israel's foreign relations during 1957 and 1958, Mrs. Meir progressively reclaimed for her Ministry the authority over most of those overseas operations which had fallen into the domain of other departments, like the Treasury and the Jewish Agency. The new, more clearcut division of authority in security matters overseas between the Foreign Ministry and the Ministry of Defense also was largely in her favor.

After Israel's grave disappointment with its Asian friends at the Bandung Conference of "unaligned" nations, Mrs. Meir focused her attention on expanding relations with the newly independent states of Africa. She visited many of them, and became the best-known white woman on the black continent. She refused to be discouraged when these new African friends often let Israel down when votes were counted at the United Nations: "Sometimes people have arguments even with those closest to them; it's not the end of the world."

Mrs. Meir is especially sensitive to the memory of the Holocaust and its implications for German-Israel relations. She refuses to speak German (which she learned in school in Milwaukee) and declares that when the question of diplomatic ties with Bonn arose, "There was a very difficult debate between my heart and my logic."

The debate between heart and logic is typical of Mrs. Meir, perhaps more than of any other Israeli leader, because she cannot easily separate the two. The steel of her will and the sharpness of her tongue cutting an opponent to the quick do not cancel the warmness of her emotions, giving her simultaneously the titles of "the Grandma Prime Minister" and "the only man in the Cabinet." She is both the traditional Jewish mother worrying over her brood and the angry prophetess calling the wrath of Heaven down upon the enemies of Israel.

Golda Meir's personal world is also painted in black and white, with almost no grays in between. If she is fond of somebody at work or in private life, she backs him irrespective of his weaknesses, mistakes or failure; if she resents somebody, she will do what she can to get him out of her sight—literally as well as figuratively speaking. Those who work with her are divided into enthusiastic admirers of a great woman and critics of a domineering, vituperative old lady.

During her nine years of stewardship of Israel's foreign affairs, people in Israel and abroad came to know the mannerisms and behavior which became so familiar after she was chosen Prime Minister: she always wears dark colors—black or gray—adorned with a carefully chosen pin; the tiny wrist watch, the hands unwrinkled even in the eighth decade of her life, the nicotine-stained fingers of a true chain smoker. Above the strong chin, the stern visage—which suddenly breaks into a warm smile.

Golda Meir does not simply object to views opposing her own. She is "amazed" that such views exist. Nor does she just reject criticism of herself or of Israel; she is "shocked" by the idea that such things are even voiced. And while other nations may have interests—just or unjust—her own country always acts out of right and virtue.

The edge and heat of her style were fully in evidence in domestic politics when she joined the battle on the side of the late Levi Eshkol against David Ben-Gurion in the bitter struggle inside Mapai follow-ing the Lavon Affair (over the responsibility for an abortive intelli-gence coup in Egypt during Pinhas Lavon's term as Minister of Defense). One version is that the deep split between her and Ben-Gurion originated in former Deputy Defense Minister (and now Minister of Communications) Shimon Peres' invasion of the for-eign-affairs domain when she was Foreign Minister and Ben-Gurion was Prime Minister and Minister of Defense. Others believe that the real cause was that Mrs. Meir shared the anger and frustration of party veterans at the promotion over their heads of Ben-Gurion's protégés, Moshe Dayan and Shimon Peres, who were relative new-comers to party struggles and achievements.

Whatever the reasons, Golda Meir was among the more extreme of the Ben-Gurion opponents in the struggle. Yet there remained a strange ambivalence in sentiment between the two leaders. For many years Ben-Gurion spoke of her as "that woman," while she would not return his curt "Shalom" when they happened to be in the same room. And, though she often said that "even Ben-Gurion cannot destroy my image of Ben-Gurion," she was one of the very few Israeli personalities who refused to join the public committee which arranged the celebrations of Ben-Gurion's eightieth birthday.

In 1965, Mrs. Meir resigned from the Cabinet, to spend the rest of her life with her children and grandchildren. But not a year passed before she was in public life again—this time as secretary-general of Mapai. In her new job she continued her old fight against the "splinterers" of Rafi, and even on the eve of the Six-Day War, she kept up her battle against Moshe Dayan. More than the late Levi Eshkol himself, she opposed the popular demand that he hand over the Ministry of Defense to Dayan. Therefore, she was considered the main obstacle to the establishment of a National Unity Govern-ment in the week before the war; in the streets of Tel Aviv there were even demonstrations by women against her. Later she claimed that "the whole campaign organized against me did not have any effect. . . . On the streets, children continued to wave their hands

in greeting . . . not one soldier refused to take a 'lift' in my car
. . . personally, I have nothing to be ashamed of. . . ."

During the negotiations over Rafi's return to Mapai, Mrs. Meir
worked hard to assure that the Achdut Ha'avodah party of Yigal
Allon, Dayan's competitor for future premiership, would merge
simultaneously into the enlarged Labor party.

In 1968 she resigned as party secretary-general and returned
again to private life. But the sudden death of Levi Eshkol brought
her to the pinnacle of her political career: fearful that a struggle
among contestants for the succession would break up the coalition
government and possibly even split up the newly united Labor
party, its veteran leaders suggested that Mrs. Meir become the new
Prime Minister.

After entering office she underwent two distinct changes: from
party politician par excellence she became a national leader. And in
the eyes of the public, which only a few months earlier had considered her a threat to national unity, she suddenly became a national
heroine whose popularity ratings soon surpassed even those of
Dayan and Ben-Gurion at the zenith of his career. (Precipitous ups
and downs in popularity have always been typical of Mrs. Meir's
standing among her countrymen.)

One of her very first acts in office was to end the unwritten ban
on smoking at Cabinet meetings, established by Ben-Gurion and
Moshe Sharett before her. On the substantive level, she reorganized
the working methods of the Cabinet plenum; most specific issues
are referred to various subcommittees, while the plenum deals with
matters of principle and serves as an appeals forum on matters
which have failed to obtain unanimous decisions in ministerial subcommittees. Personally, she does not hesitate to make drastic decisions; but when a decision has far-reaching implications, she often
asks to review it. She likes to think about her most difficult problems
at home in the evenings, consulting mostly Cabinet members and
other confidants rather than experts. When there is a major military
retaliatory action against terrorist bases across the border, she stays
awake till the small hours after midnight, awaiting her military ad-

jutant's reports on the results—and the casualties, if any—of the operation. When she manages to get away from her official Jerusalem residence on weekends to her private home at Ramat Aviv, near Tel Aviv, she enjoys puttering in her small garden.

Golda Meir's strong personality and international fame were her main assets in her four meetings in Washington with President Nixon, with whom she established close rapport. During her term of office there was a notable increase in America's military and political support of Israel. Mrs. Meir reciprocated to Mr. Nixon with words of praise which were not lost on American Jewry in the 1972 election campaign.

The fervor of her support for the struggle of Soviet Jews to emigrate and of her conviction that Israel has the right to annex sizable proportions of the territories taken in the 1967 war has its roots in a feeling that the non-Jewish world is essentially hostile to the Jews and that the Jewish people has a moral duty to fight for its and Israel's survival in face of this hostile environment. She refuses to draw maps of how much Israel wants to keep of the conquered lands before the Arab leaders are ready to sit down at the peace table. She insists that any talk must be held with representatives of the neighboring sovereign Arab countries and not with any "Palestinians" whose separate nationhood she firmly rejects.

Mrs. Meir's March, 1973, trip to Washington was a resounding success. Despite what looked at first like bad timing (she arrived a week after the Libyan airliner tragedy for which Israel was blamed by world public opinion), she obviously secured commitments for continued arms supply as well as sympathy for Israeli demands for direct negotiations with the Arabs without prior conditions.

The warmth with which she was received by President Nixon and the enthusiasm she aroused among American Jews were reflected back in Israel: more people were willing to forgive her shortcomings and the leaders of her party became even more determined in their demand that Mrs. Meir serve again as Prime Minister after the November, 1973, elections. She herself obviously still hesitated in the spring of 1973 to commit herself.

Many believe that Golda's final decision will depend on three factors: the political developments in the months immediately preceding the elections; the internal relations within the Israeli Labor party; and—last but not least—the state of her health, which has been excellent ever since she became Prime Minister.

There is a certain paradox in the fact that the more the Labor party leadership is frightened by the prospect of a "war of succession," the less public evidence there is of the backstage fighting. And, despite his public statements that he is unlikely to be the choice of those who will determine the successor, few political observers believe that the number-one contender, Defense Minister Moshe Dayan, has given up his hopes of becoming Prime Minister. In the early part of 1973, there were even signs that Dayan was becoming less passive in his quest, realizing that no one was going to hand him the prize on a silver platter.

One always has to depend on the evaluation of "friends" and "close associates" of Dayan in order to guess what he really thinks or wants to do. And they too, in early 1973, were mostly guessing. Dayan has always been a lone wolf, whether by choice or because he cannot establish intimate contact with other people. In an interview, he once said quite frankly: "I do not look down upon people; they just bore me. There is not a single person in the world in whose company I am interested unless I have something specific to tell him."

This is the less-known side of Moshe Dayan. The public in Israel and abroad know him primarily as the commander of the Israel forces in the 1956 Sinai War and Defense Minister in the 1967 Six-Day War. The older generation possibly remembers him also as a successful commander in the 1948 War of Liberation. Above all, he is known as a cool, aggressive general, stubborn in his views, and one who "knows how to talk to the Arabs."

Moshe Dayan speaks Arabic fluently and many say "he even thinks like an Arab." He was born in 1915 in Kibbutz Degania, where his parents were among the founders of the settlement. His father, Samuel, was a well-known figure in Israel farming circles and

Moshe, a sickly child, inherited his father's taciturn nature. But most of his intellectual qualities came to him from his mother, who had an extraordinarily strong character and sharp intellect. When Moshe was six, the family moved from Degania to join the founders of Nahalal, a cooperative farmers' village (moshav) west of Nazareth. Here young Dayan learned for the first time about the Arabs, both as neighbors and as enemies. At the age of twelve, he already knew how to hold a gun, and at the age of fourteen he was already one of the nightwatchmen guarding the settlement. At the age of eighteen, Dayan served as an instructor in the Haganah, and when he was twenty-two he became deputy to the legendary Captain Orde Wingate, who organized the Jewish "special night squads," a commando unit sponsored by the British to combat Arab terrorist gangs.

In 1935 Dayan married Ruth Schwartz, daughter of a well-known Jerusalem lawyer. The young couple lived in Nahalal and Moshe Dayan continued to be active in Jewish self-defense, both legal and illegal. In 1939 he was arrested while training a group of youths in the use of firearms and was sentenced to five years in prison. He busied himself in Acre jail by writing, among other things, poetry. By 1941, relations between the Haganah and the British Army improved because of the necessity to cooperate in the war against the Nazis. Moshe Dayan was released from prison and joined an Israeli unit fighting the pro-Nazi Vichy regime in Syria. In a battle for one of the bridges over the Litani River, an enemy bullet hit the binoculars he was holding to his face, shattering his left eye. From that time on, Dayan has worn the black eye patch, which has become his personal symbol.

When he was discharged from the hospital, young Dayan became an assistant to Yitzhak Sadeh, the already legendary founder of the Haganah, who at that time was engaged in planning the defense of the Jewish settlements in Palestine in case of a German invasion. General Rommel's forces were advancing in North Africa toward Egypt, and Dayan was in close contact with intelligence units of the British forces in the Middle East. He established friendship with

several British officers, who helped him in various Haganah projects, primarily in an effort to save some of the Jews of German-
occupied Europe.

In the last years of World War II, Dayan returned to Nahalal, but,
in 1947, when the pre-independence attacks of the Arabs on the
Jewish settlements became more and more bloody, he was recalled
to service in the Haganah. General Sadeh appointed him to organize the Haganah's first armored unit, composed of a few old German
tanks from Czechoslovakia which had just been secretly unloaded.
In May, 1948, the Syrians laid siege to Degania, Dayan's birthplace,
and he asked permission to command the defending forces. After
beating back the Syrians in the north, he returned to the central
region, where he commanded the armored unit that spearheaded
the troops which took Ramlah and Lod. After this victory, Ben-
Gurion asked to see the young officer. That meeting marked the
beginning of a close friendship between the "Old Man" and Dayan,
which has persisted to this day. Ben-Gurion is the only human being
whom Dayan admires.

The last months of the War of Independence witnessed the beginning of Dayan's rapid rise in the Army. After a brief stint in the
Negev, he was shifted to Jerusalem and became district commander
of the capital. He represented Israel in armistice talks with the
Jordanians under UN Truce Supervision Organization Chief General William Riley. At that time Dayan met the commander of the
Arab-held Old City, Colonel Abdallah Tel, and the two officers
agreed to establish a direct phone link across the armistice lines—
the first "hot line" of its kind. For nineteen years "Dayan's line" was
the only direct phone contact between Israel and any Arab country.

Dayan was accused at that time by leftist circles in Israel of making
a secret agreement with the British-backed Jordanians not to attempt to occupy any territory held by Jordan in Palestine, and to
accept tacitly King Abdullah's decision to annex the West Bank to
his kingdom.

In the spring of 1949, Dayan participated in the four-month-long
negotiations with King Abdullah over an Israel-Jordan peace agree-

ment. The monarch's assassination put an end to the negotiations.

In the early 1950's, Dayan was an advocate of the hard line in the argument between Prime Minister Ben-Gurion and his Minister for Foreign Affairs, Moshe Sharett. Like most Army commanders, Dayan believed that only a determined attitude on the part of Israel's military forces would prevent the reorganization of Arab strength for a second round against Israel, and that only such a posture would assure Western support for Israel. Sharett believed that a flexible Israeli attitude and readiness to make concessions would induce the Arabs to make peace with the Jewish State.

The ensuing Israeli policy of retaliation against Arab terrorist attacks evoked strong international condemnation, particularly at the United Nations, whose attitude at that time was still taken very seriously in Israel. In December, 1953, Ben-Gurion resigned as Prime Minister and retired to the Negev desert settlement of Sde Boker, but not before recalling Dayan from studies in England and making him the new Chief of Staff. It did not take long for Dayan's firm hand to produce results in raising the fighting spirit of the Israeli forces. He stressed the principle of individual initiative and the expansion of the paratroop units as the striking force of the Forces. Dayan's overall approach to defense matters closely reflected Ben-Gurion's view and was shared by the new Defense Minister, the intellectual former Secretary-General of the Histadrut, Pinhas Lavon. However, Lavon's attempt to impose personal control over the Army command, which had become accustomed to considerable independence under Ben-Gurion, progressively worsened relations between Lavon and Dayan. It was during this time that the so-called "security mishap," the failure of an Israeli operation in Egypt, occurred. The public controversy over this affair ultimately led to Lavon's resignation and Ben-Gurion's return to the government as Minister of Defense.

Nineteen fifty-five was a year of reverses for Israel. The American-sponsored Baghdad Pact was organized but Israel was not asked to join, despite hopes that its military capabilities would make it a desirable partner. The Bandung Conference highlighted the rising international stature of Egypt's General Nasser while Israel was demonstratively ostracized by the organizers of the conference. The first Egyptian-Czech arms deal was signed and there was a marked upswing in Arab terrorist activities.

Israel responded with a number of severe retaliatory raids, and the chain of Arab attack, Israeli retaliation, Arab attack continued in 1956. In that year Israel initiated its "unwritten alliance" with France, which considered Cairo the main instigator of the Arab rebellion in Algeria. Dayan visited Paris several times, accompanied by Deputy Minister of Defense Shimon Peres, and French arms began to arrive in Israel. Nasser's decision to nationalize the Suez Canal heightened the sense of imminent threat to Israel and quickened the pace of international events. Plans for a joint British-French move against Egypt began to take shape and Dayan accompanied Ben-Gurion to the final conference near Paris at which the French assured Israel of air cover for its cities in case of Egyptian bombing attempts—Ben-Gurion's nightmare in those days. Returning to Tel Aviv, Ben-Gurion came down with influenza as the zero hour approached. Dayan came to his sickbed to obtain final approval for his plans. In his *Sinai Diary*, written ten years later, Dayan recorded that he did not share the excitement of his colleagues at headquarters because he had already made up his mind that "the hour has come. We are going to war. The arguments are over. There is no other way out." Dayan's main concern upon the outbreak of war was that Israel would be compelled to cease operations before attaining its two main objectives: to smash the Egyptian forces poised against it in Sinai and break the Egyptian blockade of the Gulf of Elath. During the first two days of fighting, he was constantly on the move between headquarters and the front lines, but on the third day he stayed at the front. He remarked later that he just could not go back and leave the fighting units.

Immediately after the shooting ended, Dayan concentrated on setting up the military government in the Gaza Strip and on promoting local elements who were ready to cooperate with the Israelis in normalizing day-to-day life in the area. In those early weeks in Gaza,

Dayan learned some of the lessons which stood him in good stead eleven years later, when he laid the foundations of Israel's relations with the Arab population in the territories occupied in the Six-Day War. One of his basic tenets was that a peaceful attitude on the part of the Arab population depended on the prolonged presence of Israeli forces and that this would also influence their attitude later if and when there would be a change in the nature of the Israeli presence. Dayan tried to convince Ben-Gurion not to give in to the heavy international (mainly American) pressure to evacuate Sinai and the Gaza Strip. When it became clear that Ben-Gurion was ready to retreat, Dayan urged him not to hand over the territories to the United Nations Emergency Forces but directly to the Egyptians, in exchange for whatever commitments could be obtained concerning freedom of navigation to Elath and tranquillity along the border. "The Arabs are our neighbors, not the United Nations," he maintained. This philosophy directed him again after 1967, when he opposed any intermediaries in the attempt to establish relations with the Egyptians.

The retreat from Sinai and Gaza was a bitter pill for Dayan. Yet he could also poke fun at it. In 1957, on his way back from an official visit in Burma, he decided to spend a day at the famous Taj Mahal in India. When he arrived at his hotel, he was told that all the rooms were occupied by the entourage of Harold Macmillan, who replaced Anthony Eden as Britain's Prime Minister after London's Suez débâcle. Dayan told the manager of the hotel, "Go and tell Mr. Macmillan that the man to whom he owes his job as Prime Minister is downstairs." Macmillan immediately vacated several rooms for Dayan.

In January, 1958, Dayan completed his tour of duty and resigned from the Army. He had been a member of the Mapai in his youth and expected Ben-Gurion to offer him a top spot on the party ticket in the 1959 elections. However, when Dayan told the "Old Man" that he planned to study at the Hebrew University, Ben-Gurion praised him for his thirst for knowledge. Dayan did not last long in the classroom. He decided to become active in the party even though he did not have the faintest encouragement from Ben-Gurion.

Party officials viewed matters differently. They considered him a threat to their own positions because they expected Ben-Gurion to push him ahead. These suspicions were shared by Mrs. Golda Meir, who had disliked the defense activities of Dayan's and Peres's crew from the time of her conflict with them while she was Minister for Foreign Affairs. She became a bitter political and personal opponent of Dayan in a feud which lasted over ten years. After the 1959 elections, in which Dayan was elected to the Knesset, Ben-Gurion appointed him to the Cabinet but gave him the relatively junior post of Minister of Agriculture. It was a compromise between the party veterans (whose unofficial grouping was known as "the bloc") and the original idea of giving Dayan a prominent portfolio.

As Minister of Agriculture, Dayan succeeded in eliminating small-scale dairy farming, especially in the vicinity of the cities, and streamlined the division of labor between his ministry and the Settlement Department of the Jewish Agency. But his plan to switch to new cash crops was frustrated by the resistance of the farmers. Dayan had to learn the hard way the difference between the Army, where orders are given and executed, and civilian life, where pressures and counter-pressures not always relevant to the substance of the issue determine policy.

In 1965, when Mapai was racked by the Lavon Affair, an outgrowth of Ben-Gurion's demand for a public investigation of former Defense Minister Lavon's role in the "security mishap" that had occurred earlier in Egypt, Dayan was in no hurry to take sides. He quit the Cabinet but joined Ben-Gurion in leaving Mapai only after much hesitation. Ultimately, however, he joined the new Rafi party and was elected on that list to the Knesset. He was not very active in parliamentary life or as a Rafi leader, for that matter. Instead, he traveled abroad. His series of articles from Vietnam was syndicated in American and European newspapers, and he finished writing his *Sinai Diary*. The book analyzes with clinical detachment not only the successes but also mistakes which unnecessarily cost soldiers' lives.

Golda Meir protested that Dayan's candidness was "spilling poison on he wounds of bereaved parents."

With the increasing frequency of Syrian attacks on the northern border, Dayan became convinced by 1966 that another war could not be avoided. His views, published in a series of articles in *Ha'aretz*, were in complete contrast to the dovish attitude both of that paper and of the Israeli public in general. The atmosphere changed completely in 1967 when the Egyptians blocked the Straits of Tiran. Within a few days, the public saw Dayan as the antithesis of Prime Minister Levi Eshkol and his vacillations, which immobilized the government just as the Egyptian threat was growing daily. As the crisis deepened, Eshkol gave Dayan permission to inspect the operational plans of the Army and visit units deployed in Sinai. His appearance among the troops boosted their morale, while his familiarity with the war plans speeded his takeover of command when, a week before the war, he became Minister of Defense. Dayan also authoritatively contradicted Ben-Gurion, who felt that Israel had missed the opportunity to hit the Egyptians, and therefore should accept the closure of the Straits until a new opportunity would arise.

In the last week before the war, public pressure grew for Eshkol to hand over the Defense portfolio to Dayan. Eshkol tried to compromise, asking Dayan to become Deputy Prime Minister and his military advisor. But Dayan insisted that he become Minister of Defense. Gradually the majority of Mapai leaders joined in the demand for Dayan's appointment, and when Eshkol was left with only Mrs. Meir's backing for his refusal, he yielded. With Dayan in the Cabinet, the on-again, off-again hesitations of the government ended. There was a firm majority in favor of battle and the Cabinet gave Eshkol and Dayan the joint authority to decide on the right moment.

After the lightning victory of the Six-Day War, a debate arose over how much of the success was due to Dayan personally. There were some, like Mrs. Meir, who felt that Dayan entered the picture when everything was already prepared, and that even without him victory would have been no less speedy. Others shared the opinion quoted in the *New York Times,* that "although Dayan did not build Israel's military machine, his 'hawkishness' was its moving force." The changes which Dayan is believed to have introduced in Israel's operational plans on the eve of the war were of political as much as military significance. Dayan shifted the main aim from taking territory and occupying strategic points to the encirclement and destruction of the largest possible number of Egyptian units.

Dayan was far from enthusiastic over the idea that the Israeli forces should go all the way to the Suez Canal. He was convinced that neither the Egyptians nor the Russians would tolerate such a situation for any length of time and would act jointly to remove Israel from the Canal. "How do we get off the scaffold?" he asked after Israeli troops took the entire East Bank of the Suez Canal. This philosophy lay at the root of his plans for a division of Sinai so that the Egyptians would obtain the western half of the peninsula, "which is most important to them so that they can control navigation in the Suez Canal," while Israel would retain control of the eastern half, including Sharm-el-Sheikh, to ensure freedom of navigation to Elath. This is the origin of Dayan's notion of an "interim settlement" between Israel and Egypt.

After June, 1967, Dayan lived under the specter of direct Soviet military intervention in the Arab-Israel conflict. Therefore, he ordered Israeli pilots to avoid any shootouts with Soviet fliers or attacks on Soviet bases in Egypt, even at the height of the Israel counter-offensive to Nasser's "War of Attrition." But Dayan opposed any idea of replacing the Bar-Lev Line along the Canal with a mobile defense, lest Israel's casualties grow. Instead, he approved the bombings-in-depth of Egypt. When it appeared that the Russians had advanced their anti-aircraft missiles virtually up to the Canal, thereby raising considerably the danger to Israeli aircraft, he accepted the American-initiated ceasefire in the summer of 1970.

The success of Dayan's policies in the occupied Arab territories is not disputed even by his critics and political opponents. The basic tenets of this policy are that the Arabs are not expected to like the

Israeli Military Government, but that they can and should live peacefully under it; and, secondly, that the Arabs in the territories should fear Israeli punishment for cooperating with terrorists more than they should fear the terrorists' violence for not cooperating with them.

On the one hand, Dayan instituted a system of passive and active antiterrorist measures, including demolition of the houses of those who sheltered terrorists; on the other hand, he introduced the policy of "open bridges" between the occupied West Bank and Jordan and, through it, to many of the Arab countries.

Goods and persons move freely in both directions across the Jordan River, permitting commercial contacts between Israel and the Arab world and a growing number of Arab tourists to Israel. In 1972 over 150,000 Arabs visited Israel under the Dayan-sponsored summer-visits scheme, designed for Arabs abroad who have families in the occupied territories. Dayan also gave a free hand to local authorities to conduct their own affairs and made a special effort to promote agriculture in the territories, which had lagged behind farming in Israel's Arab villages. His success can be measured by the gradual and almost complete elimination of terrorists' presence in the territories and by the heavy participation of the population in the 1972 municipal elections on the West Bank, despite threats from Arab terrorists against all candidates.

There is one aspect of Dayan's policy which is strongly disputed by his opponents, primarily the doves in the Labor party: the large-scale employment of Arabs from occupied territories in Israeli agriculture and industry. These critics, whose main spokesman is Finance Minister Pinhas Sapir, feel that Dayan's policy will lead to gradual de facto annexation of the territories—and ultimately to the emergence of an Arab majority in the Jewish State. Rather than face this, Sapir and his friends would give up the occupied territories.

When Golda Meir became Prime Minister after Levi Eshkol's sudden death, Moshe Dayan stayed on as Minister of Defense. Relations have gradually improved between them, turning into mutual admiration, mainly because they share a hawkish approach to most aspects of the Israel-Arab dispute. They found themselves on the same side of most arguments over security and foreign-policy matters. When Mrs. Meir on one occasion expressed support for Sapir's fears of the demographic consequences of Dayan's policies, Dayan publicly demanded that the Labor party executive debate his policies. The executive preferred to avoid the debate and Dayan's policies continued to be implemented.

Employment of a large number of Arabs from the occupied territories, as well as the concept of "open bridges," is part of Dayan's fundamental idea that the most important aspect of Israeli rule is to make Jews and Arabs aware that they can live peacefully side by side.

Moshe Dayan lives entirely in the present. He does not believe in historic precedents: every morning life starts anew for him. Recently he remarked to a well-known commentator: "The trouble with you is that you know too much history." He is not sensitive to what is said or written about his much-discussed private life. (In 1972, he was divorced by his wife, Ruth.) Neither does he mind criticism of his political views, of his unorthodox driving behavior or unconventional methods of collecting archaeological artifacts. The only sphere in which he is very sensitive to criticism is his ability as a military commander.

Archaeology—digging in the field and afterward gluing together broken pottery—is his favorite pastime. He usually works sitting on the floor in a special structure, half workshop, half museum, built in the yard of his Zahala home: "This is the time when I think and deliberate," he explains.

Food is a physical necessity, not a source of enjoyment, for Dayan. Steak with vegetable salad is a favorite meal. He likes fruit: a huge bowl of apples, oranges and other fruits in season is always on his office desk. He dresses in a casual manner, verging on sloppiness. Dayan usually wears an open-necked khaki shirt and khaki pants, topped in winter by an olive pullover or sports jacket and, outdoors, with an aviator's jacket. He looks as though he were still living up to the ideal of one of his youthful poems: "To wear sandals in summer, to crack nuts at leisure and walk with a dunam-sized patch on your trouser seat . . ."

Ultimately, the crucial question determining Dayan's chances for premiership may very well be connected with that naïve poem. Are there things that Dayan considers more important in life that being Golda Meir's successor—and, if so, what is he really willing to do to get the top post?

After Mrs. Meir's visit to the United States in the winter of 1973, Labor party leaders felt confident that she would agree to run again in the autumn elections, thus staving off the fight for succession for at least another year or two. With the elections safely behind them, the Labor party machine would feel less obliged to consider popularity an important factor in choosing a successor to Golda Meir.

Such a development, of course, would work against General Dayan and possibly in favor of his perennial rival, Yigal Allon. The latter could re-emerge as the joint candidate of the machine, the doves and even the Achdut Ha'avodah faction, which is generally hawkish but in which Allon is a central figure.

It has been Allon's fate from his early years to be dogged by Moshe Dayan. Indeed, one can hardly avoid comparing the two men, similar in age, careers and obvious ambition to become the next leader of Israel.

There are many similarities between the two:

They are of the same generation—Allon is three years younger than Dayan. Both were born in farming villages in Palestine and both still have close ties to the land. Dayan owns property in Nahalal; Allon is a member of Kibbutz Ginossar.

Both grew up in the Haganah and were the fair-haired boys of Yitzhak Sadeh, its founder. In World War II both young officers fought with the British against the Vichy forces in Syria.

Both have retired several times from political life and used their retirement for studying: Moshe Dayan before the War of Independence and again when he left the army; Allon in the early 1950's and again the the early 1960's.

Both have the reputation of people who can "talk to the Arabs" in whose vicinity they grew up. When he was Minister of Agriculture, Dayan brought irrigation to Arab villages; when he was Minister of Labor, Allon build roads to some of the remotest of those villages.

The fortunes of the two parted in 1949, when Allon in effect was removed from his post as commander of the Southern Command —and Ben-Gurion gave the job to Moshe Dayan. Yet, even earlier, there had emerged some of the striking differences between the two, not only of character but also in their views and actions.

In 1949, Dayan signed the armistice agreement with Jordan— while Allon claimed that Israel should and could have continued the fighting until it had completed the occupation of the entire West Bank.

Dayan makes decisions quickly, often impulsively. Allon tends to analyze situations and make more cautious decisions.

Dayan has no personal friends and does not have the reputation of being the type who would go out of his way to help one of his supporters. Allon makes friends easily and is often ready to help his acquaintances.

Yigal Allon was born in 1918 in Kfar Tabor to the Paikovitz family, one of the pioneers of Jewish settlement in Lower Galilee. He went to an agricultural school and helped his father in farming. He joined the Palmach in his early years and in 1936 became a member of Kibbutz Ginossar. Allon served in Orde Wingate's "special squads" and within eight years, from 1941 to 1948, he rose from the rank of private to that of general and commander of the Palmach. When, before the War of Independence, the Jewish Agency adopted the policy (known in Israeli history as "the season") of hunting down members of the rightist Irgun group, Allon openly voiced his opposition and withdrew temporarily from the Palmach.

In the War of Liberation he fought on practically all fronts: first in Galilee in the north, then in the central area, and finally in the south as commander of the units which took Beersheba, reached the Gulf of Aqaba at Elath, and occupied part of Northern Sinai. Ben-Gurion, under American pressure, refused to let Allon proceed further south for another four or five days, which, in his opinion, would have been sufficient to break the Egyptian army completely and thus compel Cairo to make peace with Israel.

Allon was relieved of the Southern Command while he was on an official visit to France. The fact that his replacement was Moshe Dayan probably marked the beginning of the rivalry between the two.

In the early 1950's Allon went to Oxford to study philosophy and history. He was befriended there by the noted military analyst B. H. Liddell-Hart, and together they tried to formulate theories of guerilla warfare. In 1953 when the Israeli left was rocked by the double crisis of the Prague trial of two Mapam (the left-of-center workers' party) leaders on charges of espionage and by the attempts of one of its leaders, Dr. Moshe Sneh (who later joined the Communist party), to move Mapam toward the more extreme left, Allon was urgently recalled from England. He was asked by the Kibbutz Hame'uchad, the parent organization of his kibbutz, to concentrate on the effort to prevent a split between moderates and leftists. These efforts failed and Allon returned to his studies. When he resumed his political activities, he was appointed secretary-general of Achdut Ha'avodah, a group composed of opponents of the leftist trend in Mapam. Allon traveled to India in an attempt to explain Israel's policies to Nehru and convince him to establish diplomatic relations between the two countries. In 1960 he went to England again, this time to take courses in Near East studies, but was again called home. In 1961 he became Minister of Labor.

In the Cabinet Allon took positions which were often disliked by the more doctrinaire elements of his party. For example, his Ministry presented legislation establishing special labor courts, and other laws obliging unions to give advance notice of strikes.

On the eve of the Six-Day War in 1967, when public pressure grew for the late Prime Minister Eshkol to hand over the Defense portfolio to Dayan, Achdut Ha'avodah (and also Dayan's opponents in Mapai) urged Eshkol to appoint Yigal Allon as Minister of Defense. But Eshkol vacillated and Allon was at that time in Leningrad, of all places, at the head of an Israeli delegation to an international conference on social security. His party colleague in the Cabinet,

Israel Galili, failed to alert him to return immediately. When Allon returned, he assumed that he would be appointed Defense Minister and even went to Army GHQ to be briefed by top officers. By then, however, the demand for Dayan's appointment had taken on avalanche proportions, and when Eshkol finally yielded, the post went to Dayan. Allon missed the opportunity—some think the opportunity of his life—to assure his candidacy for premiership in the future. Typically he took this reverse quietly.

After the June, 1967, victory, Allon was the first Cabinet member who formulated a proposal for a territorial settlement which could serve as the basis for a peace agreement with Jordan. The so-called Allon plan in essence provides that the occupied areas densely populated by Arabs will be handed back to Jordan while Israel will keep a narrow strip along the Jordan River, where it can establish paramilitary farming settlements.

In 1967 many considered this too hawkish; today the Allon plan is considered by many to be too generous to Jordan.

In the summer of 1968 the late Levi Eshkol partially compensated Allon for what had happened in June, 1967: he was appointed Deputy Prime Minister. In the same year he became the first Israeli Cabinet member to build his official residence in the formerly Arab-occupied Old City of Jerusalem. He also switched his portfolio from Labor to Education, but his relations with Eshkol cooled when Allon's hopes of sharing part of the Prime Minister's real power did not materialize. Another setback to his hope of establishing himself as the next Prime Minister came when he failed to gain the support of Finance Minister Pinhas Sapir (considered one of the "kingmakers")—possibly because Sapir began to see himself as a potential candidate.

There was some redivision of authority when Mrs. Meir succeeded the late Levi Eshkol: she handed over to Allon some of her official duties, particularly as ex-officio chairman of various ministerial committees. He also became more active in matters of foreign policy, and it was widely reported that in 1970 he met secretly several times with King Hussein of Jordan in an effort to find common ground for peace negotiations. His opponents charge, however, that he is much more interested in politics than in his job as Minister of Education, in which post he has been the recurring target of numerous teachers' strikes. Allon found himself between two opposing pressures: on the one hand, demands for a larger education budget, and, on the other, tightly held purse strings in Finance Minister Sapir's hands.

Allon does not like extreme decisions. He prefers agreed solutions, even if they involve compromise. By nature he is a man of collective deliberations and collective decisions. He enjoys abstract debates and has a flair for summing up conclusions clearly and leaving the working-out of details to his subordinates.

He makes a point of attending all family celebrations of friends and can politely listen for hours to long discussions—without showing his lack of interest. He is a careful dresser but likes to appear in open-necked shirts. After official ceremonies he takes off his necktie almost demonstratively—a familiar mannerism among Achdut Ha'avodah leaders. Allon loves good food and knows exactly what wine goes with which dish. He likes the theater and is an avid concert goer.

In 1972 Allon took clearly dovish positions on many current security issues. Political observers interpreted this as yet another indication that, no matter what others thought, Allon still considered himself in the running for the premiership and wanted to consolidate his position among all elements opposing Dayan's hawkish policies.

4

The Queen's Court

PINHAS SAPIR is not only the ranking member of the top power elite of Israel and a potential candidate for the premiership: he is also the man with the most direct personal influence on people, business, the party machine and the government leadership of any person in Israel, except Mrs. Meir. He is not a charismatic personality and does not even fit the image of a "strong man." Possibly without realizing it, he is probably the closest to an American political boss, whose power stems from the ability to make other people dependent on him and his decisions.

Sapir—and only Sapir—could soften up the chairman of the Manufacturers' Association, Mark Mosevics, during a lengthy strike at the Elite Company, because Mosevics remembered how often Sapir had helped him out in the past. Sapir is the one who can assure the Labor party the votes of new immigrant towns and settlements, to which he steered new factories giving employment, or where he made one of his trusted followers secretary of the labor council, or where he found money for a new school. Members of opposition parties know that they can ask Sapir for a favor; Religious party functionaries know that Sapir will always turn up funds for a new synagogue.

He becomes furious when accused of "distributing public money" or doing favors to "buy" this or that politician or business-man. He is always ready to prove that he has not given anybody something not due to him. Indeed, his power is based on doing anything that the government has not decided on. His power comes from his direct personal involvement in dozens of affairs, big and small alike. Like an American political boss, Sapir too has the talent of creating the impression that he and only he can decide who will get a certain favor from the government and who will not, even when it is clear to everyone that the law, regulations, custom or written contracts make it clear in any case what each party's right is in the matter.

The amassing of political power based on personal involvement is not the result of a carefully planned strategy on Sapir's part. Sapir gets involved in things simply because he is genuinely convinced that only his intervention can get things moving. Like many people who are new experts in administration, Sapir has a deep-seated suspicion of delegating authority. He is never sure that things that others are asked to do will indeed be done. Endowed with almost unlimited stamina, which leaves many of his younger assistants ex-hausted each afternoon, Sapir can work longer hours than practi-cally anybody in the Israeli establishment. He certainly remembers by heart more figures than anybody else.

Sapir likes to meet people and listen to them. He loves to visit factories and development areas and devote two days a week on the average to "seeing with [his] own eyes" what is happening in the economy. These visits serve him both as an opportunity to establish personal contact with local influentials and also to recharge the batteries. Sapir, like the late Levi Eshkol, whom he resembles in many respects, is much more impressed by on-the-spot visits than by any detailed economic analysis.

His philosophy is that the important things are the buildings and the machines in them and not the entrepreneurs and their motiva-tions. This led him to support some very dubious businessmen and questionable ventures. When, years later, economists or newsmen add up the millions in government money poured into some of these enterprises, Sapir says, "So what? The plant is working, it is selling for export. So it costs some money!" And he often adds, "This is the type of investment we get. What can I do?"

Although some people claim that Sapir is a power-hunting politician, in fact his personality and his political career indicate much more complex motivations. When Ben-Gurion offered Sapir the portfolio of Trade and Industry after the 1955 elections, Sapir was very far from political life: he was not a member of the Knesset or active in any party post. Chronologically he belongs to the late Third Aliyah, that came from Poland in the 1920's, to which many of the older Israeli leadership belonged. Yet Sapir reached the upper levels of government only at the end of the first decade of Israel's independence. Until then he was known in government circles as an effective executive who could cope with complicated situations, but he was not part of the decision-making elite and remained almost entirely unknown to the public.

Sapir was born in 1908 in the small town of Sowalki in Poland. He received a religious education and went to an Orthodox high school in Warsaw. The poverty of his childhood left a deep impression on him and he frequently recalls that during World War I people in Sowalki actually had to make their clothes from old sacks. In Warsaw he joined the Zionist youth movement Hechalutz, and became one of those responsible for finances and agricultural education in the movement. He learned two things in that period: bookkeeping, and how to spend money when you don't have it. Both talents served him well when he came to Palestine and had to find funds for settlement and development projects.

He came to Palestine in 1929 and worked as a citrus picker. In the early thirties when Jewish labor unions began to fight the employment of unorganized Arab workers in Jewish citrus orchards, Sapir was among the organizers of the first picket line. For this he was sentenced to four years in prison. After he came out of jail he returned to Kfar Saba, where he organized the local bank, a housing company and the new waterworks, and for many years was one of the members of the local town council. His national career began in 1937 when Levi Eshkol put him on the board of Mekorot, the water and irrigation company serving the Jewish settlements in Palestine. Sapir continued to live in Kfar Saba, which, as his headquarters, has become a place familiar to many Israelis from numerous newspaper stories as the place where Sapir cooks up deals and spends millions before his early-morning breakfast.

Sapir organized the construction of the first pipeline that brought water to the Jewish settlements in the Negev. The development of their agriculture, based on irrigation, contributed significantly to the fact that the Negev became part of Israel in 1948. His work brought him to the attention of Ben-Gurion, who sent him to Europe as one of the illegal-arms-purchase agents. Sapir made his headquarters in Geneva and assembled around him a number of young Israeli students learning economics at Swiss universities, some of whom later became officials of the Israeli Ministry of Finance. Here again Sapir's bookkeeping talents came to the fore: buying arms in postwar Europe involved not only huge sums but also many shadowy characters and often competing claims for payment on the same delivery.

Sapir returned to Israel in October, 1949, and was appointed Director-General of the Ministry of Defense. Later he became head of the development division of the Ministry of Agriculture and was then shifted to the post of Director-General of the Ministry of Finance. The reorganization of the Ministry along the lines which guide its activities to this day is the work of Pinhas Sapir. He established a special directorate for fuel affairs, set up administrative procedures for all transactions in foreign currencies and established the departmental framework for government support of agricultural and industrial projects. These improvements created a system where, in many cases, there had been only ad hoc arrangements. They also created the basis for the government's overwhelming direct influence in practically every sphere of the private and public economy.

Sapir's work at the Ministry of Finance brought him to wider public attention for the first time. He was described as a powerhouse capable of staying at his desk for eighteen hours and meeting as many as forty people a day. His success in the Ministry of Finance brought him his first Cabinet post, as Minister of Commerce and Industry in 1955. The first two years in his new job were a period of frantic activity. It was a time when the country had to absorb hundreds of thousands of new immigrants quickly and agriculture was unable to provide jobs for most of them. New immigrant towns and settlements rose like mushrooms all over Israel and the only way to provide employment for the newcomers was to build factories in the new townships. Sapir went about this task with his unbounded energy and preference for action over deliberation.

It was at this time that the new concept of "investment per employee" became supreme and Sapir soon discovered that the cheapest investment was in textile plants. And so textile mills were built in rapid succession in Bet Sh'ean, Nazareth, Beersheba, Ofakim and Dimona—places which were not on the map ten years earlier. Sapir soon became convinced that neither the government nor the existing private entrepreneurs in the country could provide the funds or the initiative for such rapid industrial expansion. Therefore he enticed financiers from abroad and from Israel into joint ventures with the government—a system that is characteristic of Israeli economy to this very day. Here were the origins of the "big families" of the Israel economy, the large investment and industrial concerns, each of which encompasses all branches of a specific sector and operates with a mixture of foreign investment and cheap government loans approved by Sapir. The Minister also discovered quite early that these big concerns represent an important source of power that can be utilized in other projects—economic or political.

Unlike a party boss, Sapir does not make party membership or adherence a condition for his support in new business ventures. The important thing for him is his feeling that the man proposing the deal is capable of establishing the project. He also makes it a point to use existing concerns as a recruiting ground for leadership in new ventures. He realizes that, with the close links between the Minister of Finance and the concerns—even if controlled by private ownership—they cannot refuse his requests, even if they do not think a new venture proposed by Sapir will be profitable. Sapir, on the other hand, makes sure that those who "cooperate" get their compensation in one way or another—in the form of government loans or tariff protection, for example.

For a long time Sapir promoted the system of joint partnership by several concerns in any new venture. This method served both to distribute the risks and to enhance his influence, because the government usually had only a minor partnership in the new venture but was in a much stronger position if it had several partners rather than one big one. His vote could therefore tip the scales, making his advice weightier than that of the companies' directors.

When Ben-Gurion retired in 1963 and Eshkol became Prime Minister, Sapir took over the Finance portfolio in addition to that of Commerce and Industry. In 1968 he surprised everybody when he gave up his portfolios in order to devote most of his time to the Labor party: he became its secretary-general but remained a member of the Cabinet as a Minister without Portfolio. In his new task he made full use of the numerous personal contacts and innumerable personal favors he had done for party functionaries all over the country. It was probably no coincidence that at the 1969 Labor party convention, Sapir's people took over most of the key posts in the party machine. When people talk today about the levers which Sapir can use, if he wants to, to help and perhaps determine the chances of any potential candidate for the premiership, they mean the power created for himself during his term as secretary-general of the party.

But his influence in the party and its network of local branches did not end when he left the secretariat and returned to government. Nor was it diminished when he found himself in the minority on crucial questions of government policy toward the Arabs after the Six-Day War. Sapir, opposed to Golda Meir, Moshe Dayan and Israel Galili, believes that most of the territories occupied in 1967 should be given back to the Arabs. He holds this view not because of concern for the international implications of holding occupied territories: he simply prefers a smaller Israel with an overwhelming Jewish majority to a big Israel with a large Arab minority.

Sapir himself is in the minority in the Cabinet on the question of economic integration between Israel and the occupied territories. He wants to keep the number of Arab workers coming from the territories down in order to keep Israel's dependence on Arab labor to a minimum. He also wants to restrict the volume of Israeli investments in the territories. Apparently Sapir is not concerned with the possibility that his identification with the doves will lose him popularity, just as he did not worry over his image as the tax collector par excellence who became almost a folkloric figure in Israel. He does not despise popularity. But he knows that popularity as such does not represent power.

Sapir is a big, heavily-built person. Repeated attempts to keep to a strict diet represent some of the more obvious defeats of his career. His shining big bald head and his heavy walk add to his powerful appearance. His dawn-to-after-midnight schedule leaves little time for books. He goes to the theater "when they take me there" and he sometimes offends people by falling asleep, out of sheer exhaustion, during their speeches. He is not a brilliant orator but he is extremely successful in his fund-raising appearances abroad, as well as in his campaigns to get new foreign investments for Israel. For many middle-aged American Jewish millionaires, he is the equivalent of the self-made man. Since the Six-Day War Sapir has "educated" American Jews to contribute sums they would not have dreamed of giving only a few years earlier.

Sapir insists firmly that he has reached the end of his political career: he wants neither to be Prime Minister nor to continue as Minister of Finance. Not everybody in Israel is ready to believe that he will stick to this decision. In political circles Sapir is still considered one of the potential front runners to succeed Mrs. Meir. The more distant the threat of renewed warfare between Israel and her neighbors, the more economic issues come to the fore and the better are his chances.

It is said that after one of the more severe censures of Israel at the United Nations, after its retaliatory raid against the Arab village of Kibya in 1953, Abba Eban, then Israel's chief delegate at the United Nations, asked David Ben-Gurion whether the raid was really necessary. The "Old Man" replied with a smile, "I had some doubts myself. But when I read the text of your speech at the United Nations I became convinced that it was so."

This story, even if apocryphal, demonstrates three fundamental elements of the public image of Israel's present Minister for Foreign Affairs.

He is, first of all, the voice and spokesman of Israel to the nations of the world.

The most dramatic period in his career was his service as Israel's chief delegate to the United Nations when the world still took the United Nations rather seriously. Eban could utilize there to the full his exquisite knowledge of English and his great parliamentary skills.

His main strength, and his main claim to fame, comes from his oratory.

His big head, framed by dark-rimmed glasses, is the third most familiar Israeli visage in world caricature, next only to that of Golda Meir and eye-patched General Dayan. His fast walk belies the heavy impression created by his bulky frame, and he almost dashes up to the UN rostrum when his turn comes to speak. Eban keeps to a strict diet and tries to stay away from candy, which he likes very much. In his free time he plays golf either at Caesarea or, whenever he has an opportunity to do so, abroad.

An honest face, quick-wittedness and the gift of articulate expression were qualities of Abba (Aubrey) Eban from his early youth. He was born in 1915 in South Africa but moved to Britain in his childhood and studied in London and Cambridge, where he became active in the Zionist movement. In 1938 he completed his studies with distinction in classical languages and in Near Eastern languages (Hebrew, Persian, Arabic and Aramaic). At the age of twenty-three he was lecturer in Near East languages at Pembroke

College, Cambridge. He was also active in the Labor party and became chairman of its Cambridge University branch.

It was as a young lecturer that Eban met the late Dr. Chaim Weizmann, who was impressed by the erudite young man and made him his secretary.

On the eve of World War II Eban enlisted with the British Army and served as an intelligence officer in Cairo, where he met his future wife, Susan (Suzie), daughter of the well-to-do Ambache family. (Her sister, Ora, is married to General Haim Herzog, former head of Army Intelligence and former military attaché in Washington.)

In 1942 Major Eban was sent to Jerusalem to recruit Jewish volunteers for special tasks with the British Army and there established close links with the Jewish Agency and the Haganah, from which most of his volunteers came. In 1944 he was appointed lecturer at the Near East Army College of the Allied Forces, located in Jerusalem. After the war he decided to stay in Jerusalem and join the political department of the Jewish Agency.

Eban's diplomatic career started in 1947. He was a member of the Jewish Agency delegation to the UN General Assembly and worked on the drafting of the memoranda in support of the division of Palestine and the establishment of the Jewish State. His first public speech at the UN in May, 1948, was aimed against the United States: he attacked the American proposal to replace partition by a trusteeship regime. When Israel was accepted as a member of the United Nations, thirty-four-year-old Abba Eban became the youngest head of delegation there.

His speeches, his Churchillian English and his witty comments to journalists contributed greatly to increasing Israel's prestige in American public opinion and particularly among the Jews of America, who were especially influenced by his command of the English language; for many of the older generation, fluency in English was one goal they never achieved in America. He also became respected and popular among his UN colleagues and was elected Vice-President of the General Assembly in 1953, the highest office Israel ever managed to attain at the United Nations, which—at least on matters involving the Middle East—has since become dominated by the Arabs and the Communists.

In 1950 Eban was appointed Israel Ambassador to Washington, but continued to serve also as head of the Israel delegation to the UN. Dividing his time between Washington and New York, in the ten years of his tour of duty in Washington, he became the most influential figure in Israel's relations with its two most important partners: the United States and American Jewry. He laid the foundations for Israel-American aid under the Truman administration and for nuclear and military assistance during the Eisenhower administration. He traveled hundreds of thousands of miles across America to appear before organizations, conventions and colleges, and was unquestionably the most sought-after foreign speaker in America. He was especially liked by university audiences, to whom he managed to present his political message in the form of scientific lectures. By the end of his assignment in Washington in 1959, he had received honorary doctorates at several dozen American universities.

Back in Israel Eban was in a peculiar position. On the one hand his fame in America preceded him to Israel, where many shared American Jewry's admiration for him; on the other hand, he was considered too far removed from the problems and concerns of day-to-day life in the country. This feeling was not helped by his appointment as president of the Weizmann Institute in Rehovoth, an institution which was considered almost foreign by many Israelis because of the high standard of living and isolation of its staff from Israeli life.

Eban threw all his energies into the 1959 election campaign as one of the top candidates of Mapai; to the surprise of many he turned out to be one of the party's biggest crowd getters. At first he seemed to be somewhat ill-at-ease dashing around with an open-necked shirt, but even his opponents did not question that he secured quite a number of votes for the Labor ticket, especially among intellectuals. After the election he became Minister without

Portfolio in Ben-Gurion's Cabinet. Ben-Gurion had an ambivalent attitude to Eban: appreciation for his knowledge of facts but skepticism on his basic approach to issues; appreciation of his professional qualities, especially the ability to muster convincing arguments for Israel's cause, but also a bemused deprecation of his flowery style of speech, which never lost its slight British accent. Yet the Mapai leadership always agreed: you can make jokes about Eban but you cannot leave him out of the Cabinet.

When the late Zalman Aranne retired in 1960, Eban was appointed Minister of Education. In his new job he devoted special attention to problems of high school and university education but was also the originator of the "extended school day" providing additional afternoon classes at elementary schools for new immigrant children.

When the split occurred in the Labor party over the Lavon Affair (an outgrowth of Ben-Gurion's demand for an investigation of a security mishap when the Ministry of Defense was headed by Pinhas Lavon), most of the dissidents in the Labor party assumed that Eban would join them and follow Ben-Gurion out of the party. But he stayed on the side of the late Levi Eshkol and in 1963 was appointed Deputy Prime Minister.

In the 1964 elections Eban was in charge of the publicity campaign of Mapai. To the surprise of many of his colleagues, it became apparent that he was still one of the most sought-after campaign speakers. After the elections Golda Meir retired and Eban replaced her as Minister for Foreign Affairs. However, though in this position he was in his element, he did not enjoy the same prestige and influence in the government that Mrs. Meir had. During his term of office two shifts in Israel foreign policy developed: increased orientation toward America, instead of the earlier West European orientation (both politically and as a source of arms supply); and a slowdown in the earlier rapid expansion of Israel's presence in Africa.

As Foreign Minister, Eban makes excellent use of his talent to read lengthy reports quickly, summarize their essence and locate those points immediately which can be used in support of Israel's

arguments. He has found time to write books, first *My People* and
then *My Country,* both of which became immediate best sellers. (All
in all Eban has written about twelve books, including a novel, a
biography of the late Dr. Chaim Weizmann, as well as several volumes on international politics and the culture and society of the
Middle East.)

The weeks preceding the 1967 war are the most controversial
period in Eban's career. He was among those who opposed General
Dayan's co-option into the Cabinet. When French President de
Gaulle told him, "Don't be the first to start the war," Eban still
believed that he had "found understanding" on the General's part
for Israel's position. In his meetings in Washington he compelled
the State Department to acknowledge the existence in the White
House files of a 1957 undertaking to ensure freedom of navigation
in the Straits of Tiran; but his report that the United States was
planning to organize an international armada to force the blockade
was interpreted in Jerusalem as a veiled request to postpone Israel
military action against the massing Egyptian troops in Sinai.

After Israel's victory Eban was his brilliant self at the United
Nations. He led the effort to combat any resolution that would
demand unconditional Israeli withdrawal, such as was adopted after
the 1956 Sinai Campaign. His popularity at home was at a peak:
public-opinion polls indicated that 82 percent wanted him to continue as Foreign Minister, compared to only 47 percent who wanted
the late Levi Eshkol to continue as Prime Minister.

When Golda Meir succeeded Eshkol as Prime Minister, there
occurred a certain diminution in the position of the Foreign Minister: Mrs. Meir, who had held the post in the past, considers herself
an expert on foreign policy and makes decisions on matters which
the late Levi Eshkol left to his Foreign Minister to decide. Eban's
position was hurt also when the new Ambassador to Washington,
former Chief of Staff General Yitzhak Rabin, began to bypass the
Foreign Ministry demonstratively and send his reports directly to
Mrs. Meir—who did not call the Ambassador to order. Eban's dovish views put him in opposition to the more hawkish members of the
Cabinet, who failed to support him in his dispute with Rabin.

The flexible wording of drafts prepared by Eban made it possible for Swedish Ambassador to Moscow Dr. Gunnar Jarring to continue his mission as representative of the UN Secretary-General in the Middle East, at a time when an admission of failure in negotiations could have brought out considerable American pressure on Israel. Initially Eban was in a minority in the Cabinet when he claimed that Israel could not avoid using the term "withdrawal" in defining its attitude; he also proved correct in his claim that Washington fully supported Israel despite putting some pressure on it; and he also was right when he maintained that the deep-penetration air raids in Egypt during the War of Attrition (1969–70) would ultimately bring about a confrontation between Israeli and Soviet pilots. On the other hand, he was proved wrong in his estimate that unless Israel became more flexible in its conditions for a settlement, the Soviet involvement on Egypt's side would become increasingly deeper.

Eban was greatly embarrassed in the spring of 1971 when he concluded a tour of African countries with a statement that his hosts had promised not to support anti-Israel resolutions; yet a week later the Organization of African States adopted its most virulently anti-Israel declaration. His embarrassment was not helped when South Africa, Israel's supporter at international forums, became furious over a Foreign Ministry decision to contribute to the "Liberation Fund" of the Organization of African States; to add insult to injury, the organization, under Arab pressure, rejected the Israeli contribution—decided upon in Jerusalem, as it turned out, without Mr. Eban's prior knowledge. Eban's bad publicity in Israel continued when he was quoted as having said in a New York television interview that he was not interested in additional trials of Nazi war criminals. He was defended by the noted author Elie Wiesel, but the case was slow to die down and hurt Eban's image.

Eban's critics claim that he is not willing to fight for his views or for his Ministry in interdepartmental squabbles, and that he, moreover, greatly underestimates his chances of success in such confrontations. They recall that in the only major instance when Eban stood firm, opposing an attempt to take away the overseas information services for his Ministry, Mrs. Meir gave in and Eban, who threatened to resign, got his way. Eban also opposed Mrs. Meir's intention to appoint her former political secretary and later political adviser, Simha Dinitz, as the new Ambassador to Washington but withdrew his objections without a real fight. There were rumors that his decision not to fight Mrs. Meir was connected with speculation at that time that Eban might become a compromise candidate for premiership, should Mrs. Meir retire and a deadlock develop between General Dayan and a candidate of the Labor party machine.

Eban is more popular among Jews abroad than in Israel. Again, his popularity with the Israeli public is greater than among the Labor party leadership. Like Dayan or Yigal Allon, Eban too has some firm opponents in the top echelons of Israel's political hierarchy. But, unlike Dayan and Allon, Eban has very few supporters who would emerge in an all-out fight on his behalf.

Israel Galili, the senior member of Golda Meir's closest circle of advisors, is actually younger by three years than Pinhas Sapir. Yet, according to his image (and his looks) he is at least half a generation older. From Moshe Dayan, who is only five years younger, Galili is separated by at least a whole generation. The fact that Galili was born in Russia (in 1911) and came to Palestine shortly before World War I certainly contributes to his "old" image; but the primary reason lies in his character and outlook, which bracket him with the older generation.

This image would certainly hurt Israel Galili if he were running for any elective office in Israel's hierarchy. Rather than influence events directly, Galili likes to influence people who influence things. He is believed to be Mrs. Meir's closest confidant (some call him "Golda's guru"); he likes to be the *éminence grise* behind the scenes rather than be in charge of a ministry and bear parliamentary responsibility for it. He has made into a fine art the distinction between influence because of power and power because of influence —and has chosen the latter ever since he began his political career, first in the leftist Mapam workers' party, then in the further right Achdut Ha'avodah faction and finally in the Labor party.

Before the establishment of the State, Galili was for a time Chief of Staff of the Haganah and played a central role in the establishment of its elite unit, the Palmach. During the War of Independence he was number-two man in the Ministry of Defense headed by Ben-Gurion, but suddenly was dismissed by Ben-Gurion (probably as part of the "Old Man's" consolidation of power against the leftist workers' party). From that time, for sixteen years Galili avoided accepting any public office in government or in party life.

His political views changed considerably in the early fifties. In 1950 when the North invaded the South in Korea Galili denounced America's aid to the South as "foreign intervention." But in 1952, while still a member of the leftist Mapam party, he opposed his party's justification of the Prague show trials. In 1953 he was among the first, not only in his party but in the country in general, who urged Israel to adopt a policy of "active defense" in retaliation to growing armed Arab infiltration.

In 1954 Mapam split because part of its leadership opposed the continued leftward trend of Meir Ya'ari, Ya'akov Hazan and the late Dr. Moshe Sneh. The group re-established Achdut Ha'avodah (which some years before had merged into Mapam) and Galili was among those who joined it.

From 1961 Galili worked determinedly to extricate his faction from its position as "somewhere between Mapam and Mapai." Finally in 1965 Galili succeeded in formulating a joint program with Mapai, and since then has promoted the interests of Achdut Ha'avodah members in the new partnership. He gained the nickname of "the big elbow of the little partner" from some Labor party officials who were less than enthusiastic about his efforts.

In 1964 Galili re-emerged from the shadows, joining the Cabinet as Minister without Portfolio. Two years later, already a close associate of the late Prime Minister Eshkol, he was put in charge of all government information services. Yet he declined a formal appointment as Minister of Information so that parliamentary responsibility was not his but the Prime Minister's. His new role quickly became controversial not only among members of the opposition but also among many Mapai leaders who charged that Galili was trying to put his people from Achdut Ha'avodah into key posts in the government mass media. Especially controversial was his role as the de facto boss of the broadcasting services, where his entry marked the beginning of constant turmoil, resignations and disorders that have not ended to this very day.

Domestic information services, including the government press bureau, also under Galili's direction, were constantly deteriorating until they almost completely collapsed on the eve of the Six-Day War. His opponents charged that his concentration on his running fight against Ben-Gurion's and Dayan's Rafi party, even at the height of the crisis, instead of being an all-out effort to boost the self-confidence of the Israelis, backfired on Galili: a nervous and frustrated public compelled Eshkol a few days before the war to establish the broad National Coalition Government in which Moshe Dayan became Minister of Defense.

Toward the end of 1967 Galili became uninterested in the broadcasting and information services and concentrated his efforts on arranging a merger between Achdut Ha'avodah and Mapai. At the same time he took it upon himself to become the official spokesman not only of the Cabinet but also of Israel; he made public statements on some of the most sensitive issues even before the Cabinet decided its official position.

In 1969 Galili was in conflict with both Foreign Minister Eban and the entire Israel press. Eban fought successfully against what he saw as Galili's attempt to encroach upon the Foreign Ministry's responsibility for Israeli information abroad, while the press unanimously attacked him for telling the broadcasting services not to broadcast "minor border incidents" and to play down "unpleasant" operations of the Israel Army.

In 1970 Mrs. Meir wanted him to become Minister of Labor but Galili refused. He knew from experience that a Minister without Portfolio can be much more influential than a Cabinet member who has to devote his time and energy to the running of a ministry. Indeed, Galili today is free to serve as chairman of some of the more

important Cabinet subcommittees, such as the permanent committee that approves any Israeli settlement in the occupied territories
or the 1972 ad hoc committee which recommended what cuts could
be made in General Dayan's Ministry budget. Lack of departmental
responsibility also helps Galili keep aloof from interdepartmental
conflicts and controversy.

Mrs. Meir calls him "the honest man" or "a moral man," and this
indicates at least one source of his great influence. His piercing eyes
and flowing white hair give him the image of a half-prophet, half-
revolutionary. He avoids attending social functions as far as possible, and when he does come to a dinner or a cocktail party he wears
an open-necked white shirt and a rather old-fashioned suit. He likes
to come to work dressed in a dark blue shirt, which was the virtual
uniform of the labor movement in the past.

Galili's influence grew considerably after Mrs. Meir became Prime
Minister. He used to be in close touch with her during her retirement and he probably spends more time with Mrs. Meir than any
other Israeli politician. After most of the other "regulars" of "Golda's Kitchen" leave, Galili usually stays behind to sum up whatever
decisions are made.

Golda Meir considers him the intellectual among her close circle
of associates. His preference for behind-the-scenes influence rather
than formal power lends him an aura of unselfishness and lack of
personal ambition. He is gifted with great personal tact, which also
helps him to bridge conflicting views and positions in politics and
in the Cabinet. Golda often asks him to draft in precise terms various decisions which in their original form were intentionally left
somewhat vague to assure their unanimous approval. Occasionally
Mrs. Meir asks Galili, instead of the Foreign Minister, to draft an
especially important cable summarizing a government decision for
Israel ambassadors abroad.

Galili's behind-the-scenes influence is also served by the widely-
held belief that he will have a determining say in Achdut Ha'avodah
as to whom that faction will support for premiership when Mrs. Meir
retires. And nobody is prepared to swear that his support will go to

Yigal Allon, his former colleague in Achdut Ha'avodah.

The post of Director-General of the Ministry of Defense, which was held briefly in 1948 by Galili, served as a stepping stone in the career of several Israeli leaders. Each of them was influenced by the problems faced in the job but, even more, each of them molded the job in his own image. Galili saw it as a political role and did not influence the day-to-day operations of the Ministry. Pinhas Sapir, a financial and economic expert, left his mark in setting the standards for financial management of the Ministry. But there is no question that the man who left the deepest mark on the shape of the Ministry of Defense was Shimon Peres.

Epithets like "the implementer," "technocrat No. 1" and "preacher of scientification" were attached to Peres both as compliments and as criticisms throughout his ten years of service in the Defense Ministry. His friends credit him with making the research and development needed for military production into the major lever for the modernization of Israel's civilian industry. His detractors charge him with setting up Israel's "military-industrial complex" and sinking billions of taxpayers' money into it.

Above all, Shimon Peres played a key role in making the Ministry of Defense a decisive element in Israel's foreign policy for almost a decade. The roots of Israel's unofficial alliance with France lie in the war in Algeria; but it was Shimon Peres who translated this friendship into the language of supplies, armaments, intelligence and coordination which made the 1956 Sinai Campaign possible.

Shimon Peres (Perski) was born in the small town of Wishniawa in Poland in 1923, the son of a well-to-do grain and timber merchant. The family came to Palestine in 1934 and Shimon later joined Kibbutz Alumot, whose secretary he became. His political career started at the age of eighteen, when he was appointed coordinator in northern Palestine of the "working youth" movement clubs. He rose in the ranks despite the fact that he was the only functionary in the movement who did not belong to what later became the Achdut Ha'avodah faction in the Labor party. When the split in the party took place, Peres succeeded in keeping the youth movement with the Labor party and out of the hands of Achdut Ha'avodah.

Shimon Peres first appeared in the Ministry of Defense as one of the young assistants of the late Levi Eshkol, when he was Director-General of the Ministry. Here he met David Ben-Gurion, who was then the Minister of Defense (in addition to being Prime Minister) and the "Old Man" fully approved Eshkol's decision to send the twenty-seven-year-old "boy" to the United States as head of Israel's supply mission. From these two men, says Peres, he learned two priceless pieces of wisdom: from Eshkol how to distinguish between daring and adventurism; from Ben-Gurion that "what is important is what you do and not what you say." When he returned from the United States in 1952, Peres was appointed Director-General of the Ministry of Defense. He was not yet thirty when he was put in charge of a huge and growing portion of Israel's government budget and thereby became one of the most important figures in determining the direction of Israel's industrial growth.

Peres stressed the expansion of military industries and constant sophistication of their methods and products. He fostered the establishment of joint ventures between the government and private investors especially in the metal and electronics industries, in order to create a domestic supply base for Israel's defense establishment. At the same time he looked for new sources of items that could not yet be produced in Israel. In 1954, when Pinhas Lavon took over for a period as Minister of Defense from Ben-Gurion, who was in temporary retirement, Peres signed the first agreement for the supply of tanks from France. This was the first major Israeli-French arms deal. Lavon wanted to cancel it, and some political observers see this conflict as the first link in the chain of conflict between Peres and Lavon which ultimately culminated in the Lavon Affair.

Following the 1955 Egyptian-Czech arms deal the Prime Minister at that time, Moshe Sharett, rushed to Washington and Ottawa to obtain weapons. Peres, at the same time, began to build up his personal contacts in France, especially among people who had a say in the French military establishment. When Ben-Gurion returned to the premiership, the focus of Israel's diplomatic and arms-supply effort was turned to France. Peres became the chief matchmaker and was on the move between Jerusalem and Paris throughout most of 1956. His activities were resented by the then Foreign Minister, Golda Meir, whose Ambassador in Paris (Ya'akov Tsur) was left out of the picture. Peres was at Ben-Gurion's side at the secret meeting in France where the final details were arranged for the impending Sinai Campaign. For his efforts Peres was decorated with the Order of the Legion of Honor.

Peres was elected to the Knesset and thus could be made Deputy Minister of Defense. (Deputy ministers, under Israel law, must be members of the parliament.) In his new position Peres continued his former policy of expanding Israel's military production and making the results of defense research available to civilian industry. Peres was among the moving forces behind the construction of Israel's second nuclear reactor at Dimona. He also greatly expanded the scope of the weapons-research agency attached to the Ministry of Defense.

Meanwhile, relations between Peres and veterans of Mapai machine became more and more strained. When the Lavon Affair erupted in 1960, he was one of the main targets of Lavon's supporters. (His friends claim that party veterans who were obliged to accept Dayan's entry into the Cabinet in 1967 tried to use the Lavon Affair to block Peres's rise into the top ranks.) The cooling-off of French-Israel defense cooperation also did not help Peres's position. In 1963 the Russians began to supply SAM anti-aircraft missiles to Egypt but France could not provide Israel with a similar weapon. Peres went first to England and then to the United States, where he conferred with the late President Kennedy. Some time later, the United States sold the first Hawk missiles to Israel. Ben-Gurion's replacement as Prime Minister by Levi Eshkol led to a further weakening of Peres' position. He continued as Director-General of the Ministry of Defense but both in the Labor party and elsewhere there was growing criticism of Israel's continued reliance on France, which seemed an increasingly shaky source of support.

Foreshadowing the subsequent split, the "Young Turks" in the Mapai demanded in 1964 that Peres be made a member of the Committee on Foreign and Security Affairs, although until then only Cabinet members had belonged to it; Achdut Ha'avodah, on the other hand, threatened to leave the Cabinet if Peres was made a minister "through the back door." When the split in Mapai occurred, Peres went with Ben-Gurion to form the new Rafi party and became its secretary-general. Ben-Gurion and Dayan, who headed the new party, were the potential vote getters; but in the day-to-day "feeding and care" of the party, they helped very little. Peres, who a few months previously had ruled over a huge staff at the Ministry of Defense and controlled a budget totaling hundreds of millions of pounds, suddenly found himself the secretary of a small party, unable to meet its phone bills, sweating in a small office without an air conditioner.

In later years Peres began to favor the idea of reunification between Rafi and Mapai despite Ben-Gurion's opposition. Ultimately, after lengthy negotiations following the Six-Day War, during which Rafi joined the government, the three parties—Labor (Mapai), Achdut Ha'avodah and Rafi—merged and Peres became one of the deputy secretary-generals of the enlarged Labor party, with Golda Meir as secretary-general.

Peres likes to quote Ben-Gurion's saying, "There are only experts for what has happened. There are no experts for what will happen." Yet, in his demand for scientific and technological expansion, Peres insists on the importance of forecasting probable technological developments. The ability to combine an understanding of long-range trends with the know-how of setting in motion programs for their implementation is one of Peres' strong points. He has a very quick grasp of problems and has learned to avoid making the impression of intellectual superiority in order not to antagonize those who do not immediately understand what he is talking about. He can also swallow hard when his friends don't do quite right by him, as for example, after Rafi's merger with Mapai, when the second Cabinet portfolio went not to him but to Haifa union leader Yosef Almogi.

Peres made it finally into the Cabinet after the 1969 elections. Initially he was put in charge of the Ministry of Immigrant Absorption and also was asked to supervise rehabilitation of Arab refugees in the occupied territories. However, his plan for resettlement of the refugees was politely listened to but never implemented.

In 1970 he became Minister of Transport and of Posts—and one of his first actions was to change the name of the latter office to the Ministry of Communications.

The change of name did not, however, bring about improvement in the limping postal services, which probably suffer more than any other government ministry from antiquated working methods. Peres introduced modern equipment but could not introduce a system of incentive pay, which was opposed by the postal workers' union. Being Minister of Communications is still a thankless job for any up-and-coming politician.

When Mrs. Meir took General Haim Bar-Lev, who had just completed his tour of duty as Chief of Staff, into her Cabinet in the spring of 1972, many attributed this to intramural fighting in the Labor party: adding a well-liked general to the Cabinet could well serve to balance the weight of the popular Moshe Dayan.

The party machine apparently remembered the 1967 crisis, when the public demanded the inclusion of a general in the government, and they did not want to be dependent on Moshe Dayan alone, should such a crisis ever arise again.

Haim Bar-Lev's father had wanted his son, born in 1924 in Vienna and raised from childhood in Yugoslavia, to become a doctor. But the boy's love for animals led him to study at an agricultural school after the family came to Palestine in 1939. He graduated from Mikve Yisrael, one of Israel's oldest agricultural schools, in 1942, enlisted in the Palmach and stayed in uniform for thirty years. In the War of Independence he was a battalion commander and later became an Armored Corps officer. In 1952 he was appointed head of the Northern Command, but, unlike other officers who reached the level of regional commander, Bar-Lev quit after a year in favor of university studies. After he returned to active service, he was sent to Staff College in Britain and later was made head of the Training Division at GHQ.

In the 1956 Sinai Campaign Bar-Lev was in charge of an armored brigade. From then on his career prospered: in 1957, commander of all armored units; in 1961, postgraduate studies in economics and business administration at Columbia University in New York; in 1964, head of the Staff Division at the GHQ; then again Staff College in France. In May, 1967, he was urgently called home to assist the Chief of Staff, General Yitzhak Rabin, in shouldering the heavy responsibilities of the on-again off-again waiting period before the outbreak of the war. Next he became Deputy Chief of Staff, and when General Rabin resigned to become Ambassador in Washington, Bar-Lev reached the top rung of the military ladder.

Haim Bar-Lev's first months in his new office were marked by large-scale attempts of Arab terrorists to undermine Israeli control of the occupied territories. These attempts were frustrated by construction of defense fences along the Jordan River and by General Dayan's carrot-and-stick policy toward the inhabitants of the occupied territories. A greater challenge came with the beginning of Nasser's War of Attrition against Israel positions on the East Bank of the Suez Canal. The network of Israeli fortifications, where soldiers can play chess while heavy artillery fire rages outside, was built at that time. It is still called the "Bar-Lev Line." It was also during this period that the policy of commando raids against the Fatah camps and headquarters deep inside Arab territory was initiated. This period also saw the establishment of effective Israeli control over the southeastern tip of Lebanon that had been taken over by the terrorists, known as "Fatah Land."

Bar-Lev was ideally suited for command in a war of attrition: his fatherly appearance, calm voice and slow speech helped to maintain both confidence and alertness in that special situation when there was only the daily drudgery of small-scale warfare with its attendant daily list of killed and wounded. Bar-Lev also succeeded in no small measure in reassuring parents whose sons were at the Suez front that everything was indeed being done to minimize the number of casualties.

Bar-Lev, who has always looked older than his real age, never belonged to the category of dashing generals. He is an extremely cool person—mentally and physically. Nobody ever saw him rush or perspire, even on the hottest day in Sinai. His punctuality has become legendary: he always tells his driver to slow down if he feels that he will arrive too soon for a meeting or conference. He would never dream of being late, of course.

He loves dogs, and horseback riding is his favorite pastime. Unlike many of his colleagues, he used to take off his uniform and change into civilian clothes as soon as he got home. He even used to carry a civilian shirt and jacket in his car to put on if he went to a movie or to visit friends after work.

In December, 1971, Bar-Lev completed his tour of duty and in March, 1972, he became Minister of Commerce and Industry. When it became known in 1971 that the Labor party was negotiating with him on his political future, both the party and Bar-Lev were severely criticized by the press: formerly, it had been an iron-clad rule not to involve Army officers in politics while still in uniform. However, some of this criticism in party circles could be attributed to ill-feeling among veteran functionaries, who resented a man's getting Cabinet rank without going through the drudgery of years of party work. The danger of the militarization of politics was mentioned again and again, especially by politicians who felt their own chances of getting a Cabinet post diminished by "unfair competition" from the General.

Finance Minister Pinhas Sapir, who until then was also Minister of Commerce and Industry ("I'm just keeping the seat warm for Bar-Lev," he used to say), left no doubt that he would continue to make the important decisions in Commerce and Industry also for General Bar-Lev: he published a five-year industrial-development program just one day before Bar-Lev took office. Bar-Lev, on the other hand, made it clear from his very first day in office that he considered it his job to be "a father to the industrialists," that is, their voice in the Cabinet and their protector vis-à-vis the Ministry of Finance. But he never challenged Sapir's primacy in determining economic policy. Politically, Bar-Lev was in no hurry to identify himself with any group or faction inside the Labor party, as if to make sure that he remained acceptable to all elements. Indeed, some of his associates believe that Bar-Lev envisages a situation where a deadlock over succession may bring a call to the premiership to a quiet ex-general who has no enemies in any quarter.

The most controversial figure in Mrs. Meir's circle is undoubtedly the Minister of Justice, Ya'akov Shimshon Shapira. When he rejoined the Cabinet in September, 1972, after a brief retirement, the newspapers were flooded by an unprecedented stream of letters of protest. There was even speculation that if the Labor party loses some of its strength in the 1973 elections it will be due in no small measure to the unpopularity of Mrs. Meir's decision to recall Mr. Shapira to the Cabinet.

Yet even his bitterest critics admit that Ya' akov Shimshon Shapira is among the most capable members of the Cabinet. During his first years of office the Ministry of Justice completed the drafting of some most important legislation, and his extraordinary influence as counselor and advisor to the late Prime Minister Eshkol continued when Mrs. Meir took over. Much of the opposition to Shapira stems from his gruff manner and lack of a sense of what is and what is not politic for a minister to do and say. Even his admirers admit that he is a very proud man, often impatient, and inclined to statements that hurt the feelings of others and damage his own position.

Shapira, whose heavy dark eyebrows and grim visage make him a favorite of cartoonists, differs from most party politicians in one very important matter: he was never dependent on the party machine for a livelihood or for the advancement of his political career. He makes a point of "keeping distance" and never tries to be chummy to make himself popular.

Shapira was born in 1902 in the Ukraine to an old Hassidic family, which traced its origins to one of the disciples of the Baal-Shem-Tov. He studied medicine but because of his Zionist activities was expelled from school by the Soviet authorities. In 1924 Shapira made a trip to Palestine and worked as a farm laborer and later as a construction worker in Jerusalem. There he also joined a circle of young intellectuals calling themselves "the Jerusalem commune" and for the first time met Golda Meir (at that time Meyerson) and other future Mapai leaders. In Jerusalem he began to study law and was admitted to the bar in 1932. At first he joined the staff of a local firm but later moved to Haifa, where he specialized in maritime law. That expertise, together with his activity in the Haganah, made him the unofficial permanent counsel in all matters of "illegal" immigration, including defense of ships seized by the British for bringing in visaless Jewish immigrants. In 1946, when the British arrested the entire Jewish Agency directorate (which at that time was the unofficial Jewish government in Palestine), Shapira was appointed general counsel of the Agency and directed both the legal and the publicity campaigns against the British authorities.

After Israel's establishment, Shapira was appointed the first Attorney-General and served in that post for twenty months. After his retirement from government service he opened his own law firm in Tel Aviv, which soon became one of the country's most successful, counting among its clients a number of the most important Israeli companies. He continued his private practice after he was elected to the Knesset and became a prominent member of the parliamentary Labor faction.

Shapira's encounters with bad publicity are all, somehow, connected with oil. When oil was first found in the Negev in 1955, "petroleum fever" hit the country and some believed that Israel was to become another Kuwait or Saudi Arabia. Shares of oil prospecting firms shot up, including that of Lapidoth, which was the first to discover any petroleum in its concessions. Lapidoth had earlier given Shapira's office thirty thousand shares at one Israeli pound nominal value instead of cash payment for legal services. When the market boom occurred, those thirty thousand shares were worth almost one million pounds and Mr. Shapira was widely criticized for being involved in a get-rich-quick scheme. He maintained that, in fact, it was he who did Lapidoth a favor before oil was found, but under pressure of public criticism he resigned from the Knesset, a considerably embittered man.

For ten years Shapira devoted most of his time to his Tel Aviv practice, although occasionally he took on public assignments and remained active in Mapai councils. When David Ben-Gurion's demand for a legal investigation of the Lavon Affair rocked the Mapai, Shapira was among those who led the opposition to Ben-Gurion. In the heat of the in-fighting, he called the Rafi faction, composed of Ben-Gurion's supporters who had left the Mapai, "a group of neo-Fascists" and Ben-Gurion himself "a coward." These were statements that return again and again to haunt Shapira's political career. Even Ben-Gurion's opponents felt that Shapira exceeded the limits, and thus it came as quite a surprise when Levi Eshkol offered him the Justice portfolio in 1966. Curiously enough, Ben-Gurion and Shapira meanwhile were reconciled and Shapira accepted the chairmanship of the board of trustees of the college at Sdeh Boker founded by Ben-Gurion.

As one of Eshkol's and Golda Meir's contemporaries and long-time friends, it was quite natural that Ya'akov Shimshon Shapira should carry extraordinary weight in their Cabinets, not only as Minister of Justice, but as one of their most trusted advisors in domestic and foreign-policy matters. When public criticism of Shapira reached its peak over his handling of demand for a judicial investigation of alleged irregularities in Netivei Nepht, the government-controlled oil-producing company in Sinai, his earlier counsel to the government was also questioned anew. It was recalled, for example, that Shapira had advised the government to keep secret the court proceedings against editors of the sensation-mongering magazine *Bul*, who were accused of divulging details of alleged Israeli involvement with the French intelligence apparatus.

Public criticism of Shapira's handling of the Netivei Nepht investigation was exceeded by an outcry over the legal fees he awarded to the attorneys assisting the work of the commission that investigated the affair. Shapira was again the main target of the attacks and he handed in his resignation—an action unprecedented among Israeli politicians. Mrs. Meir did not appoint another Minister of Justice and ultimately induced him to return to the Cabinet despite public hostility to the move.

The position of Haifa ex-Labor boss Yosef Almogi in Golda Meir's circle is sometimes likened to that of a feudal lord whose temporary alliance with the king's (queen's) enemies is perhaps forgiven but not forgotten, but whose forces nevertheless are needed with the royal troops. Indeed, the Labor party's rule in the Haifa area in no small measure is reminiscent of the feudal system: in this case the king-lord-church triangle is replaced by positions of power in the Haifa branch of the Labor party, in the municipality and in the Histadrut. If Almogi was forgiven earlier than others who joined Ben-Gurion in Rafi, this was probably due to the fact that, even during the split in the Mapai, he seemed closer to Levi Eshkol and Pinhas Sapir than to Moshe Dayan or Shimon Peres.

Simultaneously Almogi succeeded in changing his public image considerably. The man who was well known as the representative of stevedores and port workers and whose appearance and manners were often those of a porter or crane operator, now took on a statesmanlike manner. He behaved like a wise old labor leader, far removed from the once-familiar jokes that circulated about him and his alleged lack of education.

In fact Almogi, who was born in 1910 in Poland to a scholarly Orthodox family, deliberately refused to pursue a higher education: he considered university studies contrary to his childhood ambition to become a farmer in Palestine. In 1930 he came to Palestine, became a kibbutz member and commander of a Haganah unit recruited from farm workers. At the beginning of World War II he joined the British Army and was taken prisoner by the Germans in Greece in 1941. During his four years in POW camp, he learned English from books in the camp library. After the war he returned to Haifa, became secretary of the Mapai–affiliated Hapoel Club, from whose ranks he organized a permanent group of blue-shirted ushers. Although originally organized to provide jobs at sports events and public rallies, the ushers also became the strong arm of Mapai in the Haifa region.

Almogi's national career started in 1946, when he became secretary of the Haifa Labor Council, and in 1958 he was put in charge of the Labor party's election campaign. His success brought him the job of secretary-general of Mapai, and in 1961, for the first time, he joined the Cabinet. In 1962 he became Minister of Housing and Development and focused his Ministry's activities on projects for the development of the Negev.

He joined Rafi out of loyalty to Ben-Gurion rather than for ideological reasons, and was deeply hurt when "his" Haifa did not follow him. When Almogi and Abba Khoushi (who remained with Eshkol and Mapai during the split) made peace in Haifa in 1966, this foreshadowed the reconciliation between Mapai and Rafi. Almogi became the chief intermediary between Rafi and Eshkol-Sapir in the negotiations that ultimately led to the ending of the split. In 1968 Almogi was mentioned for the first time as a candidate for the post of secretary-general of the Histadrut. His name crops up repeatedly whenever the hostility between the doctrinaire Histadrut Secretary-General Yitzhak Ben-Aharon and Labor party leadership reaches boiling point. Almogi sees eye to eye with Pinhas Sapir not only on the role of the Histadrut in Israel but also on topical political issues such as their opposition to the employment of Arab workers from the occupied territories in Israeli industry. This association may yet prove most important when the Labor party, which in the final analysis controls the Histadrut, eventually decides to replace its maverick secretary-general.

5

The Ruling Party

The basic fact which has dominated the formation of Israel's political elite is the long-standing division between ruling parties and parties of the opposition. The Labor party, under slightly varying names, and with it the Independent Liberals (formerly the Progressive party) and the National Religious party (formerly the Mizrachi and Hapoel Hamizrachi), have always been the "ins." On the other hand, Herut and the Liberal party (now linked in a common bloc called Gahal) have almost always been the "outs." The brief periods in which the Liberals (then called General Zionists) and in later years, Gahal, joined the government are the exceptions that prove the rule.

The ease with which Achdut Ha'avodah joined the Labor party after the Six-Day War indicates that essentially it belonged to the ruling side despite its extensive period of absence from the government, together with the further left Mapam party. Mapam's own joining in a parliamentary and electoral alignment with the Labor party demonstrates the limits of its participation in the regime: by its past and present role in collective agricultural farm networks and by its role in the Histadrut, Mapam is part of the establishment. But the deep ideological differences between its leftist Marxism and the Labor party's middle-of-the road socialism create a chasm between the two groups.

When Herut joined the coalition Cabinet on the eve of the Six-Day War, this was, in a way, a revolutionary change for the party. For the first time since the establishment of the State, it became a partner in ruling the country and thus altered its image as a permanent outsider, an image which had been created even before Israeli Army units shelled and sank the freighter *Altalena* carrying ammunition for the Irgun (Herut's forerunner) off the coast of Tel Aviv in 1948. The partnership between Herut and the Liberals in Gahal demonstrates that the latter essentially belongs to the opposition. Yet the inability of these two nonsocialist parties to merge, and the oft-recurring tensions between the two, indicate how unrealistic are those who hoped that the Gahal bloc would emerge as "the" opposition which could serve as an alternative to Labor.

The permanent coalition-versus-opposition status of the respective parties has molded both the mentality and the patterns of recruitment on each side. In Israel, where the possession of administrative power is of crucial importance in one's public career, the opposition parties, being devoid of such power, have found it difficult to recruit able young men into their ranks. In the ruling parties, on the other hand, status and advancement depend very much on the individual's power in his administrative job. It is no coincidence hat the only young leader who has grown up inside Herut is Knesset member Yoram Aridor, who owes his prominence to his role as one of the Herut-affiliated labor leaders on the Histadrut executive. The search for additional young leaders has led Herut to try to recruit officers retiring from the Army, where they acquired both fame and administrative experience.

The Workers' Party of Eretz Yisrael—Mapai—which is the dominant component of the present Labor party, has always stressed that it is a party of doers, a party that puts Zionist socialism into practice. Its ideological and organizational roots lie in the collective and cooperative farm movement; yet for a long time now it has been a typically urban party rather than a rural movement. Mapai's spiritual fathers were the young Zionist pioneers who came from Russia before World War I. Most of them have already died—men like Berl Katznelson, Yosef Sprinzak, Yitzhak Ben-Zvi and David Remez; the few that remain, like David Ben-Gurion, are now in retirement. (It is symptomatic of the impact of Mapai on Israel's political life that its most towering figure, David Ben-Gurion, although long in retirement, is still capable of creating a political furore or even crisis by some well-chosen remark.)

The man who was considered the "youngster" in the group, Levi Eshkol, died only after the Six-Day War. This fact points up the great cohesion of the group as a political entity, which was also the cause of the widespread feeling that Israel, though one of the world's youngest states, is ruled by one of its oldest governments. Ben-Gurion and his associates belong to what is known as the Second Aliyah, the second wave of large-scale immigration to Palestine before World War I. Those who are among today's top leadership, like Mrs. Meir and Pinhas Sapir, belong to the Third Aliyah, which came in the years after World War I. This group, which also is now on its way out, held most of the key positions in the Jewish life of Palestine and later in the State of Israel for almost fifty years. While the Second Aliyah provided primarily the ideological leadership of all the labor parties, and Mapai in particular, the Third Aliyah provided the functionaries in the party, in the Histadrut, in the Jewish Agency and, ultimately, in the government.

Identification with traditional Jewish values was always typical of the Mapai. This was one of its three ideological foundation stones and colored the nature of the other two. Ben-Gurion's frequent references to the Bible in considering current problems was an evidence of the first component; but the Labor party also stressed that its adherence to socialism and democracy came from the ancient Jewish sense of social justice and human equality.

The nationalist emphasis that typified Mapai helped it probably more than any other factor to acquire the support and loyalty of voters who are neither wage earners nor kibbutz farmers. The importance of the national component in its ideological makeup, which already was clear in its first platform back in 1925, gained overwhelming importance after World War II, when the struggle for Jewish statehood reached its climax. After Israel's establishment, Mapai favored cooperation of the socialist and capitalist sectors of the national economy in order to foster rapid economic growth. Yet in those early years the socialist sector was dominant. (In the early fifties Mrs. Meir still spoke of "creating a socialist society in our generation.") Today the Labor party promotes the Histadrut enterprises in a much more practical way—as an essential factor of its power base. At the same time party representatives in government and trade unions fully support private ventures and capital investment to help them expand Israeli industry. The party even managed to turn many of these private enterprises into effective tools of its dominance in the country.

Splits in Mapai always had personal origins. The leadership knew each other intimately for decades and thus ideological disputes could not be separated from personal ones. Typically, most of those who left Mapai temporarily in the sixties to form the Rafi party, including Moshe Dayan, did so more out of affection and loyalty to Ben-Gurion than because they shared the views and demands which earlier left him a minority in his own party.

In the early 1970's the Labor party was still in the process of trying to recover from the soporific effect of the terms of office of several party secretaries who had neither the stature nor the organizational ability to keep it an active political organization. The party machine and its institutions had no effective control over those who officially represented it in the government and in other top national institutions. This was a comfortable situation for Mrs. Meir and also for lesser figures in official positions, since it left them free to decide and act in the party, and in its name, outside the formal political framework.

Yehoshua Rabinowitz, the Mayor of Tel Aviv, represents to a great extent this type of "extra-institutional" rule of the party. Rabinowitz is a confidant and mouthpiece of Finance Minister Pinhas Sapir. His main power lies in his ability "to arrange things" and "to help people." He can do that both as the boss of the revived "Gush," the closest thing in Israel to Tammany Hall, and as the head of the largest municipal bureaucracy in Israel. But while the original Gush, or Bloc, which broke up under the stress of the Lavon Affair, was controlled by Shraga Netzer, who never held any formal office or ever emerged from behind the scenes, Rabinowitz, who inherited his mantle in the late 1960's, prefers to wield both official and unofficial power.

Through the delegates from the Tel Aviv area and his other supporters, Rabinowitz now controls about 25 percent of the members of the Labor party's central committee. This is by far the largest single bloc on the committee. But Rabinowitz also wields great influence more directly—through the various institutions and enterprises that are financed or supported to a large extent by Tel Aviv municipal budgets.

The Gush is an informal, unofficial framework and therefore has no officials or formal procedure. Its leaders usually meet on Saturday nights at the home of Rabinowitz. The meetings are closed not only to those who supported Ben-Gurion and Dayan during the split in the party, but also to younger members who have never wavered in their loyalty but are suspected of hoping to replace the outmoded party machine. The group apparently has two simple aims: one, to re-establish the unquestioned dominance of the Mapai faction in the Labor party, and, second, the creation of a "generation of continuity" molded in their own image, who will take over the running of the party machine. The Gush, most of whose members are doves in foreign policy and security matters, is also considered to be one of the main levers at the disposal of Pinhas Sapir if he wants to become Prime Minister or, at least, prevent Moshe Dayan from becoming so.

Yehoshua Rabinowitz was born in Poland in 1911 and graduated from teachers' college in Vilna. After his arrival in Palestine in 1934, he studied law and economics in Tel Aviv. He came to political life through his activity in the Histadrut framework, in which he was head of the industrial division in Hamashbir Hamerkazi, the trade unions' central marketing cooperative. His first tasks in the Labor party had to do with money and budgets, not only because the party needed urgent help in overcoming chronic financial ills but also because bookkeeping holds an abiding fascination for Rabinowitz. "Figures are my kind of dice," he says frequently.

He was elected Tel Aviv City Councilor in 1955, became Deputy Mayor in 1959 and progressively took over most of the duties of ailing Mayor Mordecai Namir. In 1962 he was put in charge of all municipal finances, and in 1969, after almost ten years of de facto mayorship, he was also officially elected Mayor of Tel Aviv.

Of all the mayors of major Israel cities, Rabinowitz is probably the least known by sight to his electorate. When he walks across the huge square in front of the modern City Hall, hardly any heads turn in recognition. This fact was probably a major consideration when his supporters in the Labor party, in the spring of 1973, quietly but effectively sabotaged a bill sponsored by the party to replace the present system of mayors' being chosen by municipal councils with direct popular mayoral election. Rabinowitz and his friends were not at all sure that he would be elected under the new system.

It would be hard to image a person more different from Yehoshua Rabinowitz than his colleague, Jerusalem's Mayor, Teddy Kollek, whose face is familiar to everyone in his city, Jew and Arab alike. Kollek tries to keep away from party activities and considers beautification of the city more important than neat municipal budgets. Rabinowitz reached his present post thanks to his rise in the party machine; Teddy Kollek won his first elections largely because he dared to contest the Labor party machine.

Everybody calls him Teddy—Ben-Gurion and the Mayor of Paris, his secretary and the chairman of the United Jewish Appeal in America. Kollek is the grand master of public relations for Israel. It is said that when he goes on one of his periodic visits to the United States he composes two lists of names: one of friends whom he does not need to see and one of friends from whom he wants something. Upon arrival, he makes a point of calling to say hello to those he does not need, lest they hear of his visit from the others and say,

"That s.o.b.—when he doesn't need me he doesn't call me!" Kollek is one of those who can "trade" in the public-relations game. For example, it was he who introduced Baron de Rothschild to Lyndon Johnson.

His flair for human relations is attributed to his country of origin: Kollek was born in courtly, light-hearted Vienna in 1911. He came to Palestine in 1934 and developed an extraordinary ability to maneuver in the maze of official and social bureaucracy of the country. One of the founders of Kibbutz Ein Gev on the eastern shore of the Lake of Galilee, he had been barely four years in the country when he was sent on behalf of the Jewish Agency to Europe. In 1942 he moved to Istanbul, which had become a base of efforts to save Jews from Nazi-occupied Europe. In 1947 Kollek went to New York as head of the Haganah mission there, to obtain arms to fight the impending war with the Arabs. Kollek concentrated primarily on the fund-raising side of the effort.

In 1950 he was appointed head of the U.S. Division at the Israel Foreign Ministry and one year later was sent as Minister to Washington. It was a time when the young State lived from one financial crisis to another and Kollek again worked primarily to obtain loans, credits and American aid.

In 1952 Ben-Gurion appointed him Director-General of the Prime Minister's Office. For twelve years Kollek held one of the most important jobs in the government bureaucracy if not the most important. Besides heading the administrative and political staff of the office, Kollek gathered under its roof different departments and services which, somehow, did not come under the jurisdiction of any other ministry, from the National Scientific and Research Council to the Israel Coins and Medals Corporation. Another of his major projects was to expand facilities for Israel's tourist trade. At the same time Kollek also went on numerous diplomatic missions, either on behalf of Ben-Gurion or as head of his entourage when traveling abroad.

As the man in charge, ex officio, of the Israel Broadcasting Service, Kollek pushed through the decision to introduce semi-commercial broadcasting on the government radio. Unlike many officials who jealously guard their empires, Kollek frequently sloughs off departments, making them autonomous directorates or enterprises. His desk at the Prime Minister's Office also served as an address for many odd and not so odd proposals and projects.

The most remarkable testimony to his talents was created by Teddy Kollek on one of the hills facing the Knesset in Jerusalem. It is the Israel Museum, fruit of his initiative, perseverance and consummate knowledge of how to arrange things in Israel and among Jewish millionaires abroad. The foundation stone of the museum was laid in 1962: for two years Kollek devoted almost all his time and energies to fund raising, organization and soliciting of works of art for the new museum. Again he used his wide acquaintance with Jewish art collectors all over the world and obtained from them some notable masterpieces. One of the most spectacular contributions was the huge sculpture collection of New York impresario Billy Rose, now displayed in a sculpture garden designed by Isamu Noguchi. In 1964 he took leave from the Prime Minister's Office to spend all his time on museum affairs: he did not have to make it leave without pay, because by that time he had accumulated some fifteen months of unused vacation in government service.

In Mapai split he joined Ben-Gurion in the Rafi faction and was the splinter party's candidate for Mayor of Jerusalem. He collected almost as many votes as the Labor party, which had ruled the Jerusalem City Hall for fifteen years. Thus, in December, 1965, he was able to put together a coalition with several smaller parties and became Mayor. Kollek has imprinted his personal style on running City Hall: new parks and public gardens, early-morning inspections of the garbage-collecting service, brighter street lamps, frequent chats with housewives and the man in the street. Being a representative of a splinter group which successfully challenged the Labor machine did not help Kollek in getting financial assistance from the Ministry of Finance—nor did demonstrative moves, such as threatening publicly to haul the Israel government to court for defaulting on municipal taxes on its properties in Jerusalem. The latter action was probably another public-relations gimmick in an effort to make Jerusalemites pay their taxes, but it netted the city coffers several million pounds.

Kollek has an attractive personality; he smiles easily and his blond hair, constantly falling into his eyes, has become a trademark in Israeli politics. But, unlike most of his colleagues, Teddy Kollek is not a good orator. He knows it and when he has to make a speech —usually with his hands in his pockets—he keeps it very brief and pithy.

Kollek's great hour came on the eve of the Six-Day War and during the days of fighting. Jerusalem was the first place where, on a municipal level, a national coalition including all parties except the Communists was formed to face the challenge of impending hostilities. This provided considerable impetus to the formation of such a coalition on the national level a week later. When the Jordanians started shelling Jerusalem, Kollek traveled through the city from dawn till past midnight in what soon became a bullet-riddled car. He went to the most exposed neighborhoods, encouraged people in the shelters and saw to it that emergency maintenance crews repaired disrupted water, electricity and sewage lines even under fire. When the shooting was over, he organized the speedy repair of all damage caused during the fighting.

Kollek was equally fast to extend municipal services to residents of the Arab parts of the city taken by the Israel forces. The integration of the Arab population of Jerusalem into the life and municipal activities of the city has become one of Kollek's central ambitions since 1967. This led him to repeated conflict with Herut and even some Religious party council members, who frequently charged him with conducting a "pro-Arab" municipal policy.

In the 1969 elections Jerusalemites rewarded Kollek for his efforts: the Labor Alignment municipal ticket headed by Kollek in Jerusalem received almost twice as many votes as the Alignment's Knesset ticket. In the early 1970's Kollek fought with the Labor party machine, which disliked his independent attitude. He was also attacked by conservationists who felt that he did not put up a strong enough fight against the marring of Jerusalem's landscape and sky-line by mushrooming high-rise apartment buildings and hotel construction.

The prototype of the party faithful and one whom the Labor party machine rewards for loyal service is Knesset Speaker Yisrael Yeshayahu Sharabi, who rose in the hierarchy first as spokesman of immigrants from his native Yemen and later as an "ethnic" representative of Israelis of "Oriental" (i.e., Near East or North African) origin.

Yisrael Yeshayahu (he dropped the Sharabi) has published numerous articles on the history and folklore of Yemenite Jews and on problems of absorption into Israel society. From his early days he always had the knack of identifying his own career with the advancing of the representation of Oriental Jews in Israeli public life. He is of small stature, dark-skinned, and has mops of hair on either side of his balding head. Even in the hot summer he wears a jacket, usually dark. Yeshayahu walks with very rapid steps and almost always carries a briefcase or a bunch of papers and magazines under his arm.

Although he was born in Sana in 1920, and came to Palestine in his early childhood, Yisrael Yeshayahu still can describe life in Yemen vividly. His studies at the Yeshiva and his acquaintance with the national poet, Chaim Nachman Bialik, helped to polish his Hebrew. Yeshayahu entered public life in the department for Oriental and Yemenite Jews in the executive of the Histadrut. There he met the late Knesset Speaker, Yosef Sprinzak, who became the young man's mentor in politics. After Israel's establishment, Yeshayahu worked on the "Magic Carpet" operation in which almost the entire Jewish population of Yemen was flown to Israel. In 1951 Yeshayahu became a member of the Knesset after Mapai obliged several other candidates higher on the list to resign in his favor. His rise in parliamentary life was strikingly rapid. One year after joining the Knesset he already headed its Ways and Means Committee, and in 1955, he became Deputy Speaker of the House. Apparently he was not fully satisfied with the pace of his advancement: in 1961 he threatened to resign in protest over "the non-inclusion of a minister of Yemenite origin" in Ben-Gurion's new Cabinet.

He attached great importance to his parliamentary work but he was equally diligent in party life. In 1962 he was appointed one of five members of an unofficial directorate of the party and was put in charge of its information and propaganda services. But in the party, too, he felt discriminated against because of his Yemenite origin and resigned from some of his duties in 1963 in protest against failure to fulfill a promise which, he claimed, was given to him earlier to make him a member of the Cabinet.

Although previously known as a great admirer of Ben-Gurion, he was among the first who lined up behind Eshkol in his split with Ben-Gurion over the Lavon Affair. Yeshayahu, who was then chairman of the standing committee of the party secretariat, demanded the right to censor speeches of all party representatives in order to keep the behind-the-scenes fight out of the public eye. Ben-Gurion refused and Yeshayahu later submitted to the party congress a draft resolution nominating Levi Eshkol rather than Ben-Gurion as the Labor party's next candidate for premiership.

His dream of becoming a Cabinet member was finally realized in 1967, when Prime Minister Eshkol made him Minister of Posts. In his new role Yeshayahu continued to see himself as a party representative. When the Director-General of the Ministry (and former Israeli scientific attaché in Washington), Yeshayahu Lavi, wanted to modernize the postal services, Yeshayahu sided with the postal workers' union against the proposed reform. Lavi resigned to become Director-General of the Ministry of Defense and still later vice-president of General Telephone and Electronics in New York. In 1968, Yeshayahu created a furore in the Israeli press when he proposed that the Labor party should "transfer" privately owned newspapers to "public ownership." He retreated under attack but revived the idea again a year later when he proposed that all newspapers get government subsidies instead of income from advertisements.

Yeshayahu is considered a faithful follower of Finance Minister Pinhas Sapir in all intraparty struggles. In 1971 he was elected secretary-general of the Labor party with the support of the Achdut Ha'avodah faction, who were promised that one of their men would be made deputy secretary-general. But after the vote Yeshayahu declared that he needed no deputies, thus creating a crisis in the party which immobilized the secretariat for over half a year, until the majority compelled him to appoint two deputies, one from Achdut Ha'avodah and one from the ex-Rafi faction.

In 1972 the post of Knesset Speaker became vacant and Yeshayahu was chosen as the Labor party candidate—but only by a majority of thirty to twenty-eight. This narrow margin reflected his decline in the party's esteem because of the immobility that characterized his term of office as secretary-general. Yet, when the decisive vote was taken, all Labor members lined up behind him. In April, 1972, he became Speaker of the Knesset and thus Deputy and potential Acting President of Israel.

In the Knesset, more than in any other public body in Israel, seniority is of prime importance. This is particularly so in the Labor party, where length of service rather than personal qualifications determine a politician's weight and position in parliamentary committees. The young Knesset members frequently complain that the seniors, who hold almost all the committee chairmanships, not only fail to assign them to important committees, but prevent any legislative initiative on their part. Some seniors recently went so far as to propose that Knesset members should not all get the same salary but that salaries should be graded according to years of service in the house.

The power of the senior Knesset members is perpetuated by the present system of national proportional elections to the Knesset. Under this system each party puts up one single list of candidates in the entire country: voters choose party lists rather than competing individual candidates whom they know. The veterans of the party machine have a dominant say on the appointments committee which puts the list of candidates together, and they make sure that they themselves obtain "safe" spots on the list to assure their re-election. The veterans, who act as a group, also have a high degree of cohesion. Thus the saying that only death parts a veteran politi-cian from his chair is only a slight exaggeration in the case of the Israel Knesset.

Typical of the young generation of Labor politicians is Yitzhak Navon, formerly Ben-Gurion's political secretary, who almost suc-ceeded in defeating the veterans' candidate, Yeshayahu, for the post of Knesset Speaker in 1972. Navon represents both the younger Labor politicians in general and those of its "Oriental" minority who have succeeded in advancing in the predominantly East Euro-pean-controlled political elite. It often seems that Navon's Sephardi background is more important to the non-Sephardi majority than to those whom he should ethnically represent.*

Yitzhak Navon was born in Jerusalem in 1921 and his attachment to the old Sephardi community of the city inspired his later success-ful play, *A Spanish Garden.* He studied Islamic culture and Arabic literature at the Hebrew University in Jerusalem and for a few years taught high school. His rather infrequent arguments with his former boss stem from his experience as a teacher: Navon disputes Ben-Gurion's claim that the Bible is a source for the inculcation of sublime moral values in youth; Navon maintains that the Bible is full of deeds that one cannot very well tell children without blushing.

Navon met Ben-Gurion for the first time before the 1948 War of Independence, when the young teacher also doubled as head of the Arab Department of the Haganah branch in Jerusalem. After 1948 Navon became political secretary of the late Foreign Minister Moshe Sharett and in 1952 moved to the Prime Minister's Office as Ben-Gurion's political secretary. For eleven years Navon was Ben-Gurion's right-hand man, admirer and advisor, and one of the few in Ben-Gurion's circle of associates who never hesitated to contra-

*Sephardi Jews are descendants of the Jews expelled from Spain in 1492.

dict the "Old Man" when he thought he was wrong. Endowed with a good sense of humor and talent for storytelling, Yitzhak Navon succeeded in being a rather difficult combination: simultaneously he was Ben-Gurion's voice and shadow and yet was a personality in his own right, whose power and influence did not depend only on being Ben-Gurion's secretary.

In 1963 he left the Prime Minister's Office and became Director of the Cultural Division in the Ministry of Education, where he was also in charge of the campaign to end illiteracy among new immigrants. It was natural that, when the split in Mapai occurred, he followed Ben-Gurion and was elected as one of the Rafi candidates to the Knesset. He was elected Deputy Speaker of the house. Throughout his party activities Navon continued in the post of director of the America-Israel Cultural Foundation, which provides subsidies for theaters and other arts. After the Six-Day War he was in the minority in Rafi, opposing the merger with the Labor party.

Navon's disappointment at his narrow miss in the election for Speaker was repeated in March, 1973, when he was a prominent candidate for the presidency of Israel. This is mainly a ceremonial office, with the President symbolizing the unity of the people and representing the State to other nations of the world. His only political function is to charge the leader of the largest party after a national election to form a new government.

When the Labor party met to nominate its candidate, Navon soon won wide support. Other political parties pledged their support to Navon, emphasizing that as a Sephardi, familiar with the problems of the underprivileged, he would be able to make a special contribution to the office.

However, the old Mapai leadership of the Labor party opposed Navon, reportedly because it disliked his past activity in the Rafi faction. Another candidate was then presented to the central committee of the party, Professor Ephraim Katchalski, an illustrious scientist of the Weizmann Institute. Still, despite pressure exerted by the party machine, Katchalski had only a narrow victory in the central committee, with Navon picking up 44.2 percent of the vote.

Navon's contemporary and another representative of the younger generation is Avraham Ofer, director-general of Shikun Ovdim, the Histadrut-affiliated housing construction company, one of the largest in the country. But, while Navon advanced in the government bureaucracy, Ofer rose through party ranks; Navon's strength lies in cultural and political matters, whereas Ofer is a businessman who has never strayed too far from the party machine.

Born in Poland in 1922, Ofer came to Israel at the age of eleven and from his early youth was active in Mapai youth organizations. In the War of Independence, twenty-six-year-old Ofer was commander of the manpower division of the Israeli Navy and later first commander of Israel's naval base in Elath.

After the war he re-entered political life and was among the first who urged Mapai to support the introduction of the district representation electoral system, in order to bring new blood into the party. Ofer has a special talent of being part of the party establishment and opposing it at the same time. He was secretary of the Tel Aviv district of Mapai when he organized a conference of the young generation in order to introduce more democracy in its procedures. In 1958 the Minister of Agriculture, Moshe Dayan, picked Ofer to reorganize poultry and dairy production and made him Deputy Director-General. His first encounter with the construction industry came in 1964, when he left the Agriculture Ministry to become director of the Ashdod Company, a privately-controlled concern engaged in building Israel's new southern port. In 1965 Ofer was back in politics as Mapai member of the Tel Aviv Municipal Council. When he was appointed director-general of Shikun Ovdim in 1967, he was obliged to resign as Deputy Mayor of Tel Aviv but continued as a municipal councilor.

On the eve of the merger of the Rafi faction with Mapai, Ofer conducted an interparty census to determine the relative weight of the three components: Mapai, Achdut Ha'avodah and Rafi. However, he did not publish the results until well after the merger.

Ofer frequently has clashed with Housing Minister Ze'ev Sharef, whose construction policies Ofer dislikes. The Housing Ministry, which builds for new immigrants, has been accused by Ofer of intentionally exaggerating the magnitude of the housing shortage. Ofer also has clashed with the Israel Lands Authority, a government authority, which he charges with withholding public land for housing purposes, thus creating an artificial rise in land values in the country.

Ofer showed his strength in the party in 1971 when he managed to obtain 44 percent of the votes in support of his candidate for the post of secretary-general of the party, Aharon Yadlin. The party machine's candidate, Yisrael Yeshayahu, was elected only by a 56 percent majority. It was due to this show of strength that Yadlin later became secretary-general in 1972.

Yadlin and Ofer are part of a loose grouping of the younger generation who are gradually taking over the most-influential political and economic posts in the country. Less-known figures in this group hold key positions in Histadrut-affiliated financial institutions while Aharon Yadlin's cousin, Asher Yadlin, is secretary-general of Hevrat Ha'ovdim, the Histadrut's holding company, and also general manager of Kupat Holim, the Histadrut health service, which covers about half of Israel's population.

Aharon Yadlin is one of the "most related" members of the Israeli elite. Besides being the cousin of the secretary-general of Hevrat Ha'ovdim, he is also married to Ada Hacohen, daughter of veteran labor leader David Hacohen, head of one of Haifa's most influential families.

Slightly built, intellectual-looking and bespectacled, Aharon Yadlin, who can make even the most abused ideological clichés sound intelligent, is the prototype of what a nice boy from a good family should be. Born in 1926 in Ben Shemen, he went to the elite Reali high school in Haifa, was a Scout leader, studied economics and sociology at the Hebrew University and was one of the pioneers who participated in the overnight establishment of eleven Jewish agricultural settlements in the Negev in 1946. Active in various educational organs of the party and of the kibbutz movement, he was elected to the Knesset and in 1964 appointed Deputy Minister of Education.

In this job Yadlin put special stress on reintroducing idealistic values in the elementary and high-school curricula. In the 1965 Labor party split he was on the anti-Ben-Gurion side of the divide and, perhaps not by coincidence, he was on Pinhas Sapir's side in 1969 when the Finance Minister first came out against Moshe Dayan's concept of economic integration between Israel and the occupied territories. When Yisrael Yeshayahu was elected Speaker of the Knesset in 1972, Aharon Yadlin took over the post of Labor party Secretary-General. He inherited a rusty party machine, with many of its branches inactive and with practically no control or influence over the behavior of Labor party representatives in Parliament, the municipalities and the Histadrut. Yadlin knew that he had to revitalize the party for the 1973 elections, but should Golda Meir consent to run again, his task will be considerably simplified.

A predecessor of Yadlin in the Labor party secretariat and another representative of the young generation is Arie ("Lova") Eliav, who has the distinction of being one of the few people who have managed to create some ideological controversy within the placid party establishment. This stir was publicized for the first time in 1972, when Moshe Dayan took the floor at a party meeting and demanded that the party take a position on the future relationship between pre-1967 Israel and the occupied territories. One of Dayan's reasons was his sharpening dispute with Finance Minister Sapir over the employment of laborers from the territories in the Israeli economy, but no less important was the debate created among party intellectuals by Eliav's book *The Beautiful Land,* in which he urged recognition of a separate Palestinian national identity and far-reaching territorial concessions as a means of achieving peace with the Arabs.

Eliav's views on Israel-Arab relations are supported only by a minority in his party and in the country. But being in the minority is nothing new to Eliav, who is accustomed to doing the unconven-

tional. Though he is an outstanding member of the younger generation in the Labor party, in his ideological values he is more like a
member of the pre–World War I Second Aliyah: while his colleagues work at politics in Tel Aviv, Eliav prefers to engage in
traditional agricultural and settlement pioneering, whether in the
Negev or as an advisor to the Iranian government. Apparently Eliav
is motivated by that inner unrest which was typical of Labor leadership a generation ago. He is also one of the few who possesses some
of the personal charisma which typified many Zionist leaders in the
early 1920's and 1930's.

Lova Eliav was born in Moscow in 1920 and came to Palestine
with his parents in 1924. He studied biology at the Hebrew University and joined the British Army in 1941. He fought in the Western
Desert and in Italy, where he first met the survivors of the European
Holocaust. For three years after the war Eliav worked on behalf of
the Jewish Agency in the Haganah, organizing "illegal" immigration
of Jews to Palestine from the entire Mediterranean area.

His reminiscences of that period are the subject of his book *Ulua*,
the name of one of the illegal ships which he commanded. Following
a stint as assistant to Levi Eshkol, who was then head of the Settlement Department of the Jewish Agency, Eliav went to Cambridge
to study farm economics and business administration.

In 1953 Eliav took on one of the most interesting assignments in
Israel: to be in charge of the Lachish project, in an empty region of
the Negev, where a group of new settlements were to be built. This
was the first fully planned regional development project in Israel.
Eliav introduced what has become the standard method in later
projects: everything had to be located on site—headquarters, offices
and residences of planners, engineers, economists and social workers, who all had to live where their work was and not in distant Tel
Aviv or Jerusalem. Thus plans could be amended and changes in
projects made at once when circumstances required. This method
is credited with the unusual success of the project. The rate of
dropouts in the new settlements of Lachish was considerably lower
than in any other settlement program implemented since 1948.

In November, 1956, Eliav made a dramatic switch of pace in his career: reviving his expertise from pre-Independence days, he commanded the secret operation, which during the Anglo-French Suez Campaign, helped evacuate the Jews of Port Said from the Egyptian city.

Yet another change occurred in his life when in the late 1950's he was appointed First Secretary at the Israel Embassy in Moscow. Attempts to establish contact with Soviet Jewry were among his duties, and the intense emotional experiences of that period are reflected in his book *Between the Hammer and the Sickle.*

In the early 1960's Eliav returned to settlement work and repeated his success of Lachish in directing the new Arad development program.

Eliav too was caught up in the internal struggle of Mapai, when he supported Levi Eshkol against Ben-Gurion. As head of the organization department of the Labor party, Eliav was in charge of ousting Ben-Gurion's supporters from the party. Yet he was no yes man even at that time and clashed with the party machine when he demanded the inclusion of younger people in top offices. He even publicly opposed the candidacy of veteran Labor intellectual Zalman Shazar for the presidency because of his advanced age.

From party politics Eliav went back to government service, first as Deputy Minister of Commerce and Industry and later as Deputy Minister of Immigrant Absorption. His appointment as secretary-general of the Labor party in 1970 created hopes among the younger generation that he would reform the ailing party machine. These hopes, however, were not fulfilled and Eliav began to devote much of his attention to ideological questions connected with Israel's control of the occupied territories. His book *New Targets for Israel* openly advocated unilateral withdrawal of Israel from the territories —even without obtaining concessions from the Arabs in return. After two controversial years Eliav quit and went back to his studies for the fourth time. He again stirred up a major controversy in 1972 with his book *The Beautiful Land,* which advocated handing over the occupied territories to representatives of the "Palestine people" as part of a peace treaty between them and Israel.

In past controversies, Eliav usually could count on the support of Shlomo Hillel, an old ally of his in the young leadership of the party. This time, however, Hillel, who currently is Minister of Police, did not share Eliav's views: while his friend has become a leader of the doves, Hillel has become much more of a hawk.

Hillel knows the Arabs as well as anybody in the present Israel leadership. He was born in Baghdad, the capital of Iraq, in 1923. He came to Palestine in 1930, studied at Tel Aviv's exclusive Herzliah high school, was active in the Scout movement and became a founder of that movement's first kibbutz, Ma'agan Michael. After World War II he joined the "illegal" immigration network and helped bring many Iraqi Jews to Palestine.

Hillel is a small, slight-looking man, taciturn by nature and by training. Some of his most daring exploits are still closely guarded secrets. Before the War of Independence he was a secret emissary in Syria and in the early 1950's headed the highly confidential Israeli group that signed an agreement with the late Prime Minister Nuri Said permitting the departure of all Iraqi Jews. Later Hillel joined Eliav in the Port Said evacuation. In the early 1960's he was elected to the Knesset. However, during his entire career, Hillel has made a point of not presenting himself as a representative of the Oriental Jew. The Labor party, of course, valued his ethnic background as a vote-getting factor in elections.

After two years of studying at the Hebrew University, Shlomo Hillel was appointed Ambassador to Guinea and to the Ivory Coast and then became a member of the Israeli delegation to the United Nations. In 1969 he became Minister of Police, and has been successful in improving the public image of the police.

6

The Histadrut Bosses
and the Parties of the Left

IN the years before the establishment of the State of Israel, the Histadrut (General Federation of Israeli Workers) served as the main power base of the ruling Labor party, which was then composed of Mapai (the Workers' Party of the Land of Israel), and the smaller Mapam, the leftist labor party. The kibbutz (agricultural collective) movement, the moshav (cooperative settlements) movement and even the underground military organization, the Haganah, all played important roles in consolidating the political power of the labor parties. However, none of these groups played as significant a role in guaranteeing labor domination before and after 1947 as two arms of the Histadrut: its economic enterprises and the labor unions.

The economic enterprises, including banks, factories, bus cooperations and even luxury hotels, could be counted upon to supply the funds for election campaigns and provide jobs for minor functionaries, while the unions, comprising more than half a million members today, helped to bring in the votes. This is the reason why, despite the constant friction between the Histadrut and the government over the latter's economic policy, social legislation and education, government leaders are careful to preserve the unique place of the Histadrut within the framework of Israel's democracy.

The Histadrut is an original Israeli creation. Even when it was established in 1920 it was more than a mere federation of labor unions. The workers incorporated in the Histadrut were first and foremost Zionists dedicated to the Jewish revival. Thus, when they felt that private employers were not building the country fast enough, or when, in the 1930's, new pioneers arriving from Poland and Germany were faced with unemployment, the workers turned the Histadrut into an entrepreneur, a force that began establishing industries, financial institutions and even its own marketing organization. Since the Histadrut enterprises never had to distribute their profits, and could always plough them back into business, their rate of growth was often astonishing.

The inevitable internal conflict between the Histadrut as an organization of wage earners and the Histadrut as an employer of many tens of thousands of workers was postponed for many years because of the strict egalitarian ethos that prevailed among Israeli workers. However, in recent years that dam has given way. Today the clash within the Histadrut is no longer only between those who demand higher wages and those who feel that the country as a whole (and the Histadrut itself) cannot afford it, but also between the different unions themselves. There are those workers, like the stevedores, the El Al Israel Airlines technicians, and even the marine officers, who feel that a general federation like the Histadrut is incapable of safeguarding their particular interests.

The harmony—or rather consensus—between the leaders of the Histadrut and the key government leaders that existed by virtue of the fact that they all belonged to the same party, the Labor party, has also come under strain in recent years as a result of three major factors:

• The inevitable dispute over jurisdiction and policy between the government and organized labor.

• The internal conflicts within the Histadrut, and the weakness of the labor federation as reflected in its inability to discipline all groups within it.

• A severe personality clash, mainly between the Secretary-General of the Histadrut, Yitzhak Ben-Aharon, and Pinhas Sapir, the Minister of Finance.

Strangely enough, in 1969, when members of the majority group within the Labor party agreed to the proposal of the minority Achdut Ha'avodah group within the party to appoint Ben-Aharon to the post of secretary-general, it was felt that his strong, independent personality would be an asset. It was hoped that Ben-Aharon would be able to restore the dwindling grip of the Histadrut over its membership and enhance its damaged prestige. Yet Ben-Aharon acted like the sorcerer's apprentice: he became a threat to those who brought about his election. The disappointment is all the more surprising because those who chose Ben-Aharon for the job had known him for the last forty-five years as an impatient, obstinate labor leader.

Minister of Labor Yosef Almogi explains the breakdown in communication between the government and the Histadrut as the result of the traditional income policy's being abandoned in favor of a controversial wage policy. During the first two decades of Israel's existence, Almogi has revealed, leaders of the Histadrut and government met regularly to discuss changes in the income of wage earners. Not only pay increases but also the tax level, government subsidies and social-welfare payments were topics of informal agreements reached in those meetings. In recent years these comprehensive agreements have been replaced by open clashes over pay increases in new labor contracts.

In order to avoid an all-out "class struggle," which Ben-Aharon sometimes advocates in his public speeches, Mr. Sapir resorted to "package deals," in which economic policy measures were worked out between the government, the Histadrut and the employers' groups. Although these agreements, worked out in February, 1970, and later in March, 1973, were severely criticized at the time, it is generally believed that they were safety valves which prevented the Israeli economy from slipping into chaos and runaway inflation.

Yitzhak Ben-Aharon (Nussbaum) is a broad-shouldered man with a thin gray mustache and burning eyes, who looks much younger than his age. He was born in Bukovina, on the Rumanian-Russian border and studied economics and political science in Berlin. When he came to Palestine in 1926 he joined a kibbutz, and in 1932 was among the founders of Givat Haim, on the coastal plain between Tel Aviv and Haifa. He joined the British Army during World War II and was one of the Palestinian officers captured by the Germans in Greece. He later summed up his war experiences in a book, published in London, called *Listen, Gentile*.

Ben-Aharon, who still has his home in Kibbutz Givat Haim, started in his public career early. In the 1930's he was an emissary of the labor movement in Germany and later served as secretary of the Tel Aviv Labor Council. He was one of the founders of Mapam, which originally was a merger between his own Achdut Ha'avodah faction and Hashomer Hatzair, a Marxist Zionist group (Achdut Ha'avodah later broke away from Mapam). He was Minister of Transport between 1959 and 1962.

It was Golda Meir who reportedly selected Ben-Aharon (over Yeruham Meshel and Yosef Almogi) as secretary-general of the Histadrut. Yet, soon after these elections, he embarrassed the government by supporting the extreme demands of the Ashdod port workers, thus causing the resignation of Haim Laskov, the director of the Ports Authority. Using fifty-year-old socialist terminology, Ben-Aharon demanded a new division of wealth in the country and at the same time suggested that the power base of the Histadrut be strengthened.

Since then, Ben-Aharon has come out in support of nearly every demand for wage increases, rejecting only wildcat strikes, such as those of the Lod airport workers and the El Al technicians. In the spring of 1972, after the Histadrut had signed an agreement containing "indicators" for the wage scale of that year, he supported unions whose demands exceeded these indicators by far and also opposed government moves against strikers in essential services.

When the Prime Minister, Golda Meir, intervened in the spring of 1972 in a wage dispute in the canning industry, and prevented a strike by suggesting a compromise, Ben-Aharon resigned in protest against government intervention in Histadrut affairs. However, three days later he was back in his job, but not before Golda Meir and Pinhas Sapir themselves asked him to rescind his decision and carefully organized groups of workers staged "spontaneous" strikes on his behalf.

Ben-Aharon was less successful in the summer of 1972 when he supported the strike of two thousand workers of the Elite food-products concern. The strike was settled seven weeks later with the workers obtaining very few of their original demands. Time and again, Ben-Aharon would appear before the striking Elite workers to raise their morale. However, their employers, who had large stocks of their products with which they supplied the markets, were not in a hurry to give in. This was one of Israel's few strikes that did not end with a victory of the workers.

In his speeches, Ben-Aharon often warns against "reactionary capitalism" of the "privileged few" and says that unless social justice is implemented the country is doomed. The Minister of Finance, Pinhas Sapir, a target of many of Ben-Aharon's attacks, bitterly rejects the "demagogic" use of facts and figures by the Secretary-General. He and Mrs. Meir often accused Ben-Aharon of "inciting" the workers.

People who know him have noticed the two faces of Yitzhak Ben-Aharon. At his desk and in small groups, the Secretary-General is a charming, polite man, cultured, with a good sense of humor and a way of expressing his opinions quietly and eloquently. However, when the same man stands on a podium, he gets excited and delivers orations at fever pitch.

To those of Ben-Aharon's opponents who claimed that he caused disharmony in relations between the government and the Histadrut were added in early 1973 others who were antagonized by his political ideas. To the surprise of many of his colleagues, including his associates in the Achdut Ha'avodah faction, Ben-Aharon came out in favor of Israeli withdrawal from the occupied territories, perhaps even before peace is achieved. He argued that increased dependence on Arab labor may be more detrimental to Israeli society than exposure to Arab military attacks.

Despite his fierce criticisms of personalities and institutions, Ben-Aharon is annoyed when he himself comes under attack. He complained to the Broadcasting Authority when a satirical television program made fun of him. He also demanded the dismissal of the editors of *Davar*, the Histadrut-owned daily, when an article criticizing him appeared in the paper.

During his first years as secretary-general of the Histadrut, Ben-Aharon said that he would not seek another term in office and planned to retire from public life after the 1973 elections. However, as the elections to the Histadrut and the Knesset drew nearer (both are scheduled to take place in the fall of 1973), there were an increasing number of indications that Ben-Aharon would like to be re-elected as secretary-general of the Histadrut.

If Sapir had had his way, the leadership of the Histadrut would probably have gone to Ben-Aharon's deputy, Yeruham Meshel. In his personality and views Meshel seems to be the opposite of the present secretary-general. Although he started out as a union leader at the time when struggles over wage increases were popular, in recent years he has shown himself an advocate of the view that workers as well as employers must adhere to wage agreements. He believes that workers can gain much through compromise and quiet diplomacy. In the last decade Meshel's position in the Histadrut has gradually become stronger because of his success in handling wild-cat strikes and obtaining concessions for workers at the negotiating table rather than on the picket line.

Yeruham Meshel, who was born in Pinsk, Russia, in 1912, became an agricultural laborer when he arrived in Palestine in 1933. He then became a construction worker and began his union activity in 1936, when unemployment hit the labor force. He became secretary of the Building Workers' Union in Tel Aviv and later, during World

War II, was an official in the Union of Arab and Jewish Workers who worked in the British Army camps. At that time, he organized his first strike.

Shortly before the establishment of the State in 1948, Meshel entered union work on the national level. At first he was in charge of all the industrial workers' unions and later, in 1961, he became director of the Trade Union Division of the Histadrut, a department which represents the Histadrut in all labor negotiations.

Although Meshel's prestige as a national figure was far less than that of Ben-Aharon (this was the reason why he did not get the number-one job in the Histadrut when Labor party leaders were looking for "a strong candidate"), his reputation as a skillful negotiator has not suffered. On the contrary, it has been frequently demonstrated that when there is a knotty labor situation no one but Meshel, the quiet, patient, undramatic negotiator, can find a solution satisfactory to all sides. Thus, when in February, 1973, twenty thousand engineers and technicians threatened to cripple the economy with a strike, it was Meshel who found a formula to satisfy most of their demands which, at the same time, would not provoke other groups to put forth similar demands.

One place of work where Meshel is known, but has very limited influence, is the port of Ashdod, which is ruled—through the Committee of Stevedores—by Yehoshua Peretz. Peretz, a young union leader, who possesses almost charismatic control over his associates, represents a new generation of labor leaders who did not grow up in the Zionist movement and who know very little about socialist ideology.

Peretz, an immigrant from Morocco who at one time registered for emigration to Canada, showed enormous talent in exploiting inherent weaknesses in the Histadrut, in understanding the potentialities of the television camera, and in manipulating the utter dependence of the whole economy on small groups of workers, such as his own stevedores' union, to their benefit.

Another of Peretz's talents was to recognize the conflict in 1969 between the impetuous new secretary-general of the Histadrut and

the equally stubborn Haim Laskov, the director of the Ports Authority, who soon proved to be the weaker of the two when he was not
given full government backing for his opposition to the workers'
demands. The victory of Peretz over Laskov brought him into alliance with Ben-Aharon. The picture of the bearded, balding steve-
dore, who openly advocates opportunism as a method of attaining
his ends, hugging and kissing the aging doctrinaire socialist represents the new age in the Histadrut.

Yehoshua Peretz, who was born in 1938, arrived in Israel with his
family in 1950 and served in the Army after working as a blacksmith
in Dimona. His colleagues in Ashdod like to tell stories about his
service in a commando unit, whereas in point of fact he was a cook.
After Peretz was released from the Army, he found work in the
construction of the new port of Ashdod. There he led his first
sitdown strike, when he was one of the forty workers who demanded
a permanent job in the port, although their contracts specifically
stated that they were hired for construction work only. When the
government showed lack of resolution and preferred to give in
almost without a fight, Peretz learned his lesson. He realized that
in Israel of the 1960's noisy demonstrations, clever handling of the
media and organization outside the framework of the Histadrut
could produce better results than traditional labor negotiations.

Peretz also realized that the fact that his port workers were mostly
immigrants from Morocco and that many of them lacked education
was not a weakness but rather an advantage in their confrontation
with the Histadrut and the government. He likes to pose as the poor,
uneducated worker who is baffled by the complications of industrial
society, although he, and not the traditional leaders, has in fact
learned how to manipulate the mass media, above all television, to
his advantage.

The strength of Yehoshua Peretz and the weakness of Ben-
Aharon were best demonstrated in 1968, when Peretz, as chairman
of the Ashdod Port's Workers Council, appeared in a Histadrut trial
for breach of discipline, and cleverly turned the trial into a mockery.
His victory was complete a year later when the new secretary-gen-

eral of the Histadrut, Yitzhak Ben-Aharon, gave his backing to Peretz and his port workers.

While labor leaders of the old generation, who grew up on Zionist and socialist traditions, like to appear as workers whose blue shirt (the movement uniform) is waiting to be donned on the day they give up public service, Peretz is not embarrassed when it becomes known that he is demanding special privileges for himself. Thus, even when the news spread in 1972 that Peretz had obtained two apartments in Ashdod financed by public funds, and that he needed the second apartment because he has a mistress, in addition to his legally wedded wife, his public image did not suffer. In the March, 1973, election to the Stevedores Union, he scored an overwhelming victory.

While there may be similar Yehoshua Peretzes in other Israeli communities, he himself has won recognition, albeit grudging, as a national figure. It is understandable therefore, that Histadrut leaders would like to get him out of Ashdod, not only in order to "kick him upstairs," but also to use him as a vote getter and manipulator on the national level. Peretz himself still hesitates to leave his Ashdod power base. He realizes how important he is to various personalities and political parties and is determined to exact the highest price for his services.

While Peretz has made his uncouthness and artificial naïveté a trademark, Shaul Ben-Simhon, the first Moroccan-born labor leader to break into the Israeli establishment, paved his way by acquiring a certain polish and learning the methods of operation of the Israeli elite. Ben-Simhon, a tall man with wavy graying hair, has learned from experience that the Israeli establishment does not tolerate constant clashes, but rather accommodates each group, including the opposition, and provides for each of them according to their size and nuisance value.

As one of the early leaders of Rafi, the faction that was established around the leadership of David Ben-Gurion at the time of the 1965 split in Mapai, Ben-Simhon belongs to an exclusive club which also includes Moshe Dayan, Shimon Peres and Yosef Almogi. In recent years, he has mobilized the support of the Moroccan Jewish community, both in Israel and abroad, and forged it into an impressive power base.

Shaul Ben-Simhon, born in Morocco in 1930, was "lucky" to reach Israel in time to join the Palmach, which thus makes him part of the elite group in the younger generation which fought in the War of Independence. His public career, like that of Yehoshua Peretz, began in Ashdod in 1958. Although his activities in Ashdod were interrupted when he was sent to North Africa on a mission (and was wounded there in an accident), he built up his power base there and became secretary of the Labor Council.

Ben-Simhon utilized the split in the Labor party to his advantage and brought many North Africans into the newly-established Rafi party. At the end of 1965, following his success, he headed Ashdod's municipal coalition. However, soon afterward he left Ashdod to represent Rafi in the central committee of the Histadrut. When Shaul Ben-Simhon clashed with the secretary-general of the Histadrut, Ben-Aharon, he proved that he no longer needed the good will of the old-timers of the party. His success in organizing a world convention of North African Jews in 1972 proved that Ben-Simhon is a national figure who cannot be overlooked.

In 1968 the three factions of the labor party, the old guard Mapai, the pro-Ben-Gurion splinter group Rafi and the slightly more radical Achdut Ha'avodah merged into one party. Although the party now presumably talks in one voice and differences of opinion on the future peace settlement with the Arabs and other crucial issues no longer are based on old factional lines, nominations of the party's candidates for various posts are still often influenced by this background. Each faction carefully guards that no other faction gets more than its share of nominations.

Yet the acute internal tensions within the Labor party and even serious ideological differences between such doves on foreign policy as Pinhas Sapir and hawks like Moshe Dayan are hardly likely to cause a new split. Likewise, Mapam, the Zionist-Marxist party which since 1969 has formed an "alignment" with the Labor party and appears jointly with it in all elections, in recent years has been plagued by internal conflicts and yet is in no immediate danger of falling apart.

The backbone of Mapam has always been the collective settlements formed by its socialist youth movement Hashomer Hatzair. Although today the majority of Mapam's supporters live in the cities, the veteran leaders of the party (correctly called "the traditional leadership"), come mainly from the Hashomer Hatzair kibbutzim. Many of them are aging idealists who in the 1920's and early 1930's advocated the "revolt of youth" and the establishment of a classless society coupled with a Jewish revival in the historic homeland of the Jews.

Despite constant internal friction, including the recent splitting-off of a dissident group that formed the Israel New Left, the "traditional leadership" of Mapam has been able to steer the party through the years through stormy ideological conflicts. Thus, in the early 1950's, the party broke with Stalinism only after one of its leaders, Mordecai Oren, was tried in Czechoslovakia for espionage and alleged complicity in the "Slansky Conspiracy." He was released only after spending several years in a Prague prison. USSR political and military support for the Arabs caused further disillusionment in Mapam with the Soviet regime.

In recent years, however, internal strife has taken the form of more than simple ideological conflict. In many cases there was open jousting for power in the party, with groups of young leaders demanding a larger role for themselves, often rationalizing their demand by calling for "rotation" in the party leadership. At the December, 1972, Mapam convention the young activists scored an impressive victory when the principle of rotation was adopted and when Meir Ya'ari, the undisputed leader of the party for over fifty years, stepped down. However, early in 1973 Ya'ari was replaced as secretary-general of the party by another member of the traditional leadership, Meir Talmi. A number of resolutions adopted by the convention, such as one referring to a continued alignment with the

Labor party, and de facto agreement to creation of Israeli settlements in the occupied territories—a move which Mapam had previously opposed—increase the likelihood that Mapam will continue to participate in the coalition cabinet to be formed after the 1973 elections.

Despite his retirement at the end of 1973, Meir Ya'ari remains the father image of Mapam. He led his party for a longer period than any other political figure in the Western world, trying to merge the principles of Zionism with the dogmas of Leninism. It is said of his ideological orthodoxy that it is a virtual extension of the Hassidic spirit in which he grew up in his parents' home in Galicia. His opponents refer to him as the "Mapam rebbe."

Ya'ari, born in 1897, was a leader of the Hashomer Hatzair movement, which was inspired by such back-to-nature protagonists as the Russian Lev Tolstoy and the Zionist dreamer Aharon David Gordon. Later the movement turned to prophets such as Marx and Lenin. Ya'ari himself studied in Vienna with the founder of psychoanalysis, Dr. Sigmund Freud, and was an officer in the Austrian army in World War I. When he arrived in Palestine in 1920, as the leader of a group which was in many ways the forefather of today's hippies, he dreamed of something like "Biblical socialism."

Like the party he led, Ya'ari's ideological beliefs, always emphatically held, changed somewhat throughout the years. The biggest shift was probably in 1953, following the arrest and trial of Mordecai Oren, when he declared, "We have freed ourselves from dependence on the Soviet Union." Yet, in all his five decades of leadership, Ya'ari has been steadfast in his belief both in Zionist ideals and in egalitarian socialism.

If Ya'ari was the Moses of Mapam, Ya'acov Hazan was his Aaron. Friends since youth, both drew their strength from the thirty thousand members of the seventy-five kibbutzim of Hashomer Hatzair (Ya'ari is a member of Kibbutz Merhavia and Hazan of Kibbutz Mishmar Ha'emek). Hazan may have been the junior member of the Mapam leadership team, but he knew how to fight for his own opinions, especially in recent years, when he showed himself more "nationalistic" in favoring participation in a Labor government. He also clashed with Ya'ari over the ideological theses published by the latter in 1971. Hazan demanded "to make it clear to the Soviets" that Israel would fight if Russian troops invaded Israel on the side of the Arabs.

Ya'acov Hazan, born in Brest-Litovsk in 1899, may have left ideological primacy to the senior member of the leadership team, but he played a more important role in formulating the party stand on economic and social issues. He had great influence in developing the educational standards of the Hashomer Hatzair movement.

Ya'ari and Hazan have served in the Knesset continuously since the election of the first parliament in 1949. However, they refused to serve in any government, preferring that party representatives chosen by them become ministers, deputy ministers and other political functionaries of the State. They felt that their own influence over the State and the party would be better served by this "indirect rule." Only once, in 1948, did Hazan break that principle, when he agreed to serve as member of the Israeli Delegation to the United Nations.

The change that occurred in 1973 in the leadership of Mapam was basically biological, due to the advanced age of Ya'ari and Hazan rather than to any ideological change. Instead of a team of two, it now looks as if leadership will be entrusted to a team led by the new secretary-general Meir Talmi. The team itself is composed of three groups: representatives of the kibbutzim (the Minister of Immigrant Absorption, Nathan Peled, and the Israeli Ambassador to Austria, Yitzhak Patish); the Mapam representatives in the central committee of the Histadrut (prominent among them, Aharon Efrat); and the leaders of the urban groups of Mapam (such as Minister of Health Victor Shemtov).

Ideologically, the new leadership of Mapam reflects three shades of thinking: (a) the followers of the "general line" of Ya'ari and Hazan who call for a continued alignment with the Labor party while preserving Mapam's independence in social and economic issues; (b) the leftists who demand that the party take a harder line in the alignment and leave the coalition if their demands are not met; (c) those who advocate merger with the Labor party.

The leftists, who include many of the young leaders who have emerged in recent years, are quite vociferous. However, this group represents no more than a third of the party members. This explains, therefore, the victory of the moderates in Mapam at the December, 1972, convention.

Of all the personalities in Mapam's new collective leadership, the one who has the best chances of inheriting at least part of the power left behind by the Ya'ari-Hazan team is Nathan Peled, the Minister of Immigrant Absorption. He himself is a member of a kibbutz and for many years served as secretary-general of the Hashomer Hatzair kibbutz movement. In addition, he served in the United States on behalf of his party and for six years was in the Israeli Foreign Service, as Ambassador to Austria.

7
Nationalists, Clericalists
and Opposition Parties

THE stable division between the parties in power and parties of the opposition that characterizes the Israeli political scene, despite small temporary fluctuations, reflects the conservatism of Israeli voters. Not in a single election that has taken place in the first twenty-five years of the existence of the State of Israel has there been any significant deviation in the division of votes among the three major blocs of parties: the Zionist Labor parties, the religious (clericalist) parties and the right-of-center parties. Even the one occasion in the early 1950's when the right-of-center General Zionists made a spectacular gain was an exception to the rule rather than a new trend.

Mapai (the forerunner of the Labor party), which has been the ruling party in every Cabinet since the establishment of the State, never succeeded in securing a majority with its own votes or together with the other labor parties. It always had to choose between forming a coalition cabinet with the religious parties or with the center parties.

In most cases partnership with the Mizrachi and Hapoel Hamizrachi (the two parties later merged to become the National Religious party) was preferred to partnership with the General Zionists (who later became the Liberal party). It is hard to state exactly why this choice was always made: perhaps it was the influence of the personal relations of Mapai leaders with religious leaders, such as the late Moshe Haim Shapira, that dated back to pre-State days, or, perhaps, Mapai realized that deals with the religious parties meant fewer concessions. Until the eve of the Six-Day War in 1967 the rightist Herut party was considered "unqualified" for partnership in a coalition cabinet.

The framework of relations between the political parties, their leaders and the central government can be described as resembling an atom whose nucleus is Mapai, with all the other parties moving around it like electrons. The closer the orbit of a party is to Mapai (which has become the Israel Labor party) the more chance it has to be accepted as a coalition partner. The closest orbits to the center of gravity, the Labor party, are those of the National Religious party and the Independent Liberal party (which at one time was known as the Progressive party). In the second group of orbits one can find parties which have on occasion joined the coalition, but not always. They include the ultra-Orthodox Agudat Israel and Poalei Agudat Israel, and the leftist labor Mapam and Achdut Ha'avodah (before it merged with Mapai). The third group of orbits include those parties which rarely join the coalition cabinet, the Liberals and Herut (which meanwhile have formed an alignment called Gahal), and the outer orbits are those of parties that will never be included in any coalition cabinet: the two Communist parties and the tiny Ha'olam Hazeh and Free Center parties.

According to research by Dr. Dan Horowitz and Dr. Moshe Lissak of the Hebrew University on the power elite before the establishment of the State Mapai gives concessions not only to the coalition parties but also to the opposition parties for accepting its decisions, however reluctantly. The payment made by Mapai allows access to the political and representative assets which Mapai controls by virtue of its being the leader of Israeli sovereignty and by also distributing the economic support raised from Jews in Israel and abroad to all groupings, according to their strength.

The control of Mapai over all channels of government in the State stunted the development of leadership possessing status and national prestige in all the other parties, especially the opposition. The only personality of national stature in Gahal who has been in opposition since the struggle for Statehood is Menahem Begin, but he belongs to Herut, which is the less-suitable partner in the Gahal alignment for partnership with the Labor party. And in Herut Begin belongs to the more extreme component, that of the Irgun Zvai Le'umi veterans.

The Herut party was formed immediately after the establishment of the State by the leaders of the Irgun Zvai Le'umi, the right-wing nationalist illegal resistance movement during the British Mandate. The party leadership was constituted from among former commanders of the Irgun, headed by Begin, and included Shmuel Merlin, Hillel Kook, Eliahu Lankin, Shmuel Tamir, Ya'akov Tamir, Haim Meguri-Cohen, Yohanan Bader, Arieh Ben-Eliezer and Haim Landau. Only when the veteran leaders of the former Revisionist party, the nationalist grouping that was in opposition to the majority Zionist organization (and were the original followers of Ze'ev Jabotinsky), began to voice criticism of the new leadership were they co-opted into the executive of the new Herut party. They included such well-known figures as Benjamin Avniel, Arie Altman, Yosef Schofman, Shimshon Yunichman and Ze'ev Jabotinsky's son, Professor Eri Jabotinsky.

Yet, as soon as the Irgun faction felt its position sufficiently firm among the traditional nationalist-Revisionist electorate, it began to eliminate the old Revisionists. This was the beginning of what has become a "tradition" in Herut: some of those who dared criticize Begin's leadership were shunted to the side quietly, others after conflicts that led to outright splits, while yet others were eased out of any post of influence. The latest to go is former Air Force Chief General Ezer Weizman, whom the party co-opted and even sent to the Cabinet during its brief period of post-1967 coalition membership. Herut hoped that Weizman, nephew of Israel's first President and one of the most popular generals, would be a real vote getter, particularly among the younger generation. Yet, when he was led into a showdown with Begin, he too had to go.

Today, Herut has practically no young people and has not a single leader of the "intermediate generation." Of the original founders of the party, only two have remained at the top: Begin and his unquestioningly faithful follower, Haim Landau.

Menahem Begin himself is, in a sense, a rarity among Israeli political leaders. He is a new immigrant, having arrived in the country only in World War II. Begin was born in 1913 in Brest-Litovsk, studied law, and was the last head of Betar, the nationalist-Revisionist youth movement, in prewar Poland. The Russians, who divided Poland between them and the Germans, arrested Begin and sent him to a concentration camp in the far north. He was released when he joined the Polish Army formed under the Stalin-Sikorski agreement; as an officer of that force Begin arrived in Palestine in 1942. He was immediately contacted by the disarrayed Irgun leadership and offered the post of Commander, but Begin refused to violate his oath of allegiance to the Polish flag. Only in 1944 did he finally go AWOL, go underground, become the head of the Irgun and call for a Jewish revolt against the British in Palestine. For years he was number one on the most-wanted list of the British, who offered ten thousand Palestine pounds for his capture, but never succeeded in finding him.

When the State was proclaimed, Begin emerged from the underground and called on his followers to obey the laws of Israel. (This could not be taken for granted, since the leaders of the new State came from the Labor parties and the Haganah, bitter foes of the Irgun during pre-Independence years.) It was due primarily to Begin's influence that civil war in the infant State was avoided when Ben-Gurion ordered the destruction off the coast of Tel Aviv of the freighter *Altalena,* which carried arms for the Irgun, at that time still an independent fighting force in the war against the Arabs.

But Begin came very close to urging a revolt against the Israel government in 1952, when the Knesset debated the draft of the reparations agreement with West Germany. On the floor of the House Begin warned, "There will be no negotiations with Germany! Over less important issues, nations went to the barricades!" Outside the Knesset, thousands of his followers tried to storm the building but were dispersed by the police. The Israeli public did not follow his call and the reparations agreement was approved, becoming one of the main sources of economic development of Israel in the fifties. That speech—and the stones hurled by demonstrators against windows of the Knesset—revived popular suspicions of Herut and helped keep it beyond the pale of political respectability for another fifteen years.

Begin's fiery oratory is in complete contrast to his extremely polite manners and considerate personality. He rarely raises his voice in private and still kisses ladies' hands in the best tradition of prewar Polish officers. He always refers to Ze'ev Jabotinsky as "my mentor and teacher," but while the Revisionist leader had the soul of a poet (he wrote both poems and dramas), Begin has the soul of a lawyer. He is interested only in foreign policy and security matters and has little interest in or grasp of domestic politics or economics. Begin wrote two books of memoirs: *The Revolt,* about Irgun's struggle against the British; and *White Nights,* about his years in Soviet concentration camps.

From 1955 onward, Begin repeatedly tried to create an alliance between Herut and the General Zionists (later called Liberals), the other major nonsocialist party of the country, in order to extricate the party from its political isolation. Yet it was not until 1965 that the Herut-Liberal bloc (Gahal) was formed, with Begin as its chairman. Two years later, on the very eve of the Six-Day War of 1967, Herut finally breached two decades of political ostracism: Gahal joined the Government of National Unity with Begin as Minister without Portfolio but with the prestige—if not the status—of Deputy Prime Minister.

Begin did not hide his satisfaction at being, finally, a member of the government. He saw himself as the guardian of the National Unity coalition and even mediated in disputes between Moshe

Dayan and the late Prime Minister Eshkol. But, most of all, Begin
saw his presence in the Cabinet as that of a watchdog over the
"territorial integrity" of enlarged Israel: already in 1967, when
other spokesmen insisted that Israel would not retreat from the
newly-occupied territories without a formal peace treaty with the
Arabs, Begin stated again and again that "not an inch of the land
of our fathers must be handed back" to the Arabs.

Being "in" rather than permanently on the outside apparently
was good for Herut: the 1969 election saw a considerable increase
for Gahal and it was given six seats in the new coalition Cabinet.
Begin preferred to remain Minister without Portfolio—underscoring his special status in the Cabinet. When, in 1970, the Cabinet
majority voted to resume negotiations with UN Special Envoy Gunnar Jarring, Begin compelled Gahal to quit the coalition: he interpreted the Cabinet vote as a decision to retreat from the occupied
territories. This was the nearest Begin came to defeat among his
own supporters: the decision to leave the coalition was made by a
slim 117 to 112 majority in the Gahal executive.

Among those who openly opposed Begin's line in that vote was
Ezer Weizman, then recently appointed Minister of Transportation.
Weizman was "parachuted" (in Israeli political slang) from the
GHQ of the Army to the Cabinet table. Herut was short of leaders
of national stature and Weizman knew that his military career was
approaching its end: he had reached the post of head of the General
Branch, the number-two job, and usually the stepping stone to the
job of Chief of Staff; however he was left in no doubt that he would
not get the number-one post. Becoming a Cabinet member for
Herut, with which he had both ideological identification and past
associations, seemed an auspicious start to his political career.

Ezer Weizman has been for most of his life the *enfant terrible* of the
Israeli establishment, one of the few people who approach something of an upper-class type in the basically egalitarian Israel society. His father, Yehiel Weizman, was one of the wealthiest businessmen of Haifa (he had the first private automobile in the
country); his uncle, Dr. Chaim Weizmann, was president of the

World Zionist Organization and became the first President of Israel. Ezer's wife is the sister of Ruth Dayan, until her recent divorce the wife of General Moshe Dayan. (The relations between Ezer Weizman and Dayan are part of contemporary folklore. Ezer calls Dayan "der Araber"—the Arab—an allusion to his unpolished behavior; Dayan grew up in a farm village with Arabs as his neighbors. Ezer's friends claim that when the question of Weizman's appointment to the post of Chief of Staff was discussed Dayan did not put up a fight for his brother-in-law.)

Weizman, a perennial optimist and among the most colorful figures in Israel leadership, has a witty but sharp tongue. Its cuts have left not a few scars on people whose support later could have helped in the attainment of his military and political ambitions. Instead, his quick barbs have contributed to an image of light-headedness and even occasional recklessness, and obscured to some extent his immense contribution to the development of the Israel Air Force as one of the smoothest, most effective striking forces in the world.

Ezer Weizman was born in Haifa in 1924. At the age of eighteen he made his first solo flight, "and in my heart I remain a solo flier to this day," he remarked twenty-five years later. Flying his black-painted World War II Spitfire is still his hobby. He volunteered for the British Army and in 1943 was in the first group of young Palestinians sent for fighter-pilot training in Rhodesia. Weizman served in North Africa and India and, after the war, went to study aeronautical engineering in England. There he also was active in the Irgun, but on the eve of the War of Independence returned to Palestine and helped to organize the air arm of the Haganah, which became the core of the fledgling Israel Air Force.

At the beginning of the war, he was sent to Czechoslovakia to ferry old Messerschmitts to Israel and soon flew one of them in the first sorties against the Egyptians, whose columns were approaching Ashdod. In 1950, at the age of twenty-six, he was appointed Chief of Operations of the Air Force and only a year later was sent as one of the first two Israelis admitted to Staff College in Britain. After the

1956 Sinai Campaign, in which he flew fighter missions, Weizman was appointed head of the Air Division—the second rung from the top on the Air Force ladder—and in 1968 became Commander of the Air Force.

Weizman played an important role, together with Shimon Peres, in translating the unwritten French-Israel alliance into a flow of French aircraft in the late 1950's and in the first half of the 1960's. But, more important, it was Weizman who instilled the tough fighting spirit in the pilots and set the exacting demands for perfection of performance by both air and ground crews which were credited with the smashing success of the Israel Air Force in the very first hours of the June, 1967, war. In that war, however, Weizman was no longer with the Air Force: he was head of the Staff Division of the GHQ, having turned over the Air Force to his hand-picked successor, Mordecai ("Motti") Hod. In his new post, Weizman played an important role in pushing through approval for the daring idea of an all-out initial annihilation attack against the Egyptian Air Force on the ground; the fact that he knew what could be expected of the pilots and their planes gave special weight to his arguments. Yet, when he claimed that six hours would suffice to destroy the entire Egyptian Air Force, this was viewed as another one of his exaggerations. Three hours after zero hour, he phoned his wife and told her: "Baby, the war is over!"

He stayed in the Army for another two years. When he left to become a Cabinet member, he was given the Transport portfolio and inherited the conflict between the Ashdod stevedores, backed by Histadrut Secretary-General Ben-Aharon, and Ports Authority head General Haim Laskov, his former boss as Chief of Staff when both men were still in uniform. Weizman stole the show from Ben-Aharon: he showed understanding for the workers' demands and held luncheon meetings with their union chiefs in popular restaurants, gaining more popularity as representative of a right-wing party than many a Labor minister had ever won. He also gained the good will of the influential bus cooperatives by supporting some of their fare-increase demands, while the religious parties appreciated his opposition to demands for public transportation on the Sabbath. This wide popularity, plus his good relations with Golda Meir (based on their common opposition to any major evacuation of territories taken in the Six-Day War), reportedly contributed to the determination of the Labor party machine to end Gahal's participation in the government.

While on questions of the occupied territories and other security matters Weizman closely followed Begin's line in the Cabinet, he did not hesitate to vote against him on other subjects, including Begin's effort to cancel the first official visit by Foreign Minister Eban in West Germany. Nor did Weizman share many of the views of his brother-in-law, Defense Minister Dayan: he particularly rejected Dayan's fears that the Soviets would actively intervene against Israel during the 1969-70 peak of Nasser's War of Attrition along the Suez Canal. Weizman's son, Shaul, was severely wounded in that phase of the war. Weizman related later that the question that came to his mind when his son's life hung in the balance was "What did we do wrong that our children too must go on fighting?"

After Gahal quit the government, Weizman became one of the directors of the Maritime Fruit Carriers, the fast-growing shipping company of veteran Herut leader Ya'akov Meridor. (Mila Brener, Meridor's partner and right-hand man, is married to Weizman's cousin.)

Being a private person for the first time after almost thirty years in uniform or in office enabled Weizman to speak out even more openly in public on political and military matters. His criticism both of the conduct of the Six-Day War (in which, he claimed the deep-penetration air raids in Egypt should have been even more forceful and reach even deeper into Egypt) and of the "interim settlement" with Egypt led him to confrontations with General Dayan. Some of his judgments were refuted by events: in the summer of 1970, for example, he claimed that Egypt had won the War of Attrition (which, in fact, resulted in crucial Egyptian defeat) and that the resumption of fighting was imminent.

His aggressive views, as well as his world outlook based on an admitted sense of inherent Israel superiority over the Arabs, have helped to create an image of Weizman as the prototype of the nationalistic-chauvinistic Israeli of the 1970's.

The 1969 entry of Weizman into the Cabinet both reinforced and symbolized the ascendant influence in Herut of the business faction, headed by industrialist Joseph Kremerman, over the "proletarian" wing of the party.

Kremerman's power in Herut is said to be based on two factors: his considerable personal wealth is an important source of financial support for the party; and his second wife is the daughter of the veteran Herut leader and shipping and business magnate Ya'akov Meridor. In fact, however, his financial skills in handling Herut's perennial budgetary crises as party treasurer are probably more important a source of influence than his personal donations. When party veterans complain to Begin about Kremerman's views or actions, Begin usually defends him by saying that "the man carries the heavy burden of raising the funds needed for the party on his shoulders."

Joseph ("Yoske") Kremerman was born in Haifa in 1926. He joined the Irgun, studied first in Tel Aviv, then in the United States (business administration) and again in Tel Aviv, where he got his law degree. Almost from the beginning of his party activities, he dealt with finances, and for years has served as head of Herut's Budget Department. In 1960 he was elected to the Knesset, but his irregular attendance earned him there the nickname of "the absent-est member" of the House. When Herut and the Liberals formed their joint bloc, they decided to close down their respective faltering dailies and put out a joint morning paper. When it, too, failed to show signs of any vitality, it was Kremerman's decision not to guarantee any further bank loans to the paper that led to its folding.

The Herut party machine knows that money for their day-to-day work—if not for their next month's salaries—depends on the fund-raising (or credit-raising) efforts of Kremerman. It was he who decided—and the party assented—that Herut's third Cabinet member should be Ezer Weizman rather than veteran party leader Yohanan

Bader. It was Kremerman and his supporters who, at the 1970 party convention, forced the veterans to elect Ezer Weizman as chairman of the executive, the number-two post after Begin. Slowly, by putting his supporters into key posts in the party machine or in the district office, and by winning some of the old-timers in the party bureaucracy to his side, Kremerman was building up his influence as the strongest behind-the-scenes figure in Herut.

Yet, when Ezer Weizman openly clashed with Begin at the 1972 convention, Weizman and his supporters lost out and Weizman had to resign as chairman of the executive. In an all-out showdown, most delegates (including Kremerman) felt they owed more loyalty to Begin than to newcomer Weizman. This defeat also marked a loss of influence—at least temporarily—for Kremerman, who became less active in the party and devoted more of his time to his extensive business affairs, centered around the Petah Tikva plywood factory Etz Lavud and interests in a Formica factory in Canada as well as flour mills and a construction subcontracting firm in Israel.

Joseph Kremerman and Ezer Weizman represent the intermediate generation of leadership in Herut. The only visible representative of the young generation of leadership is Knesset member Yoram Aridor, chairman of the Blue-White (Herut) faction on the Histadrut executive. Aridor, who carefully disguises his boyish looks with an ever-serious expression, considerably strengthened his position in the party in 1966 when he did not join other younger representatives who quit Herut with Shmuel Tamir and Eliezer Shostak to form their Free Center party. Aridor's oratory often echoes the pathos that typifies veterans of Herut, but the contents of his speeches reflect much more logical analysis and argumentation than the traditional Herut emotionalism.

Aridor was born in Tel Aviv in 1933, and studied economics and political science at the Hebrew University in Jerusalem, where he also earned his law degree. Though he was active in Herut's student movement, his rise in the party began in 1961, when he was elected to the central committee of the party, followed by his election in 1963 to the party executive. In 1966 he won an important political test case when the courts ruled against the validity of party switching by municipal councilors. In Israel's multiparty system it has repeatedly occurred that when several opposition parties manage to gain a local majority and join forces to elect the mayor, the dominant Labor party entices an opposition councilor to switch loyalties and give his swing vote to the Labor candidate. Aridor was elected to the Knesset in 1969 and already as a freshman proposed some advanced legislation, such as government compensation to defendants in criminal cases if they are found innocent, or broadening the power of the courts to intervene in administrative decisions by government agencies. His bill making cheating in union voting a criminal offense failed by a single vote, despite extreme opposition by the Histadrut.

There are not even a few of the younger leaders like Weizman, Kremerman or Aridor in Herut's partner in Gahal, the Liberal party. The veteran leadership—once among the most important in the nation—reached positions of influence, but during the last years of the pre-independence period had already departed from the scene: figures like Peretz Bernstein, Joseph Sapir, Ezra Ichilov and Israel Rokach are no longer among the living and no one approaching their stature has emerged in the party. Thus, when the Liberals too were given three seats in the 1967 National Unity government, they also had to look outside their home-grown leadership for at least one of their three candidates. But while Herut picked Ezer Weizman, a popular young ex-general, the Liberals chose Aryeh (Leon) Dultzin, their representative on the Jewish Agency executive, who had immigrated from Latin America only a few years before and was hardly integrated into the life of Israel. When Gahal quit the government, Dultzin (who never gave up his post on the Agency executive) quickly returned to his previous job.

It is quite possible that if he had not clashed with Begin in 1966 young and brilliant Tel Aviv lawyer Shmuel Tamir would now be the number-two man in Herut and possibly also in Gahal, instead of leader of the small, two-man Free Center party, which he formed when he left Herut. Tamir, born in Jerusalem in 1923 to the prestigious Katznelson family, was active in the Irgun Zvai Le'umi from his youth and at the age of twenty-five was deputy commander of the Irgun in the Jerusalem area. Arrested by the British, he was sent to detention in Kenya, where he acted as spokesman of the camp inmates.

Released upon the establishment of the State in 1948, Tamir was among the founders of Herut and began an impressive legal career, in which he often managed to combine the role of attorney with his political views. In Israel's initial years of economic austerity and rationing, he frequently represented private industries in court, charging the Labor-controlled Ministry of Supplies with discriminatory practices in raw-material allocations.

Tamir gained national prominence in the so-called Kastner trial. Dr. Israel Kastner was a wartime leader of Hungarian Jewry who sued for libel a Jerusalem pamphleteer who accused him of collaboration with the Nazis. Tamir, who took on the defense of the pamphleteer, managed to turn the trial from a libel suit by Kastner into a political trial of Kastner's superiors in the Zionist leadership and the Jewish Agency, whom he accused of a "conspiracy of silence" in the face of Hungarian Jewry's annihilation.

Again, as defense attorney for a group of young students, he turned a libel suit against them by then Deputy Police Chief Amos Ben-Gurion (son of former Prime Minister David Ben-Gurion) into a political trial aimed against the prosecution and the Labor party establishment.

In 1965 Tamir was elected to the Knesset on the Herut list, but within a year began to oppose Begin's leadership and was among the organizers of the Free Bloc in the party. When Gahal was formed, Tamir demanded that his group be organized as a separate third component of the Herut-Liberal partnership. This was rejected and Tamir formed the new Free Center faction in the Knesset.

After the Six-Day War Shmuel Tamir was among the first to demand that Israel refuse to withdraw "one inch" from the occupied territories. In his speeches he proved to be more extreme even than Herut, demanding the death penalty for Arab terrorists

and approving many of the exploits of Rabbi Meir Kahane and his
Jewish Defense League, which were often criticized even by Begin.
He supported the integration of Arabs into the Israel economy but
opposed the open-bridges policy of Moshe Dayan.

As a member of the Economic Committee of the Knesset, Shmuel
Tamir proved himself to be one of the government's most vociferous critics. His attacks were especially forceful on issues where his
legal training came in handy. In the case of the mismanagement of
the failing Autocars company, Tamir succeeded in turning the Economic Committee of the Knesset, with the help of its chairman, into
an American-style congressional investigating committee.

Shmuel Tamir is also a vehement opponent of any attempts to
change the Israeli electoral system designed to hurt small parties
such as his. In this campaign his efforts are almost parallel to those
of another unique Israeli figure, one who should be placed at the
opposite end of the political spectrum—Uri Avneri. The editor of
Ha'olam Hazeh, a weekly magazine which is a combination of political crusading, scandal, sex and nudity, Avneri won the votes of his
magazine's readership as well as of many other young Israelis in two
successive Knesset election campaigns. In 1969 his party even won
two seats in the Knesset; however Avneri and the second member
to be elected, Shalom Cohen, later parted ways.

Avneri, who was born in Germany in 1923 and arrived in Palestine
in 1933 (his speech still bears a slight German accent), was for many
years "the child prodigy" of the Israeli press. He made his mark in
two books written immediately after the 1948 War of Independence
in which he reflected the heroism and at the same time the anti-
heroic sentiment of the younger generation. He fought in the famous "Samson's Foxes" unit against the Egyptian invaders. He
later joined the staff of the daily Ha'aretz, where his writing won him
popularity. In 1954 he purchased the magazine Ha'olam Hazeh (This
World), hoping to turn it into an Israeli Time magazine. However,
Avneri gave the magazine its peculiar mixture of content when he
added sex and scandal (admittedly for circulation purposes) and at
the same time turned it into a vehicle for expressing his left-wing
political ideas.

Although many of his readers are, like him, veterans who have shown heroism in battle, a large percentage of his readership are Oriental Jews who are more inclined to extreme attitudes toward the Arabs. Uri Avneri has developed an ideology of the "Semitic partnership" between Jews and Arabs in the Middle East. In 1963 he was among the organizers of the Arab-Jewish committee that called for the abolishment of military government in the Arab-populated areas of Israel. After the 1967 war, Avneri became an outspoken proponent of the "Palestinian entity" and called for the establishment of a Palestinian state on the West Bank. His book *Israel without Zionism* won him popularity especially among New Left groups in Europe, who see in him a spokesman for the "other Israel" and the hope of a new anti-establishment force in Israel. However, Avneri's supporters outside of Israel would probably be less enthusiastic about his statements on patriotism and heroism, which do not coincide with their way of thinking.

Avneri went into politics almost by chance, in 1965, when he accused the Knesset of preparing a new libel law which he thought was directed against him. He mobilized the workers of the magazine and personal friends into a makeshift party which surprisingly enough won him enough votes to send him to the Knesset.

In the Knesset he has proved himself to be one of its most conscientious members, rarely missing a session. He bitterly attacks what he considers blatant manifestations of the Israeli establishment: organized religion, big business, militarism and chauvinism. Israeli leaders often become subjects of venomous attacks and ridicule in *Ha'olam Hazeh*. One of Avneri's favorite targets is the Minister of Defense, Moshe Dayan, whom he has exposed on various occasions, attacking his affairs with women, his yen for archaeology—which according to Avneri is theft of national property—as well as Dayan's attitude toward the Arabs in the occupied territories.

Uri Avneri is no doubt one of the most controversial figures in Israeli politics. Even his fiercest opponents admit that he has added a fresh element to Israeli political reality; at the same time, his staunchest supporters will agree that his following will never turn into a mass movement.

Echoes of Uri Avneri's anti-establishment revolt were heard in the early 1970's in one of the most deeply-entrenched establishment groups, the National Religious party. For a number of years there had been a strange division of labor in that party: the older leadership held positions in the government while the younger leaders were active in the party wards, in the religious kibbutzim and in the youth movement. At the party convention in February, 1973, the young leadership for the first time successfully challenged the old leadership, which for many years was the loyal and often silent partner of the Labor party in successive coalition cabinets.

The split in the leadership of the National Religious party (which was formed following the merger of Hamizrachi and Hapoel Hamizrachi, both Religious Zionist parties) came after the 1970 death of party leader Moshe Haim Shapira, who was a unifying factor not only in his own party but also in the government. For example, Shapira was instrumental in May, 1967, in convincing Prime Minister Levi Eshkol to bring Moshe Dayan into the government and make him Minister of Defense. Today at least five factions are jousting for power within the NRP. One group is headed by Cabinet Ministers Yosef Burg and Michael Hazani, another by Minister Zerah Warhaftig, a third represents the religious kibbutz movement, and yet another group represents young party activists. One of the largest groups within the party is headed by Yitzhak Raphael, who considers himself the heir of Moshe Haim Shapira.

Yitzhak Raphael (Werfel), born in Poland in 1914, married the daughter of Rabbi Yehuda Leib Maimon, the late leader of Mizrachi. His family background, Hebrew University education and boundless energy soon helped his rise within the party. His ambitious drive for a ministerial post was almost fulfilled in 1961 when he became Deputy Minister of Health. Even his numerous opponents admit that Raphael showed talent in running the Ministry, which for many years had been completely passive, leaving initiative in the health-care field to Kupat Holim, the Histadrut sick fund, and other institutions. Yet Raphael became indirectly involved in a bribery scandal in the planning of a new hospital and was forced to resign.

His controversial reputation probably harmed him in 1970 when the party secretariat decided by a margin of one vote to select Michael Hazani and not Raphael for a government post after the death of Moshe Haim Shapira. After his defeat, Yitzhak Raphael concentrated on foreign affairs and became one of the NRP's most outspoken hawks, objecting to any cut in the defense budget and any withdrawal from the West Bank, and demanding larger investments in the Jewish settlement at Hebron. Raphael often has voiced criticism of his own party's role within the Cabinet.

Yitzhak Raphael's hawkish ideas are similar to positions taken by young leaders of the NRP, among them Chicago-born Dr. Yehuda Ben Meir and the articulate sabra Zevulon Hammer, who have become the most outspoken representatives of the young members of the party.

Hammer, who was born in 1935 in Haifa, studied at Bar-Ilan University, served as a tank officer during the Six-Day War, and was instrumental in organizing the young members of the party, many of whom are graduates of the B'nai Akiva youth movement, into a powerful political faction.

Hammer, who entered the Knesset in 1969, became a real threat to the party leadership early in 1973, when his faction won 23 percent of the seats at the party convention and succeeded in passing a number of resolutions that embarrassed the old leadership. Among these resolutions was one that objected to withdrawal from any part of the West Bank and another that would prevent the party from joining a coalition cabinet, unless the Law of the Return is changed so that only those who are born Jews or are converted by Orthodox rabbis are recognized as Jews (the existing law does not specify that only Orthodox conversion is accepted).

Although the wording of the resolutions was later somewhat softened, it is generally believed that because of the obstinate stand taken by Zevulon Hammer and his young hawks, the National Religious party may not join the coalition cabinet after the 1973 elections. At the very least it may demand a much higher price for its support of Labor policies.

One of the major disputes in the National Religious party in 1972 was over the position of the Chief Rabbinate and the party's interference in the election of the Chief Rabbis. Traditionally there are two Chief Rabbis in Israel, one representing the Sephardi community and the other the Ashkenazi. At the time of the Turkish rule over Palestine and later during the British Mandate, the Chief Rabbis had a special position as "religious dignitaries" representing the Jewish community. Since the establishment of the State, their position has been more controversial, especially because some of the more extreme Orthodox groups, such as Agudat Israel, have always challenged the religious authority of the men who served as Chief Rabbis. For Agudat Israel the Moetzet Gedolei Hatorah (Council of Torah Sages) is the supreme authority for religious and even political decisions.

The National Religious party, however, not only saw the need for the Chief Rabbinate but was actively involved in the selection of candidates, seeing the positions as one of the party's traditional centers of power. Many Israelis believe that the constant disputes over the Chief Rabbinate, the petty infighting between the rabbis themselves, and the close association between political-clerical issues and religious-moral issues have all but destroyed the authority of the Rabbinate in the eyes of most Israelis. Only in the Hasidic sects, each of which has its hereditary Rebbe whom its members admire and whose authority they accept unquestioningly, do rabbis still wield the influence they traditionally held in Jewish communities before the establishment of the State of Israel.

Rabbi Shlomo Goren, who was elected to the Chief Rabbinate of the Ashkenazi community in October, 1972, is a product of this prolonged infighting. Yet, at the same time, his supporters believe that he will gradually acquire enough moral authority as well as the necessary political backing to restore some of the traditional glory to the position of Chief Rabbi. Shlomo Goren, former Chief Army Chaplain and later Chief Ashkenazi Rabbi of Tel Aviv, has an unquestioned ability to synthesize the old traditional ordinances of the Halacha (religious law) with the needs of modern reality.

Goren, of medium height, with a long gray beard, showed a knack for the dramatic during his long service in the Army (where he held the rank of major-general) as when he blew the shofar (the ceremonial ram's horn) on top of Mount Sinai after it was captured by Israeli troops in June, 1967, as well as good feeling for publicity when he saw to it that photographers were present when he prayed at the sacred Western Wall when the Old City of Jerusalem fell to the Israelis on June 7, 1967.

He is given credit for his unyielding efforts to provide all Israeli war casualties with Jewish burial and, at an earlier stage, for causing the abandonment of a plan to form special Army units of Orthodox soldiers. Instead, Goren saw to it that kosher food was supplied to all Army units. At the same time he helped to find ways of adjusting religious regulations to Army routine and needs. He also showed flexibility in enabling widows of fallen soldiers to remarry even if the death of their husbands had not been established as required by Jewish law.

Goren, born in Poland in 1917, arrived in Palestine in 1925. He studied at the Hebron Yeshiva and at the Hebrew University in Jerusalem. He was among the founders of Kfar Hasidim, an Orthodox agricultural settlement near Haifa, and wrote a number of research studies in Jewish law. (Following the Apollo moon landing he organized a special symposium to study the question whether the traditional monthly blessing of the new moon should be said by persons on the moon.)

Goren's first bid for the position of Chief Rabbi was in 1966, following the death of the late Chief Rabbi, Yitzhak Halevi Herzog. However, at that time he lost by a narrow margin to Tel Aviv Chief Rabbi Isser Yehudah Unterman. Goren ran again against the octogenarian Unterman in 1972 after a dramatic struggle within the Orthodox camp.

One of Goren's first moves upon becoming Chief Rabbi was to appoint a special tribunal which enabled a brother and a sister to marry their chosen partners, even though they had been declared "bastards," who, according to Jewish law, are children of a married woman by someone other than her husband, and are not allowed to marry "eligible" Jews.

The case, which was a tragic result of the Holocaust (the mother of the "bastards" did not know her first husband was still alive), created bitter feelings in Israel against the Rabbinate and religion in general. Yet, in solving this case, Goren diminished some of the pressure but did not solve the basic problem of updating religious laws which no longer fit present circumstances. He also bitterly antagonized the extreme Orthodox circles, who refuse to accept his authority.

Goren believes that, given time, he can modernize religion and at the same time impose the rule of Halacha, the religious law, on the broad masses of the Israeli public. At the same time he may be tempted to try his hand at wielding secular authority as well. His influence on the National Religious party was said to be growing even after his election to the Chief Rabbinate.

8
The Insiders

O<small>F ALL</small> the expressions that journalists use to hide the origins of their information, expressions like "informed sources" and "political circles," the expression that raises most eyebrows and whose meaning is vaguest is "sources close to . . ."

Who are those sources? What is their position in the Israeli establishment? Are they powerful enough to influence the decisions of ministers? Are there those who can "pull strings" behind the scenes in Israel? What is the base of their power?

In general it can be concluded that the Israeli top elite does not have confidential advisors possessing intellectual influence on those entrusted with authority. A phenomenon like Professor Henry Kissinger does not exist in Israel.The influence of "sources close to the minister" is often the influence derived from physical closeness to the people in power. This is "government by telephone," as it is called by public-administration experts, meaning that often those around the cabinet ministers decide whether or not to let telephone calls go through to them. Many of the Israeli insiders do not even enjoy the position of *chef de cabinet,* as it is known in Europe. European *chefs de cabinet* often have decisive influences over the timetable of their ministers. They not only decide whom the cabinet minister will see and when, but also add their comments to letters they select for him to read. These aides prepare résumés of the daily press and give opinions on almost every document that reaches the ministers' desks. Needless to say, their influence is often considerable. Israeli cabinet ministers, on the other hand, are mostly too busy and their approach to their jobs too unsystematic for them to delegate authority to the directors of their offices. It is often easier to get the minister himself on the telephone to make an appointment or to stop him in the corridor of the Knesset than to refer the matter to him through his aides. In an article on Simha Dinitz, the former political advisor of Golda Meir, Sylvie Keshet, an Israeli journalist, wrote that the Minister of Finance, Pinhas Sapir, once complained: "I call him the first time, he is busy; I call him a second time, he does not answer. I get mad. I pick up the phone to Golda at home and tell her, 'Perhaps you can get me an appointment with your Simha?' This is the way I can get to talk to him."

The Israeli bureaucracy does not appreciate those who have no executive powers. Thus those close to cabinet ministers often choose to utilize their influence in order to get an executive appointment, such as department head, division head or even director-general of the ministry. This administrative position does not prevent them from being called from time to time to the cabinet minister and asked their opinion on appointments or bringing before him suggestions on topics that are outside their immediate field.

But even if there is no clear-cut class of insiders in the Israeli bureaucracy, there are a limited number of senior officials whose main source of power is "inside information," based on the fact that they are present when important decisions are made. There are also positions, especially some close to the Prime Minister and in the Foreign Ministry, where the importance of the man is decided not by the scope of his administrative responsibilities but in accordance with the Minister's readiness to listen to his advice and act accordingly.

While each ministry, including those with administrative or economic spheres of activity, has its own insiders, their influence is felt
most in those ministries whose main function is policy-making. This
is why the personalities who appear in this chapter are drawn from
the Prime Minister's Ministry and the Foreign Ministry.

In the spring of 1968, when Michael Arnon was about to conclude
his service as Consul-General in New York, he was offered the post
of head of the Israeli information services. Arnon (who was called
"Mike" even when he served as Israeli Ambassador in Ghana—and
the Ghanaians said that they did not know any ambassador by the
name of Arnon) turned down the offer, preferring to be appointed
Secretary to the Cabinet.

At first glance, the powers of Secretary to the Cabinet seem limited; even as the official government spokesman who reports the
weekly Cabinet meetings to the press, he is restricted in what he may
divulge. Leaks about the Cabinet meetings usually come from the
ministers themselves. Yet Mike Arnon selected this post because of
its closeness to the decision-makers. As a born journalist there
seems to him to be no place as interesting as the Cabinet chamber,
even if many of the stories he hears there never see print. The
ministers have learned to appreciate Mike's quick ability to grasp a
situation, his ability to phrase complicated communiqués, as well as
his unusual talent for telling jokes. It seems that he finds it easy to
remember not only the vast range of information on topics that the
government deals with, but also the anecdotes which he meticulously collects from the many people whom he meets constantly.

Tall and somewhat stout, Mike makes the impression of an ul-
traconservative, not only with his meticulous dress, but also with his
antediluvian crewcut. He has a mischievously clever smile. Although
he works long hours, he always finds time for gossip-laced conversations flavored with humor.

His rise in the Israeli public service was fast. Born Michael Gar-
funkel in Vienna in 1924, he came to Palestine at the age of thirteen
and was a reporter on the *Palestine Post* before the establishment of
the State. In the Foreign Ministry he has served as official spokes-

man, press attaché at the Embassy in London, Director of Information Services in Washington, Director of the Information Division
of the Foreign Ministry, Ambassador to Ghana and Consul-General
in New York—all in less than twenty years.

He tries hard to give status to his present position. In his weekly
meetings with the press, he succeeds in maintaining good humor,
providing no more information than absolutely necessary. He
knows, however, how to give away hints that are picked up by some
journalists, who fully realize that these hints are intentional. With
Mike there are no accidents.

During the two periods of his service in the United States, Arnon
won popularity as a speaker in meetings of the Israel Bonds Ogani-
zation and the United Jewish Appeal. This success in after-dinner
speeches is shared with Mike by a former colleague in Prime Minister Golda Meir's office: Simha Dinitz, Mrs. Meir's political advisor
and Director-General of her office, who in the spring of 1973 assumed the post of Israel Ambassador to Washington.

It is difficult to imagine an odder combination of personalities
than the aging Prime Minister and the relatively young advisor, who
is not a former kibbutznik and does not even have a "movement
background"—a quality that she appreciates in the people that sur-
round her. Simha Dinitz, who was born in Tel Aviv in 1929 to
well-to-do parents, served in the Jewish Settlement Police, in the
Givati infantry brigade and the Military Police during the War of
Independence; he began his "diplomatic career" as a nightwatch-
man at the Israeli Embassy in Washington while working his way
through political-science studies at Georgetown University. After
receiving a degree there and marrying his American-born wife,
Vivian, he returned home to Israel and entered the Foreign Service.

He was soon discovered by Golda Meir, then Foreign Minister,
and served as Director of her office from 1963 to 1966. During this
period a special relationship developed between Mrs. Meir and her
young assistant. When she left the government, Simha Dinitz was
appointed Minister at the Israel Embassy in Rome. In 1968 he was
moved to Washington as Minister in charge of Information Services.

But, before the Dinitz family could unpack their bags, he was called back to Israel. Levi Eshkol had died and the new Prime Minister, Golda Meir, wanted Simha Dinitz as her personal advisor.

Following the death of Dr. Ya'akov Herzog, the brilliant Director-General of the Prime Minister's Office and close advisor to three Prime Ministers, Dinitz became Director-General in addition to his role as advisor. The strength of Dinitz does not lie in analyzing complicated political situations or in giving political advice: he is more of a troubleshooter and serves Mrs. Meir by representing her in consultations with groups of advisors. Dinitz has a unique talent for reading her mind and states her positions with clarity and intensity. He can simplify complicated issues and has a keen understanding, not only of political topics, but also of the personalities behind them. He sometimes would be with Golda for as much as twenty hours a day, attending her late-night "Kitchen Cabinet" sessions.

Even the severest critics of Simha Dinitz admit that he is outstanding in the social sphere. He is a brilliant raconteur and the life of a party. The ease with which he handles social responsibilities is expected to be of great assistance to him in his capacity as Irsaeli Ambassador in Washington, a role he assumed at the end of March, 1973.

The man Golda Meir chose to replace Dinitz as her advisor and Director-General of the Prime Minister's Office had often been consulted on foreign-policy matters before replacing his predecessor. He is Mordecai ("Motke") Gazit, who in March, 1973, moved to the Prime Minister's Office from the Foreign Ministry, where he was Director-General.

Gazit, among the first diplomats of the Foreign Ministry, served as Golda Meir's political secretary between 1957 and 1960. He then served in London, Burma, and Washington. When he returned to the diplomatic service in 1970 after a brief stint in the Ministry of Immigrant Absorption, it became apparent that the Prime Minister wanted the advice of Gazit, who was then Deputy Director-General in charge of North American affairs in the Foreign Ministry.

Gazit's long working day is devoted mostly to the study and

preparation of working papers on current political issues. Throughout the years Golda Meir has learned to appreciate Gazit's
thoroughness in digesting political documents and preparing extensive analyses.

Mordecai Gazit (Weinstein) was born in Constantinople in 1922
and came to Palestine in 1933. He received a master's degree in
archaeology at the Hebrew University. At that time he joined the
first training course for diplomats that was conducted in anticipa-
tion of the establishment of the State. When the course was over in
1947, its graduates were all called to active military dv y. Gazit, who
became a company commander, was sent with his men to relieve the
besieged defenders of the Jewish quarter in the walled Old City of
Jerusalem. Before he was able to assume his post as garrison commander, he was severely injured and taken out on a stretcher when
the Old City fell to the Arabs. However, he recovered in time to
assume the post of brigade intelligence officer and only after the war
moved to the Foreign Ministry.

Journalists hardly ever get scoops from talking with Mordecai
Gazit, but a background talk with him is helpful in writing "think
pieces," as analytical articles are called in journalese. Gazit himself
has taken time out during his career to write articles and lecture on
Israel foreign-policy issues. He can be brilliant and most convincing
in conversation; on other occasions, he can be withdrawn to the
point where it is difficult to believe that diplomacy is his profession.
Yet his pleasant appearance, his analytic mind and his ability to
express unconventional ideas helped to win him the admiration of
his associates as well as State Department officials with whom he
came in contact during his five years in Washington.

Gazit's successor as Deputy Director-General in charge of North
American affairs in the Foreign Ministry was Ephraim ("Eppy")
Evron, formerly Israel's Ambassador in Canada. One story of how
he obtained the Ottawa post is based on a note which Prime Minister
Levi Eshkol allegedly received, asking him to move Evron to Canada
from his new ambassadorial post in Sweden, if possible. "I miss him
and I would like to have him closer to me," the note is said to have

stated. It was signed by Lyndon B. Johnson, then President of the United States.

Even if this story is apocryphal, there is no doubt that the close relations between Eppy and the late American President—relations that were established before Johnson came into the White House, when Ephraim Evron was the Histadrut representative in the United States—were unusual for any diplomat serving in Washington. Yet this closeness of contact was not out of the ordinary for Eppy, who struck up similar friendships with leaders of the British Labour party who were in power when he was Minister in the Israel Embassy in London.

While for Mordecai Gazit diplomacy means policy analysis and discretion, Ephraim Evron has mastered the art of personal relations. His success in this field is surprising, since, contrary to the American concept of public relations, he is not the man for back-slapping and handshaking. He does not stand out in a crowd, but in small groups he is an expert in quiet, meaningful conversation. He brims over with knowledge of detail and is quick in sizing up the man to whom he is speaking. He is short and thin with a slightly reedy voice; his forehead is high and his hair thinning. He has a shrewd smile and tells his friends inside stories that prove his closeness to the decision makers.

Evron was born in Haifa in 1920, studied for a while at the Hebrew University in Jerusalem and served in the British Army between 1941 and 1946. He served in the Haganah intelligence and was wounded in the Battle of Jerusalem in 1948. In 1949, when he entered the Foreign Service, he became political secretary of the then Foreign Minister, Moshe Sharett.

Sharett was not the only personality with whom Evron worked closely. Between 1951 and 1953 he was political secretary of Prime Minister David Ben-Gurion and later director of the office of Pinhas Lavon, then Minister of Defense. However, when the controversy over the Lavon Affair broke (involving an Israeli spy ring in Cairo that was uncovered in 1955), Evron succeeded in maintaining a safe distance.

His biggest success in making contacts was probably in London, where he "relieved" the leadership of the Labour party of their anti-Israel complex and was among the frequent house guests of Prime Minister Harold Wilson. In his post at the Israel Embassy in Washington, he was aided by his close association with the U.S. Ambassador to the United Nations at that time, Arthur Goldberg, whose acquaintance he made when Goldberg was legal counselor of the AFL-CIO.

In the course of the years, Evron has managed to antagonize quite a number of senior Israeli officials. They criticize his "personal" diplomacy as enhancing not only the interests of the State of Israel but also the welfare of those who engage in it.

One Israeli diplomat whose influence on Israeli foreign relations has extended beyond his official assignments is Asher (Artur) Ben-Natan. He is a tall good-looking man whose white mane of hair and Viennese accent make him resemble a German aristocrat more than the Jewish fighter he was, charged at one time with rounding up Nazi criminals in postwar Europe.

Asher Ben-Natan successfully steered his way through the pitfalls of the job as Israel's first Ambassador to West Germany, but he has stumbled over a number of mines in his second diplomatic post, perhaps no less dangerous, as Israel Ambassador to France. He assumed this role after the imposition of the French arms embargo and the deterioration of relations between Israel and France.

Ben-Natan's name began to appear in the press in the days when he served as representative of the Ministry of Defense in Paris in 1956 and later back in Israel, when he was Director-General of that Ministry. He was known to be close to Moshe Dayan and Shimon Peres. When, in June, 1965, Prime Minister Levi Eshkol decided to appoint him Israel Ambassador in Bonn, the then Foreign Minister, Golda Meir, was not convinced he was the right choice. His name was too closely associated with defense matters and cloak-and-dagger activities.

Ben-Natan knew how to talk harshly with the Germans. Half a year after his arrival in Bonn, he told a German audience that he was

aware of anti-Semitism in Germany although it was cleverly camou-
flaged. He even told the Germans that he did not believe the new
generation to be "totally different" from their elders because of
their education or upbringing. At one time he refused to meet the
Mayor of Würzburg because of his Nazi past.

Toward the end of his mission in Germany, Ben-Natan often had
to confront antagonistic leftist German youth, who had taken up the
fashion of promoting the Palestinian cause. New Leftists at Nurem-
berg University prevented him from lecturing, shouting, "Al Fatah,
al Fatah," in unison for ninety minutes. In Hamburg, fist fights
broke out between supporters of Israel and supporters of the Arabs,
who were determined to prevent Ben-Natan from speaking. In
Frankfurt, police had to intervene when students tried to break up
a meeting where he was about to appear. Even cool-headed Ben-
Natan (it is said of him that "his boiling point is 150 degrees Centi-
grade") often found it difficult to remain calm under the pressure
of such abuse and attacks.

His "toughness" in his relations with Germans was only one side
of his policy. He understood Israel's vital interest in developing
normal relations with West Germany and attacked the hypocrisy of
Israeli individuals and groups on this matter. When he completed
his mission after three years, he summed it up in original fashion:
he published a collection of three hundred letters that German
citizens had sent to him during his service as Ambassador, which
illustrated the complicated web of relations between Israel and Germany.

Asher Ben-Natan was born in Vienna in 1921. When he was
eighteen he was dropped off the Palestine coast by a small ship
bringing "illegal" immigrants, and joined a group of pioneers who
later set up their own kibbutz at Dovrat in lower Galilee. Mobilized
for Haganah activities, he was about to be dropped behind German
lines in World War II when the plan was canceled. Instead he was
attached to a unit that investigated Nazi crimes.

After the war, he arrived in Austria armed with the credentials of
a foreign correspondent. The stories which he filed were mainly

scoops in which he was personally involved: smuggling Jewish refugees across borders and bringing them to Mediterranean ports from where they sailed to Palestine, as well as tracking down Nazi criminals. Adolf Eichmann was his first target. The photograph of Eichmann taken in 1938, which Ben-Natan obtained from the Nazi criminals' mistress, helped to identify him when he was finally located in Argentina in 1958.

In 1947 Ben-Natan went back to his kibbutz, but not for long. He joined the Foreign Service, took time off for studies in Geneva and even went into business in Africa. In 1956 he was sent back to Europe as representative of the Ministry of Defense. Those were the honeymoon days in Israeli-French relations. In Paris at that time he found a completely different atmosphere from that he had to face five years later, when he arrived as Ambassador to France.

"The French do not see themselves responsible for the death of six million Jews," said critics of Ben-Natan in Paris, when it seemed to them that the new Ambassador was still continuing the hard line he had used in Bonn.

Another ambassador who has earned a reputation for his "undiplomatic" speeches is Yosef ("Joe") Tekoah, Israel's Ambassador to the United Nations. This properly dressed gentleman, with his thinning red hair sleekly brushed down, is know as Israel's "angry Ambassador." He pours his wrath on the Soviet Ambassador in polished English, spoken with a Russian accent.

Tekoah's tough language has helped to raise his prestige in Israel, a front he considers no less important than the "glass palace" on the banks of New York's East River. He likes to compare the UN to a corporation in which Israel holds one out of the 130 shares of stock. Since at least half of the other stockholders automatically support every anti-Israel resolution, Israel has no chance of rationally convincing either her opponents in the world organization or the countries which vote with the Arabs out of narrow selfish interests. If Israel can't win votes, Tekoah believes, it must at least protect its prestige through a proud stand.

Tekoah is one of Israel's most experienced diplomats. However, when Swedish General Carl Van Horn, who headed the UN Middle East Truce Supervision Organization in the 1950's, described Tekoah as "a member of the reptilian order," he reflected the impression the hard-headed diplomat makes on Israel's enemies.

Tekoah's boiling point is also very high. He can sit quietly without reflecting any emotion in the hall of the General Assembly or the Security Council, listening to the most abusive anti-Israeli speeches of the Arab representatives. Even when he gets up to present his emphatic reply, it often looks as though for him it is really just a performance. In fact, he considers the UN a wrestling ring where the purpose is to overwhelm your opponent, without forgetting that it really represents an illusionary lineup of strength and not reality itself.

Yosef Tekoah (Tikochinsky) grew up in an international atmosphere. He was born in Shanghai in 1925 to a family that had moved there from Russia. After the capture of Shanghai by the Japanese, his family arrived in the United States, where he later studied international law at Harvard. Soon after the establishment of the State of Israel, he joined its foreign service.

His many diplomatic posts have included assignments as Ambassador to Brazil and the Soviet Union, as well as liaison officer to the Truce Supervision Organization in Israel. He is one of the few heads of delegations in the UN who do not need a translator to understand the invective of the Soviet representative, since Russian is his mother tongue.

Tekoah had hoped that his diplomatic experience, his popularity at home and the support of Foreign Minister Abba Eban would help him obtain the post of Ambassador to Washington. However, in November, 1972, Mrs. Meir preferred to give the appointment to Simha Dinitz.

On security matters, foreign ministers and prime ministers depended in the past on the Ministry of Defense for advice. Recently the Prime Minister's staff was strengthened by the addition of an advisor on special affairs. He is Aharon (Arele) Yariv, who, when he retired from his post as head of the Intelligence Branch of the Israeli Army General Staff in September, 1972, took off his uniform but did not change his profession. In fact, he continued to collect, compile and draw conclusions from intelligence reports.

The man who headed Army Intelligence for eight years, a longer period than anyone before him, was born in Lithuania in 1921. He arrived in Palestine in 1935 and shortly after finishing high school joined the British Army, where he reached the rank of captain in the Jewish Brigade. After the war he joined the training course for diplomats of the Jewish Agency, but was called to Army duty and served as battalion commander in battles of the War of Independence.

Like other senior Israeli officers, Aharon Yariv (Rabinovich) moved to the position of chief of Army Intelligence via Washington, where he served as military attaché between 1957 and 1960. When Yariv became chief of Army Intelligence in 1964, the branch had to contend with ever-growing Russian military intervention in Egypt. Until their departure in August, 1972, the Russians in Egypt constituted a new challenge for the Israeli Intelligence Services.

Yariv was a frequent visitor at Cabinet meetings, where he reported on national security. His personal relations with Mrs. Meir and with the Minister of Defense, Moshe Dayan, developed during those years. When the time came for him to retire from the Army, the Minister of Defense asked him to become his political advisor. The suggestion was seen by many as an indication that Dayan was grooming Yariv to be his successor as Minister of Defense. However, following the murder of the Israeli athletes in Munich in September, 1972, Mrs. Meir felt the need for an advisor on security measures and chose Yariv for the post.

9

Liaison to World Jewry

Jacob Tsur, chairman of the board of directors of the Jewish National Fund, once claimed that the JNF has the right to undertake tasks of a national nature such as building roads, planting trees and participating in Israel's land policy. This right, he said, may look like an infringement upon Israel's sovereignty, but it is hardly surprising to anyone who thinks (as he does) that Israel belongs not to its inhabitants but to the Jewish people as a whole.

This demand by Jacob Tsur is a kind of rearguard action in a struggle that has been going on for a quarter of a century over the division of labor between the government of Israel, the Jewish Agency, fund-raising organizations and other groups who see themselves as representatives of the Jewish people in the land of Israel. In fact, during the first years of the existence of the State, the "institutions of the Jewish people" functioned almost parallel to government authorities: duplication in the fields of health services, welfare, education, housing, agricultural settlement and afforestation created considerable friction and waste as well as a series of ideological conflicts.

In the course of the years most of these clashes between parallel administrative units have been settled, and duplication limited, so that the problem hardly ever disturbs Israelis and Jewish organizations in the Diaspora today. Even on a sensitive topic like the handling of immigration, a division of functions was agreed upon between the immigration department of the Jewish Agency and the Ministry of Immigrant Absorption. When disputes over jurisdiction flare up from time to time, they are quickly settled. Just as the representatives of opposition parties have their share in the Israeli establishment so do the "representatives of the Jewish people," whose place in the ruling body of Israeli society now seems assured.

During the period of friction and duplication between institutions of the State and institutions representing the Jewish people, the leaders of the latter had a lower status than the government elite and lacked a clear-cut position in Israel's power structure. Since the Six-Day War, however, a change can be noticed: as the division of labor became clearer there emerged a group of people in Israel whose power basis is the representation of world Jewry.

At the time of Israel's establishment, personalities in the first ranks of the pre-State Zionist leadership were given positions of national responsibility: second-rank members had to be satisfied with posts in the Jewish Agency, the Jewish National Fund, Jewish Foundation Fund and other organizations.

At least part of the friction between the government and the Jewish Agency was personally motivated: many leaders of the Jewish Agency felt frustrated because they had not been given positions in the government framework. Moreover, the main function which was presumably left for them—liaison between the Jewish people and the State of Israel—was often assumed by the government leaders themselves. Even during the crucial years preceding and immediately following the establishment of the State, the main burden of mobilizing the support of the Jewish people for the young State was undertaken by national personalities such as Moshe Sharett and Golda Meir. Since then, Israeli leaders like the first two Finance Ministers—the late Eliezer Kaplan and Levi Eshkol—and the present Finance Minister, Pinhas Sapir, have made direct appeals to the hearts and pockets of Jews abroad. Crucial decisions on fund-raising and relations with Jewish organizations have often been made in government ministries and not by the authorized bodies of the Jewish Agency.

Through the years new leadership has developed in various Jewish communities and new organizations such as Israel Bonds and the Jerusalem Economic Conference have been established. Their leaders have developed direct relations with the heads of the Israeli government without the intervention of the Jewish Agency or any Zionist body. Samuel Rothberg, who was honored by Prime Minister Golda Meir in Miami Beach during her March, 1973, visit for "twenty-five years of leadership and service to the Jewish people," did not grow up in the Zionist movement. Even the fact that Israeli personalities like Giora Josefthal and one-time Prime Minister Moshe Sharett moved from the government to take up central roles in the Zionist movement was not enough to change the fact that those charged with liaison with world Jewry have played a minor role in the Israeli power structure.

However, the fact is that since the Six-Day War of June, 1967, the various fund-raising organizations have collected sums each year that are several times higher than previously. Few remember that during the first two decades after the establishment of the State, the budget of the Jewish Agency was no more than $100-120 million a year. In 1972 the Jewish Agency budget totaled more than $400 million.

This new reality was interpreted in organizational terms in 1971 when the Jewish Agency was reconstituted and the representatives of the non-Zionist fund-raising community were incorporated into its leadership. The expansion of the Jewish Agency's base has also strengthened the position of those Israelis who fill liaison positions between the State of Israel and world Jewry. Among them are Moshe Rivlin, Uzi Narkiss, Mordecai Bar-On, Aryeh Dultzin, and, until his death in July 1973, Aryeh Pincus.

Before his sudden demise in Jerusalem, Aryeh (Louis) Pincus—originally a South African lawyer, who serves as chairman of the

Jewish Agency executive. As an Israeli who immigrated after having been president of the South African Zionist Federation for eight years, Pincus represented a new phenomenon in the Israel power elite: a leader who derived his influence by virtue of being "Mr. World Jewry" in Israel at the same time that he represented Israel to the Diaspora.

The position, molded in its present form by Pincus himself, entails fund raising, conferences and emergency meetings in support of Soviet Jews and those in Arab lands, immigrant absorption in Israel, and projects in aid of South American Jewry. All these are subjects in which the chairman of the Jewish Agency Executive has a significant voice.

Pincus was first elected treasurer of the Jewish Agency in 1961. When Moshe Sharett, who became chairman of its Executive after serving as Israel's foreign minister and prime minister, died in July 1965, Pincus succeeded him. In accepting the office, Pincus, who earlier had been director-general of El Al Airlines, gave up his Tel Aviv law practice.

At the time Louis Pincus became number one in the Zionist movement, it was undergoing one of its most difficult periods. Israel was suffering from an economic recession, and immigration, the lifeline which has nourished the Jewish State since its inception, had virtually come to a standstill. The income of the Jewish Agency had reached a low ebb and Pincus had to consider dismissing more than a thousand employees. At that time he encouraged the Zionist movement to adopt a new slogan, "Facing the Diaspora," meaning that not only the fate of Israel is important but also Jewish consciousness and self-determination of Jews, wherever they are, must be preserved at all costs.

The Six-Day War marked a turning point. Aryeh Pincus perhaps lacked the magnetism and charisma that were necessary for establishing a new Zionist movement, but his untimely death left a gap at a crucial moment. Pincus had succeeded in forging a coalition of the Jewish organizations that support Israel, a coalition concentrated around the Jewish Agency. Jews in the Diaspora, especially in English-speaking countries, appreciated his devotion and sincerity. In Israel he was admired as someone who could obtain aid for Israel and had the support of world Jewry.

There is a clear division of labor between Aryeh Pincus as chairman of the executive and Moshe Rivlin, the director-general of the Jewish Agency: Pincus handled relations with Diaspora Jewish organizations while Rivlin spent more time on liaison with the Israeli authorities. To their teamwork goes much of the credit for the reassertion of the Jewish Agency's role as the main Jewish representative body in Diaspora Jewry in Israel.

Moshe Rivlin was born in Jerusalem in 1925 to a well-known old family. Although he received an Orthodox education, he joined the labor movement as a young man and spent time in a kibbutz in northern Galilee. Rivlin served in the Haganah intelligence service and later as a major in the Army. In the early 1950's he served in New York as Consul in charge of liaison with Jewish groups, where his knowledge of Yiddish was an asset. Upon his return from New York he became head of the Jewish Agency's information department.

In 1958 Rivlin became secretary-general of the Jewish Agency and in 1966 its director-general, a post that did not exist previously. His election in 1971 as an associate member of the Zionist executive elevated him from the professional staff to a position of lay leadership.

A number of other sabras have followed Moshe Rivlin to involvement in Zionist affairs. Among them is Colonel (Reserves) Mordecai ("Moraleh") Bar-On, formerly chief education officer of the Israeli Army, who was elected head of the Agency's youth department in 1968. Bar-On, a tall blond sabra, was born in Tel Aviv in 1928. He attended the first officers' course of the Israeli Army in 1948. He was a company commander in battles against the invading Egyptian Army in the south and was wounded when his unit blocked the advance of Iraqi troops from the east.

After the war Bar-On chose an Army career. He was sent for two years of study at the Hebrew University in Jerusalem and later received a master's degree in international relations and Middle Eastern studies from Columbia University. In 1956 he was aide-de-camp to the chief of staff, General Moshe Dayan.

When he was in New York as a student, Moraleh Bar-On "discovered" the Jewish people, confronting for the first time the spiritual problems of Jews outside Israel. Bar-On, who was raised as a nonobservant Jew, began to attend synagogues, eat kosher food and study Jewish philosophy. On a later occasion, when someone asked how Bar-On's return to religion permitted his driving a car on the Sabbath, he was told: "Moraleh found his way back to Judaism but not to the Rabbinate. . . ."

When he left the Army in 1968 and was elected to the Jewish Agency executive, Bar-On explained to a journalist: "I knew that someday I would leave the Army. I knew that I did not want to become manager of a business firm and the academic world also did not attract me. Jews and their future hold a special fascination for me."

Uzi Narkiss, who was appointed in 1968 as head of the immigration department of the Jewish Agency, is still finding his way. While Bar-On has moved his power base to the Jewish world, Narkiss is still very much part of the top Israeli elite, where he was dubbed the "Conquerer of Jerusalem" during the Six-Day War.

Narkiss, born in Jerusalem in 1925, was one of the commanders of the pre-State Palmach, the commando unit of the Haganah, and took part in the bloody battle for Jerusalem in the 1948 war. He reached the rank of brigadier general in 1961. Narkiss was commander of the Israel Army's Central Command in the June 1967 war, when his troops overran the West Bank of the Jordan, including the Old City of Jerusalem.

When Narkiss chose to handle problems of immigration upon his retirement from the Army in 1968, there doubtless was an ideological element in his decision. Yet, for men like Narkiss, there always exists the problem whether liaison work with Diaspora Jewry will not in fact sidetrack his ambitions inside the Israeli establishment.

Aryeh Dultzin, the treasurer of the Jewish Agency, came to Israel as a Zionist leader from Mexico and integrated into Israel's political life. His position as one of the leaders of the Liberal party is enhanced by his activities as liaison with Jews abroad.

10

From Policy Making to
Execution

WHEN the Knesset passed the National Insurance Law in 1955, it entrusted parliamentary responsibility for its execution to the Minister of Labor, who also is the Chairman of the National Insurance Institute. Yet Ministers of Labor spend little of their time looking after the National Insurance Institute, which administers social security in Israel. The law is very specific about who should get benefits and how much; very little remains for any initiative by the Minister of Labor.

The National Insurance Institute therefore has evolved into a semi-independent body headed by an official whose status is somewhere between that of a bureaucrat and a policy maker. He is only one of several members of the Israeli elite who enjoy this somewhat peculiar position. Each of them has reached that rank of lower-echelon policy making in a different way. Some have the backing of the law, whereas others have acquired the positions by virtue of their strong personalities.

There are a number of fields in Israel where there is a constitutional and practical vacuum. In many instances a cabinet minister plays the role of an administrator and in other cases top-level civil servants decide on principles which are in effect policy making. The

Knesset discussed this dilemma fully in 1962, when the Minister of Justice, Dr. Dov Joseph, refuted the demand of the Attorney-General for special status, one which is not subordinate to the Minister of Justice. A legal committee headed by Justice Shimon Agranat ruled against the Minister and the Cabinet supported this ruling. The Attorney-General is thus not part of the Civil Service, but an authority of his own. Similarly, the Bank of Israel Law grants special status to the governor of the Bank of Israel, who is also called "Economic Advisor to the Government," although parliamentary responsibility for the Bank of Israel rests with the Minister of Finance.

Dr. Giora Lotan, for example, who was the first Director of the National Insurance Institute until his retirement in 1968, saw his responsibility mainly as administrator of the law. However, his successor, Dr. Israel Katz, is convinced that his function is to formulate and advocate new social policy. He believes that he must do more than see to it that old-age pensions are paid on time: he feels they must be adequate to provide minimum subsistence.

As Dr. Israel Katz sees it, National Insurance payments are not a single answer to poverty. He utilizes his position to alert Israeli public opinion to the dangers of social gaps and the needs for other measures to eliminate social inequality. In 1971, when Israeli public opinion was shocked by the violent demonstrations of a small group of underprivileged youth calling themselves "Black Panthers," Katz condemned them for resorting to throwing Molotov cocktails, but felt that their protest was of value. It brought many serious social problems to the attention of the public.

The charges made by Dr. Katz often infuriate the Cabinet Ministers: "He talks too much," Prime Minister Golda Meir once said. And the Minister of Finance has called him a troublemaker and instigator, and termed a "dirty lie" the claim made by Dr. Katz that 250,000 Israelis live below the poverty line. The odd thing about this is that nobody dares to remove Dr. Katz from office: on the contrary, his influence on social policy making has been considerable.

Katz was born in Vienna in 1927 and reached Palestine just before

World War II. He studied social work at Columbia University in New York, received his doctor's degree from Western Reserve University in Cleveland and served for a number of years as the dean of the School of Social Work at the Hebrew University in Jerusalem. By using his current position as a power base, he no doubt has given new meaning to the role of the National Insurance Institute, a role any successor will find difficult to ignore.

In 1962 it was decided that the Attorney-General is to be appointed by the government and only the government may dismiss him. In 1968 the government appointed Meir Shamgar to this position. He is a strong Attorney-General, who is not willing to forgo any of the authority granted to him by Israel's unwritten constitution. He heads the State's prosecution, has the authority to order the opening or closing of files. He has the right to appear in court in any case, even if the government is not a party to it, and take a stand in it. The Attorney-General is also responsible for legislation involving the government and he advises it on legal matters. For example, when Knesset member Menahem Begin accused the government of exceeding its authority when it declared its willingness to start negotiations on an interim Suez Canal agreement, claiming that this contradicts a specific Knesset resolution, the government asked for Shamgar's legal opinion. In his report, Shamgar stated that there was nothing amiss in the government's decision in early 1972 to seek an interim settlement.

The Attorney-General is also asked from time to time to make special investigations (e.g., "Is there organized crime in Israel?"). He also heads special committees charged with studying legal problems. When Minister of Justice Ya'akov Shimshon Shapira resigned in June, 1972, leaving the country without a minister for several months, most of his authority was transferred to Meir Shamgar. There were even reports that he might replace Shapira as Minister.

Meir Shamgar (Sternberg) was born in Danzig in 1925. He reached Palestine in 1939 and was a student at the Hebrew University in Jerusalem when he was arrested in 1944 for anti-British activity in the Irgun Zvai Le'umi, and exiled to Eritrea. He began studying law in detention camp and later completed his studies in Jerusalem and London. He was appointed Attorney-General after serving as the Israel Army's Chief Judge Advocate.

Despite his political background, Meir Shamgar has proved himself a most convenient Attorney-General for the Labor coalition. His decisions rarely conflict with government policy: they are carefully worded and anchored in legal theory. He is often mentioned as a possible candidate for a cabinet post.

The Israeli legislative process is based on the gradual development of a written constitution. This is done by the passage from time to time of special laws called constitutional laws, which together will eventually become the Israeli Constitution. Meir Shamgar has enriched Israeli legal literature by preparing two draft constitutional laws—one dealing with legislation and one dealing with the law courts. The latter will grant the Israeli court system maximum independence and the power of judicial review over legislation—a privilege which the present law, derived from English Common Law, does not provide.

Moshe Sanbar (Sandberg), who was appointed governor of the Bank of Israel, Israel's central bank, in November, 1971, also belongs to this small group of appointed policy makers. Sanbar succeeded the venerable David Horowitz in this position. Horowitz, a pioneer of the Third Aliyah, the wave of immigrants that arrived in the years immediately following World War I, was the founder of the Bank of Israel and governor during its first seventeen years. He carefully built the prestige of his position; the essence of his monetary policy is expressed in his famous saying, perhaps apocryphal, "If I were not hard, the Israeli pound would be soft."

Sanbar, who is not one of the founding fathers—he arrived in Israel in 1948—faced two problems when he became governor of the Bank of Israel. His first challenge was to live up to the reputation Horowitz had developed in the international financial community; the second was to overcome his background as Pinhas Sapir's right-hand man, which made people fear that he would not be independent enough in his new position.

The meteoric rise of Moshe Sanbar in the Israeli government hierarchy, before he left to become governor of the Central Bank, was outstanding, even for a country like Israel, where young economists often reach positions of great responsibility within a short number of years.

Born in 1926 in Hungary, Sanbar was sent to concentration camp by the Nazis. His experiences in the camp were described by him in a book, *Year without End,* which received a prize from Yad Vashem (the Holocaust Memorial Foundation). He arrived in Israel while the War of Independence was being fought and was immediately sent to the Latrun front, where he was wounded in battle and even erroneously reported dead. Later he joined the first class at the Hebrew University that studied economics under Professor Dan Patinkin, and received his master's degree in 1953. Even before he finished his studies he went into research. One of his papers so impressed Ze'ev Sharef, then in charge of Internal Revenue, that he asked him to join his staff. Sanbar soon became Deputy Director of Internal Revenue and later economic advisor to the Minister of Finance. His last appointment in the Civil Service was that of Special Assistant to the Minister of Commerce and Industry. Since the Minister, Pinhas Sapir, was also Minister of Finance, Sanbar was virtually Deputy Minister but did not get the title because to be Deputy Minister he would have had to be a Knesset member.

Just like Horowitz before him, Sanbar believes in the independence of the Bank of Israel. In 1972, as the country's economy was slipping into an inflationary spiral, Sanbar insisted on a strong anti-inflationary stand and recommended measures that sometimes irked his former boss, the Minister of Finance. In public appearances Sanbar is careful not to clash with the government's policy. Yet he realizes that differences of opinion are inevitable. The role of the Bank of Israel, as seen by David Horowitz and Moshe Sanbar after him, is to act like the law of the parallelogram of forces. With the government pulling in one direction, the Central Bank must pull in a different direction, in the hope that the resulting policy will be a middle course.

As Deputy Minister of Finance, Dr. Zevi Dinstein also belongs to the group of inside policy makers and, in fact, since 1965, he has been a Knesset member. Yet Dinstein's whole personality is that of a high-powered executive. Even when he has to reply to questions of Knesset members—one of the few political responsibilities with which the Minister of Finance, Pinhas Sapir, entrusts his deputy— he does so almost mechanically, often overlooking the political mines hidden in the dry factual material being debated.

Dinstein's insensitivity to political dangers and his eagerness for action almost destroyed his public image during the Netivei Nepht affair in 1972. Although the official committee of inquiry, which studied scandal charges against the government-owned oil company, found that most of the accusations against the company were without foundation, Dinstein's laxness in supervising the company's affairs was criticized.

If Dinstein had not persisted in public service and had gone into private business, as did many of his colleagues in the senior Civil Service in the early years of Statehood, he probably would have been offered a most lucrative position. Foreign businessmen have often expressed their admiration of the man whom they describe as "a human dynamo" for his quick perception and enormous capacity for work.

Dinstein, who was born in Tel Aviv in 1926, was "mobilized" into public activities in 1947 when Pinhas Sapir, then on an arms-purchasing mission in Europe, recruited young assistants from among the Israeli students at the University of Geneva. He had barely mastered French before he was discovered by Shaul Avigur, Sapir's predecessor in the job, and was soon involved in the transactions which assured Israel its defense weapons in the crucial early months of the struggle.

When Dinstein returned to Israel he became liaison officer to the American foreign-aid authorities, Controller of Foreign Exchange and later the official in charge of Israel's oil economy. At a time when the young democracy was getting more and more involved in crippling bureaucratic red tape, it needed someone like Dinstein who was ready to assume responsibility for quick decisions and for seeing a project through.

As Controller of Foreign Exchange, for example, Dinstein had a say not only in imports and exports, but also in mobilizing investments and fostering relations with many foreign contributors to Israeli projects. Although he gave up his position as head of the Investment Authority in 1970, when he disagreed with Sapir on the administration of foreign investments, he nevertheless maintained his association with Israeli big business through his election in 1972 as elected chairman of the board of the Industrial Development Bank of Israel, a quasi-public institution in charge of financing industrial expansion.

Dinstein moved into the camp of policy makers in 1965 when the Prime Minister and Minister of Defense, Levi Eshkol, received the resignation of his Deputy Minister of Defense, Shimon Peres. According to Israeli constitutional law, a cabinet minister does not have to be a Knesset member but his deputy must have a seat. Therefore Eshkol saw to it that Dinstein was included in the Labor party ticket for the coming elections. He soon after became Deputy Minister of Defense, an assignment which he described as "sitting on a galloping horse." Dinstein did not serve long in this capacity, since Moshe Dayan, who took over the Defense portfolio in the tense days preceding the June, 1967, war, made it clear that he did not want a deputy. Yet Dinstein did manage to introduce several changes, especially in defense procurement.

Dinstein became Deputy Minister of Finance and was re-elected to the Knesset in 1969. He became less and less involved in urgent issues of economic policy and devoted most of his time to the Industrial Development Bank and to the running of Israel's oil economy. Matters such as the Sinai oil wells, which supply more than two-thirds of Israel's oil needs, the Eilat-Ashkelon pipelines, the Israeli-owned tanker fleet, the Haifa and Ashdod refineries, as well as oil prospecting in Israel and abroad, all fall under his jurisdiction.

Another Deputy Minister apparently only at the beginning of his climb to the top is Gad Ya'acobi, the Deputy Minister of Transport. In 1973 he was involved mainly in problems of road safety, traffic congestion and endless negotiations with the bus cooperatives, which seem to be perpetually demanding higher fares.

The great turning point in the life of Gad Ya'acobi came in 1965 when he decided to go into politics, representing the Rafi splinter group of the Labor party in the central committee of the Histadrut. For a young Israeli with an academic background and administrative experience the decision to go into politics is not easy. Other young economists leave government service to become technocrats in the private sector or government companies, where they have both power and a considerable increase in salary. However, Gad Ya'acobi consulted his former boss in the Ministry of Agriculture and political mentor, Moshe Dayan, and decided to take the unusual road (for members of his generation) of politics.

Ya'acobi speaks softly but with self-assurance. He is not one of those young politicians whose loyalty to old-timers obtains them safe seats in the front benches of the political parties. Yet he is also not a "professional revolutionary." He was willing to serve as deputy secretary of the Labor party when it was reorganized after the Six-Day War. Yet he does not hesitate to clash with Pinhas Sapir and even Golda Meir, as when things he said during a visit to Washington were not to their liking.

Ya'acobi is better educated and more hard-working than most young people in his party. At the beginning of his political career it looked as though he had tied his fortunes to those of Moshe Dayan and Shimon Peres. Today he needs them less and less. He knows how to use the news media to his advantage, and his relaxed manner of speaking on television projects much better than the old-fashioned style of some of his older party colleagues.

His persistent fight for changes in the election system was seen by some old-timers as a personal publicity campaign. Yet it ended with a surprising victory in July, 1972, when his bill passed its first reading in the Knesset and came closer to enactment than ever before. In his deliberations with leaders of the country's bus cooperatives, Ya'acobi has proved himself a hard nut to crack.

Ya'acobi was born in 1935 in Moshav Kfar Vitkin, where his parents are members of the cooperative settlement to this day, working in their orange groves and chicken run. He was active in the moshav youth group, studied at Tel Aviv University and also attended a seminar on marketing and price policy at the London School of Economics. His close relationship with Moshe Dayan began in 1959, when Dayan coordinated the election campaign among young people of the Labor party, and Gad Ya'acobi was one of his co-workers. When Dayan became Minister of Agriculture at the end of 1951, he offered Gad Ya'acobi the post of Director of his office and spokesman of his Ministry. This job gave him his first contacts not only with the country's press but also with decision makers in the government, the agricultural establishment, as well as in the Histadrut. In 1963 Dayan surprised many of the veteran officials in the Ministry when he appointed Ya'acobi head of the Agricultural Planning Center. At first some of the older members of the agricultural establishment resented the appointment of the hard-working young man, whom they considered too much the Minister's fair-haired boy, but he soon won their confidence.

Ya'acobi's decision to go into politics in 1965 was a difficult one, not only because it was somewhat "revolutionary" for his generation, but also because he followed Dayan into the small, short-lived Rafi splinter group. His gamble paid off, and in 1969 he was elected to the Knesset and became Deputy Minister half a year later.

The fine distinction between policy making and administration is sometimes blurred in Israeli reality. A position which is clearly that of an administrator, like the Civil Service Commissioner, sometimes assumes political significance because of the considerable power the holder of this position wields.

The Civil Service Commissioner is more than the employer of fifty-three thousand government workers; labor contracts signed by him also apply to workers in government companies, municipalities and other public services. The number of all these employees reaches a quarter of a million, or a third of all salaried workers in Israel. According to the law, the Commissioner appoints government officials and is also allowed to dismiss them. He is charged with supervising the efficiency of the government service and is the official advisor of the government in all problems of manpower administration.

During the early years of Israel's existence, stubborn efforts, backed by public opinion, were made to depoliticize the Civil Service. Today, when a new cabinet minister is appointed, he may bring with him his director-general, his personal secretary and his driver, but may not dismiss anyone who has Civil Service Status.

However, when the position of Civil Service Comissioner became vacant in 1964, the selection of the new candidate was not made by the Minister of Finance, who according to the law is his immediate superior, or even by the Cabinet as a whole. The decision reportedly took place at the home of the Mayor of Tel Aviv, Yehoshua Rabinowitz, the unofficial power behind the ruling Labor party.

Vehement press criticism of this selection was directed not so much against the man who was chosen, Ya'akov Nitzan, as against the manner in which the selection took place. Yet, if someone in the Labor party expected this appointment to return Israel to the spoils-system practices of the early years of independence, there was a disappointment in store for him. It is likely that even if Nitzan had wanted to turn the clock back he would have found it impossible. And yet, while Nitzan is unable to make political appointments at will, the very fact that he represents the government in all contract negotiations leaves to his discretion issues which are not of a purely administrative nature but are definitely questions of policy.

Nitzan, who acquired the nickname of "Ritchie" when he was on the Haganah staff, is a short, determined man who can be smiling and friendly in his social contacts, but tough—and his opponents claim even ruthless—in his official capacity, when dealing with personnel problems. Even those who claim to have been hurt by him admit that he is a clever and efficient administrator.

Part of Nitzan's "meanness" may be a result of the impossible job he has to fill. Apparently the Cabinet Ministers want him to be the bad guy saying "no" to groups of workers demanding higher wages. This often enables the ministers themselves to be magnanimous and make concessions after the hard line taken by Nitzan has broken the defenses of the workers.

Ya'akov Nitzan, born in Poland in 1921, came to Palestine at an early age. He served on the permanent staff of the Haganah before the establishment of the State and later served in the Army and in the Ministry of Defense. Between 1958 and 1961 he was Consul in charge of administration at the Israel Consulate-General in New York. Upon his return home he became Administration Chief of the Foreign Ministry. He held this job until he was appointed Civil Service Commissioner.

Wherever a shocking affair of mismanagement or waste of public funds is exposed, Israelis automatically raise the question "Where is the State Comptroller?" In fact, the Israeli State Comptroller, like many holders of similar positions in other countries, is not involved in execution of policy. His warnings are not designed to prevent certain actions from taking place, but to criticize malpractices after they have occurred. His reports are expected to prevent the repetition of the malpractices.

Although the two first Israeli State Comptrollers, Drs. Siegfried Moses and Yitzhak Ernst Nebenzahl, were careful not to exceed their authority lest they antagonize the executive branch thereby, the position of the Comptroller has grown in political power through the years. The State Comptroller is neither above nor even outside the Israeli establishment; he is part of it. Perhaps this is so because the Comptrollers, understanding the peculiar nature of the Israeli establishment, realize that changes in it take place as a result of the delicate give-and-take process and not through a frontal clash.

When the present State Comptroller, Dr. Nebenzahl, was elected by the Knesset in 1961, the choice was between him and Ze'ev Sharef, who had the support of the Labor party. Nebenzahl was backed mainly by the National Religious party. However, if there was a political overtone to his election, it was soon forgotten. The Comptroller, who in 1971 was elected to his third five-year term of office, was careful neither to show party favoritism nor to step too much on the toes of those in power. Sometimes topics that deserve his criticism are mentioned in the State Comptroller's report, but in such an obscure way that only those closely associated with the topic really understand what Dr. Nebenzahl has in mind. When government Ministers ask him not to mention certain items in his report, they usually claim that exposure will harm the country's defense and economic interests. The Comptroller sometimes is sympathetic to such claims.

It can be argued that just because Dr. Nebenzahl is careful to avoid rifts between his office and the executive branch the latter is more ready to adhere to his admonitions. It is also clear that the very existence of the State Comptroller has influenced those in the executive branch to avoid doing things wrong. The thorough, somewhat stiff German upbringing of the first two Israeli State Comptrollers apparently has influenced the restrained style of their reports, which have as few adjectives as possible and are different from the very expressive emotional style of political life in Israel, usually more reflective of Eastern European and Middle Eastern traditions.

When Dr. Nebenzahl became State Comptroller, he had to resign from no less than fourteen honorary positions, including membership on many boards of directors, as well as the rank of honorary Consul of Sweden in Jerusalem.

Yitzhak Ernst Nebenzahl was born in 1907 in Frankfurt-am-Main and studied at the Universities of Berlin, Frankfurt and Freiburg. Upon his arrival in Palestine in 1933, he went into business.

As a young man in Germany he was the leader of an Orthodox Jewish youth movement, and at one time he was a National Religious party candidate for Mayor of Jerusalem, but he really never was active in politics. A tall, distinguished-looking man, he is usually extremely polite, although those who work for him claim that Nebenzahl can be stubborn and tough when the occasion arises. He was criticized when he insisted on building a house for himself and members of his family in a choice spot in the Old City of Jerusalem overlooking the Western Wall. However, Nebenzahl claimed that this was the realization of his dreams, and the matter was dropped since the construction was undertaken with the consent of the authorities.

In 1971, the Knesset requested Dr. Nebenzahl to take on another assignment, that of Ombudsman, Commissioner of Public Complaints.

A year later, a separate Ombudsman for the armed forces was appointed. At the suggestion of the Minister of Defense, Moshe Dayan, General (Res.) Haim Laskov, one of Israel's distinguished soldiers and public servants, was chosen. Until then, a soldier who felt that he had been wronged could file a complaint against his superior officer, but had to present the complaint to the commanding officer, who then transferred it further. Now any soldier can send his complaint straight to Laskov.

Important as this position may be, it is obvious that Laskov's still considerable influence on Israeli public affairs is not based on his present position so much as on his uncompromising personality, and on senior posts he has filled in the past. Even opponents of Haim Laskov, who consider him lacking in the flexibility needed for public office, admire the courage and idealism he has demonstrated all through his life.

Laskov is not associated with any political party. Yet even if members of the establishment do not accept his opinions and consider his standards too high, they see in him their conscience. They are very satisfied if he approves of what they are doing.

Laskov has always been an outstanding figure in the Israeli elite. He became a major in the British Army and a senior officer rising to Chief of Staff of the Israel Defense Forces. He is an efficient administrator who loves the Bible and is an admirer of the British poet Rudyard Kipling.

Laskov, born in Russia in 1919, came to Palestine as a child. The Laskov family was very poor, living in an Arab neighborhood of Haifa; during the Arab riots of 1929, the father, who was driving a horse and cart, was killed when Arabs stampeded his horse. Despite conditions at home, Haim went to Haifa's Reali high school, where he had a scholarship, and was educated together with the sons of the well-to-do. His schoolmates used to bring him sandwiches. In order to prolong the life of the shoes which he inherited from his older brother, he used to walk barefoot to school, carrying the shoes in his hand, putting them on only when he entered class. He was a lively boy, an industrious, brilliant student. Yet he was sensitive and bashful, working his way through school and supporting his mother at the same time.

During the last year in high school, Laskov gave lessons to other pupils. Later, when he joined the British Army during World War II, he used to put aside money from his meager pay in order to repay his high school tuition.

When Laskov was at school, he joined the Haganah and there met Captain Orde Wingate, who at that time organized the "special night squads" of Jewish fighters to repel the attacks of Arab marauders. Wingate, who was the spiritual father of many of the leaders of the Israel Army, and a founder of its strategic principles, left a deep impression on young Laskov.

During the 1948 war Laskov was a battalion commander in the bloody battles of Latrun, and later fought in the Galilee. He rose to the rank of general and for a short period even served as Commander of the Air Force. He then was sent for two years of study to Oxford—a period which he still considers the happiest in his life. He studied for such long hours that his eyesight was impaired, and he now has to use glasses. Upon his return to Israel, Laskov began to organize the Israeli Armored Corps. His Panzer theory proved itself in the Sinai Campaign of 1956, when Israeli tanks smashed Egyptian fortified positions for the first time, a feat which they repeated eleven years later. In 1957 he became Chief of Staff and retired three years later.

At first Laskov was bewildered without uniform. "The Army is the only thing with which I can identify personally," Laskov told a friend. Yet when he was asked to become the Director of the Ports

Authority, which was organized at that time, he submerged himself in the job with the same enthusiasm he gave to military command. The man who proposed Laskov for the Ports Authority post was the Minister of Transport at that time, Yitzhak Ben-Aharon. Seven years later Ben-Aharon brought about Laskov's resignation, after Laskov came into conflict with the port workers, especially the leader of the stevedores, Yehoshua Peretz. Ben-Aharon, who then had become secretary-general of the Histadrut, gave his backing to the workers and Laskov had to go.

The central character of this conflict was no less "proletarian" than other members of the Israeli elite. He opposed the workers, not as a representative of the haves, but as a believer in the principle that work contracts have to be honored. Laskov realizes the dangers inherent in a confrontation between technological democracy and the relatively small pressure groups which control key sectors of the economy.

Another Chief of Staff who clashed with the establishment in his first civilian post was Yitzhak Rabin. His five years as Israel Ambassador in Washington were marked by an unprecedented improvement in relations with the United States. Almost parallel to this was a gradual deterioration in the personal relations between the Ambassador and the Foreign Minister, Abba Eban, as well as with senior members of the Foreign Ministry staff.

Yitzhak Rabin has gone a long way from his days at Kadoorie Agricultural School in Lower Galilee, where his leadership ability was first noticed, to the occasion when President Nixon praised him in the warmest terms in March, 1973, and jocularly offered him a post in his administration. A Washington *Post* editorial once called Rabin "Israel's undiplomatic diplomat": in fact, he proved himself an unusual diplomat who expresses his beliefs in clear and simple terms and tells journalists what other diplomats only hint at in coded messages.

Rabin has his own concept of the role of Israel's top representative in Washington: he feels that the Ambassador should be part of the Israeli policy-making team and not only the blind implementer of instructions from Israel. When Eban and other members of the government in 1972 felt that Israel should stay aloof from partisan conflict in the U.S. elections, Rabin felt that a second term for Richard Nixon would be best for Israel and therefore that Israel should aid in achieving that objective. He also believed that Israel did not have to fear a re-evaluation of American policies after the 1973 presidential inauguration. The triumphal visit of Golda Meir to Washington in March, 1973, seemed a complete vindication of Rabin.

Despite his obvious success in Washington, Rabin returned to Israel a somewhat chastened man. He had hoped to be given a cabinet position at an earlier stage and in fact was promised one two years before his return from Washington. Golda Meir could not fulfill her promise at the time, when she encountered unexpected opposition in the Labor party machine to the appointment of Haim Bar-Lev as Minister of Commerce and Industry. She feared antagonism to the appointment of another "general" and Rabin, arriving in Israel just before the 1973 election campaign, was forced to start his political career as an ordinary candidate. Yet many believe that his position in the next government is assured.

Yitzhak Rabin, who was born in Jerusalem in 1922, was one of the outstanding representatives of the 1948 generation, the young men who showed utmost devotion and military capability in the crucial battles at the time of Israel's establishment. His father, Nehemiah Rabin, was one of the relatively few American volunteers in the Jewish Legion of World War I to settle in Palestine. His mother, Rosa Cohen, was one of the commanders of the Haganah until her untimely death in 1939.

In 1947 Rabin was the commander of the Second Battalion of the Palmach, which defended the water-supply line to the Negev. In 1948 he commanded the Harel Brigade, which fought in besieged Jerusalem and prevented the city from falling into Arab hands. His first diplomatic assignment was in 1949 as a member of the Israeli delegation which negotiated the armistice agreement. In 1964 he became Israel's seventh Chief of Staff and commanded the victorious Israeli forces in the Six-Day War of June, 1967.

Another bastion of power in the Israeli establishment is the Israeli Supreme Court, both in the field of implementation and in policy making. Supreme Court decisions sometimes cause controversies and Supreme Court judges—like Judge Zvi Berenson—in the case of Friday-night television broadcasts, and Judge Alfred Witkon, in the Netivei Nepht case, found themselves at the center of public disputes. However, the image of the Supreme Court as an independent and uncompromising authority remained untarnished.

One of the outstanding Supreme Court judges is Haim Cohn, a jurist who incidentally won an international reputation in theological circles for his study entitled *The Trial and Death of Jesus*. He is also a public personality who heads the Council for Jews in Arab Countries and the Jerusalem Foundation, which raises contributions for the improvement of Jerusalem. He is a brilliant former Yeshiva student who has antagonized Orthodox circles by his opinions on Jewish religious law.

Since the establishment of the State of Israel, Haim Cohn has served in many positions in the Israeli legal bureaucracy, including Director-General of the Ministry of Justice, State Attorney, Attorney-General and Minister of Justice. He was appointed to the Supreme Court in 1960 and his opinions in scores of court rulings have served as landmarks in the Israeli legal system.

Cohn, a tall bald man with an eagle nose, has represented Israel on a number of international bodies, including the UN Committee on Human Rights. His speeches show not only a vast fund of knowledge, but also considerable rhetorical gifts.

Born in Lubeck, northern Germany, in 1911 to a rabbinical family, Cohn combined secular education at the Universities of Munich, Hamburg and Frankfurt with a rabbinical education at the Jerusalem Yeshiva of the revered Chief Rabbi Kook. When he completed his legal education in 1937 he began practicing law in Jerusalem.

Despite his Orthodox background, Judge Cohn often clashes with the Orthodox establishment. Remarks made by him in a speech at the Hebrew University in June, 1963, caused Orthodox leaders to demand that he be brought to court for insulting their religious sensibilities. He attacked the rabbis for refusing to register as Jews the children of non-Jewish mothers who immigrated to Israel with their Jewish husbands. In reply to vehement attacks, Haim Cohn said, "I am a Jew out of my free will and pray for the day when there will be no more discrimination among Jews based on the origin of their mothers."

Cohn has often advocated penal reform. He has suggested, for instance, that criminals who are given jail sentences of less than nine months should work in prison all day and be allowed to go home in the evenings. In his book *The Trial and Death of Jesus,* he discusses the execution of Jesus from the point of view of Jewish and Roman law. His conclusion is that the judgment of the Church, that the Jews were responsible for the death of Jesus, has no foundation in the reality, custom or law that prevailed at that time.

11

The Top Administrators

WHEN the secretary of Avraham Agmon, the Director-General of the Ministry of Finance, is signaled by her boss on the outside line while he is simultaneously talking on the inside phone, she knows that the man talking with Agmon has convinced him to give him an appointment. Trying to fix the time, she nearly gives up, when she finds that somehow the appointment can be squeezed into her employer's crowded schedule.

The Israeli top administrator, it seems, does much more than any job analyst thinks possible. Avraham Agmon learned this expertise at doing more each day from his mentor and superior, the Minister of Finance, Pinhas Sapir. He also has subconsciously adopted many of Sapir's mannerisms, expressions and ways of thinking. Even the accent of the Minister of Finance, reminiscent of his Polish mother tongue, creeps into Agmon's speech, and like his Minister he is always meticulously dressed. According to the tradition which crystallized after Sapir vacated the position of Director-General of the Ministry of Finance in 1955, Agmon deals little with taxation. He usually is more involved with the Bureau of the Budget and the functions of the Accountant-General. He also has added to his duties the responsibility of dealing with foreign investors and heads the Israeli team of negotiators with the European Economic Community.

No one can claim that Agmon is less devoted to his job than his predecessor, or that he lacks the formal education and experience needed for one of Israel's top administrative jobs. Yet he is one of those who, as "the new generation of administrators," have become the target of criticism. It is said of them that they are "wearing shoes too big for their feet" and that they lack personal stature commensurate with the responsibilities entrusted to them. It is also claimed that the top Israeli administrators are mere technicians who see every problem, big or small, through the eyes of the bureaucrat.

During the first years after Israel's establishment, the Civil Service attracted many political party functionaries and others who performed services for the Jewish community of pre-State Palestine. They saw in their Civil Service jobs recompense for many years of devoted service. The top administrative jobs also attracted personalities from the private sector who were willing to go into government service, not only because they saw this as a civic duty, but also because only the government could offer such a wide scope of activities. Industry, the banking system and insurance companies in those days were insufficient challenges for administrators who felt that they could do more.

In the course of the first quarter century of Israel's existence, these two types of administrators have gradually disappeared from the ranks of the Israeli Civil Service. The party activists were dropped one by one in the slow process of depolitizing the Civil Service. Today, a new cabinet minister can no longer bring with him a great number of party loyalists and offer them government jobs. In many cases the arriving minister does not even appoint a new director-general, an appointment that he is allowed to make according to the Israeli Civil Service Code.

As for the recruits from private business, they too no longer consider the Civil Service a sphere of unlimited opportunities. The Israeli economy has grown in twenty-five years. Industrial firms, branches of multinational companies, financial concerns and shipping companies all afford young Israelis today a scope of operations which is often even wider than that of a government ministry. Instead of the Israeli Civil Service recruiting its executives from private business, the private sector itself often obtains its top administrators from the ranks of the Civil Service.

Yet, while top administrators are constantly leaving the Civil Service, Israel has developed a corps of administrators who see government service as a lifetime career.

It is true that these men may lack the kind of experience that is gained through participation in the business world. (It is said of the late Levi Eshkol that he once interrupted one of his assistants, who made a complicated and highly theoretical suggestion: "Young man, have you ever made a dollar in your life?") They may lack the contact with political forces in the country which many of the early officials did have, but they seem to be more professional and to have had more formal education than many of their predecessors. Many foreign visitors, exasperated by the apathy and deliberate, bureaucratic approach of the lower echelon of the Israeli Civil Service, admire the devotion that characterizes most of the top administrators.

There have been a number of scandals through the years involving corruption in the Israeli Civil Service: the State Comptroller recently complained about "manifestations of Ottomanism" in the Israeli administration. Yet experts who are familiar with the Israeli government have come to the conclusion that the top echelon of administration is "cleaner," more idealistic and hard-working than in many countries of Western Europe. By Middle Eastern standards, the Israeli Civil Service is, of course, unique. Some feel that it is one of Israel's secret weapons in the decisive military victories over the Arabs.

The Budget Division of the Ministry of Finance has served as the breeding ground for many top bureaucrats in the economic field. For many years this unit has attracted the most capable economics students at the Hebrew University in Jerusalem. Dutch-born and trained Dr. Ya'akov Arnon, one-time Director of the Division, and for many years Director-General of the Ministry of Finance, has been the instructor and guide of the "budget boys." Most of them are young sabras, whose work in the Budget Division provided the opportunity of translating their theoretical knowledge of economics into practice. At least five of the top administrators mentioned in this chapter are "graduates" of the Budget Division of the Ministry of Finance.

Avraham Agmon also started his career in the Budget Division, although he used to disappear from time to time to do stints in the Foreign Service, serving in embassies in Eastern Europe. The ease with which he moved from one assignment to another and his rapid advance in the hierarchy is typical of Israel's top Civil Service administrators. Yet, unlike many of his colleagues, Agmon is not a sabra. He was born in 1928 in Bialystok, and spent the war years in the Soviet Union. He reached the shores of Palestine in 1947 on a ship bringing "illegal" immigrants, and was wounded resisting the British soldiers who captured the ship. His mother and brother were transferred to an internment camp in Cyprus, but he was allowed to be treated in a Haifa hospital. Half a year later, when the State of Israel was established, he joined the Israeli Army and was again wounded, this time in the Negev campaign.

In 1950 he began his studies at the Hebrew University in Jerusalem, working his way through school as a postal clerk. In 1954, after having served as secretary of the Students' Union, he joined the Budget Division in the Ministry of Finance. Subsequently he started his diplomatic career, first as Second Secretary of the Israel Embassy in Moscow, then as First Secretary in the Israel Embassy in Warsaw, and later in Moscow again. In between those assignments he dealt with budgets and figures.

As Director-General of the Ministry of Finance, Agmon is charged with finding answers to some of the most urgent of Israel's economic problems. However, the fate of Soviet Jewry is still one of his main preoccupations. The cool administrator can get highly emotional when it comes to the problem of aiding Jews behind the Iron Curtain.

When Agmon became Director-General of the Ministry of Finance in January, 1970, he was succeeded as Director of the Budget Division by Arnon Gafni, who is not only himself an alumnus of the division, but also a second-generation top Civil Servant. His father, Simha Gafni, who started his career in the British Mandatory administration, reached the top as Internal Revenue Commissioner.

Arnon Gafni, tall, handsome and very serious, was born in Tel Aviv in 1932. He led a somewhat sheltered life, entering government service immediately after completing his university education. Yet he broke away once, when he served in the Ports Authority and later became manager of the Port of Ashdod. He claims that this experience of coping with difficult labor relations and the burden of daily administration prepared him for the task of top man in the Budget Division.

For Arnon Gafni, like his father before him, the Civil Service is not just a stepping stone to another career, but an end in itself. Similarly, the Accountant-General in the Ministry of Finance, Haim Stoessel, who also carries out government policy in Israel's capital market, has few ambitions apart from his work. In fact, it is difficult to imagine that the long hours he puts in at the Ministry of Finance enable him to find out whether the grass is really greener on the other side.

When the Civil Service was first constituted in 1948, many senior Israeli officials simply started at the top. However, Moshe Neudorfer, who as Internal Revenue Commissioner collects more than a third of Israel's gross national product in the form of taxes, belongs to the growing group of Israel's top administrators who came up through the ranks. In fact, Neudorfer, who was born in Poland and came to Palestine as a child, started working as an errand boy in Bank Leumi at the age of fourteen. Soon afterward, he became a clerk in the newly organized Income Tax Bureau of the British Mandate. His first salary as a government official was three Palestine pounds a month. He obtained his formal education while working: he passed the London Matriculation Examination in 1943 and became a certified public accountant twenty years later. On two occasions he studied in the United States.

As a taxcollector, Neudorfer's attitude is professional, almost detached. He leaves the thinking about the tax burden to the politicians and only indicates how much and in what way taxes can be collected. Yet he is not unaware of the human element involved in his profession. Every file is a drama, telling a story of conflict and passion, he says. He admits, however, that in his few free hours he prefers to read detective stories.

Neudorfer's teammate in the Internal Revenue Division is Ya'akov Tamir, the Income Tax Commissioner. He too, was born in Poland, and had to go to work soon after arriving in Palestine. Yet, while earning his living, he managed to obtain degrees both in law and accountancy from the Hebrew University in Jerusalem. Despite the burdens of his work and constant clashes with his "clients," Tamir is a lively extrovert. Many stories he tells belong to the category of income-tax jokes.

Neudorfer and Tamir, with their assistant, Dr. Ben-Ami Zuckerman, began in 1970 to prepare Israel for a major tax reform, the introduction of the value-added tax (VAT), which has already changed European fiscal policy. According to plans, the tax reform will be introduced in 1974. Whether or not it succeeds will be a test of the professionalism which Israel's internal-revenue system has developed in its twenty-five years of existence.

Professionalism is also the key word in the image that has been created by Gideon Lahav, the Director-General of the Ministry of Commerce and Industry. His public statements are often cryptic and technical. He prefers to make his voice heard in closed meetings with officials of his Ministry or with industrialists. It is this quality of leaving politics to the politicians that has enabled Gideon Lahav to serve under three ministers, the late Yosef Sapir, Pinhas Sapir, and Haim Bar-Lev, without clashing with any one of them.

Tall, thin Gideon Lahav is a quick thinker and, unlike many of his colleagues, does not believe that the government should control every aspect of the economy.

Like many others in the Israeli executive elite, Gideon Lahav obtained all of his professional experience in the government. He arrived in Palestine from Germany at the age of three, studied economics at the Hebrew University in Jerusalem, served in the Budget Division of the Ministry of Finance and even did two stints of Foreign Service in Geneva and Yugoslavia. He believes in reducing government protection for Israeli industry. When asked what to do with "sick" industries, he once said, "There are those patients who only need aspirin to get well; others may need artificial limbs; but there are some which are terminal cases and the sooner we realize it, the better."

Simcha Soroker was most surprised to find, upon becoming Director-General of the Ministry of Communications, that his new realm was not just another government department, but a vast industry employing over fourteen thousand workers. The development of Israel's telecommunications services, both internal and external, requires huge annual investments. It has been Soroker's assignment since his appointment in 1968 to transform the Ministry into a modern enterprise, operating the most sophisticated electronic equipment available.

The appointment of Soroker, who was born in Jerusalem in 1928 and grew up in Rehovot, was severely criticized, since he had no technical background. He too, is a "graduate" not only of the Hebrew University of Jerusalem but also of the Budget Division of the Ministry of Finance, which he directed for a number of years.

Soroker is a serious man (even too serious, some believe), and since he took over his job, he has been studying electronics and communications, squeezing the studies into his very few free hours. Soroker also supervised the construction of Israel's satellite ground station as well as the expansion of its cable communications with the world.

The problems of the telephone service, computerized planning and the deficiencies of the mail distribution system are Soroker's chief preoccupations. He is almost naïvely disinterested in the politics involved in such a large government unit and seems content to leave the limelight to the Minister of Communications, Shimon Peres.

While Soroker is a representative of the new, technical type of director-general, Hanoch Givton, the Director-General of the Ministry of Tourism, has a much stronger influence on policy making in his Ministry. He acquired this post not only because of his standing in his Minister's party, the Independent Liberal party, but also as a result of his previous jobs, which included that of Director-General of the Israel Broadcasting Authority.

Hanoch Givton (Ovsianko) was born in Poland in 1917 and came to Palestine in 1935. He graduated from the Hebrew University in Jerusalem and in 1945 began working in the radio service, which is government-owned. His first post was as an announcer; he later confided, "As I was reading the news, dictated to me by the British Mandate authorities, I became determined that one day I would write different news bulletins myself." While working in the official station, known as "Jerusalem Calling," Givton organized the underground broadcasting of the Haganah. In the 1948 siege of Jerusalem, he was spokesman for the Haganah in the beleaguered city. He served in the Israeli Broadcasting System with several interruptions until November, 1967, when he was removed at the insistence of the Cabinet Minister in charge of the Broadcasting Authority, Israel Galili, following a bitter public dispute.

After he became Director-General of the Ministry of Tourism in 1970, Givton immersed himself in the new assignment, emphasizing mainly its public-relations aspect, in order to enable Israel to overcome the negative influence of Arab terrorist attacks on tourism. His greatest success lies in the fact that, despite the unsettled conditions in the area and worsening inflation, the number of tourists arriving in Israel each year has been gradually increasing since 1967. Critics have pointed out that Givton and other members of his Ministry pay less attention to the economic aspects of their work: a more rational plan for investment in hotels and the training of personnel for Israel's growing tourist industry.

The return of Hanoch Givton to the ranks of the top Israeli bureaucrats, after three years of "exile" at the Israeli delegation to the United Nation in New York, is not unique in the Israeli administration. It may be almost impossible for deposed party functionaries to make a comeback, but this is not true for administrative posts. Thus General (Res.) Meir Zorea (Zarodinsky), who was out of the public limelight for almost fifteen years, came back in 1972 as the Director-General of the Israel Lands Administration.

Meir Zorea ("Zaro") had returned to public notice half a year earlier when he was appointed to the Witkon Committee investigating charges of mismanagement in the government-owned Netivei Nepht Oil Company. Unlike the two other committee members, who always dressed in dark business suits and ties, he sat in the committee hearings dressed in an open-necked golf shirt. He looked almost bored as he listened to long, often tedious deliberations. Yet, when the committee tendered its report, the General, who had traded in his official car for a tractor and the brass buttons of his uniform for a kibbutz member's work clothes, again had a surprise in store. His minority report was a sharply-written analysis of those involved in Netivei Nepht, including a reprimand for the Deputy Minister of Finance, Dr. Zevi Dinstein, for not having kept closer watch over the events in the Sinai oil fields.

Zorea, whose brutally frank language in describing certain cabinet ministers in a press interview almost cost him his position before confirmation of the appointment, took over one of the most sensitive and problematic units of the Israeli Civil Service when he became head of the Lands Administration.

This office was established at the end of the 1950's, following a compromise between the government and the Jewish National Fund, which before the establishment of the State bought land in Palestine for the use of Jewish settlers. According to the compromise, the Land Administration was to administer both the land which the Israeli government took over from the British Mandate authorities and Jewish National Fund lands. At the same time it was agreed that forests belonging to the government and forests planted by the Jewish National Fund should be administered by the Jewish National Fund.

While the government has the decisive influence in the Lands

Administration (having a majority on the board), the fact that JNF representatives sit on its board enables them sometimes to block government policy. Thus, when the first Director of the Lands Administration, the late Yosef Weitz, opposed a government decision on the sale of government land, he refused to execute the policy and successfully blocked the government. The Land Administration controls about 92 per cent of Israeli land and in recent years has become a decisive factor in urban development and in the apportioning of land for housing projects. Its board is headed by the Minister of Agriculture, and some of the most painful decisions the Administration has reluctantly had to make in recent years have concerned the converting of agricultural into urban land.

The economic boom conditions of the early 1970's caused land prices to soar, especially around the main cities. Pressures on the Lands Administration to allocate land for development purposes multiplied. When Zorea took over the Administration in 1972 from the aging Yitzhak Levy, he had the task not only of revamping the Byzantine bureaucracy of Land Registration and Rent Collection, but also of setting up standards for land allocation and real-estate development. His background as a tough, uncompromising administrator, who is "loyal" to agriculture and at the same time aware of the needs of urban development, should prove to be an important asset in this assignment.

Meir Zorea was born in Rumania in 1923 when his parents were on the way from the Ukraine to Palestine. He grew up in Haifa and was among the founders of Ma'agan Michael, the first kibbutz established by the Israel Scout movement. He served in the British Army during World War II and reached the rank of captain. In the 1948 war he was a battalion commander on the Jerusalem front and, after studies in England, became the founder and first Commander of the Israeli Staff College. His last Army assignment was that of Chief of Operations.

Zorea retired from the Army following a mishap when a surprise mobilization exercise on April 1, 1959, created panic in the public, which was unaware of the fact that this was merely an exercise. A public-inquiry committee appointed by then Prime Minister David Ben-Gurion found Zorea and another general responsible for the faulty execution of the mobilization exercise. Zorea rejected the criticism and, in his direct way of speaking, told the surprised Ben-Gurion, "I am resigning because you and your people have left me no choice; you are throwing me out of the Army." Zorea went back to his kibbutz and only thirteen years later was recalled to public service.

Zorea is by no means a typical military man. Similarly, the appointment of General (Res.) Elad Peled as Director-General of the Ministry of Education and Culture in August, 1970, cannot in any way be considered part of a militarization of the Civil Service. Although Peled commanded a group of divisions during the Six-Day War, he is far from being the prototype of the Army man. The serious-looking, bespectacled native of Jerusalem had won the nickname of "the intellectual general" long before he decided to devote himself to the field of education.

In fact, he entered the Ministry of Education almost accidentally. In 1968, as he was about to retire from the Army, Peled was offered a number of posts and even considered an academic career. However, he chose the Israel Electric Corporation, where he was slated to become director-general. Two years later, however, when faced with a struggle for power in the Electric Corporation, he resigned unexpectedly and took up the offer of his one-time Palmach commander, the Minister of Education, Yigal Allon, to join his Ministry.

Like Simcha Soroker in the Ministry of Communications, Elad Peled found the Ministry of Education at a crossroad. The huge increase in budgets which the Knesset voted in 1970 for education required not only a quantitative change—the addition of thousands of new classes in all parts of the country—but also a far-reaching qualitative change. The educational reform planned by the late Minister of Education, Zalman Aranne, was only in the early stages of implementation when Peled came into the Ministry. The reform, designed to improve the quality of education given to all groups of the population, required not only budgets, but also revamped organization, differently trained teachers and solutions for many theoretical and practical problems of education.

When the repeated victories of Israel over her Arab neighbors are studied by foreign experts, they invariably come to the conclusion that it is the quality of the individual Israeli soldier that makes most of the difference. Israel realizes that its future depends on maintaining these high standards. The chief danger is the lower educational achievements of children of immigrants from Asian and African countries. If the gap between the standard of education of those groups and the standard of education in the more advantaged sections of the Israeli population is allowed to widen, a disaster on a national scale could be in store.

With the Attorney-General belonging more to the ranks of the policy makers, the two top administrators of the Ministry of Justice are its Director-General, Zvi Terlo, and the Government Attorney, Gabriel Bach. Bach, a sharp courtroom lawyer, won international attention as the associate of the former Attorney-General, Gideon Hausner, in the Jerusalem trial of the Nazi war criminal Adolf Eichmann. He was also noted by the world press in the winter of 1969, when he defended Mordecai Rahamim, the Israeli security man who shot dead one of the Arab attackers of an El Al plane in Zurich airport.

Gabriel ("Gabi") Bach, who was born in Berlin in 1927 and grew up in Jerusalem, studied law in London. Representing the Israel government in cases in which the State is a party, Bach has shown himself a tough prosecutor, although he himself claims he is a defense lawyer at heart. He admits that what keeps him in government service is the fact that he can choose his cases and pick those which he considers most interesting.

One of those special cases was that of the alleged underworld czar Meir Lansky, who requested refuge in Israel but was refused as a result of an extensive study conducted by Gabriel Bach.

For Bach, strict adherence to the principles of law and order is not a matter which is subject to argument. He does not consider himself a "conservative" or as belonging to a different generation when he demands respect for the law. In this respect Bach resembles another executive of the Israeli legal system, Shaul Rosolio, the Chief Inspector of the Israeli police. Although he himself is friendly and usually soft-spoken, Rosolio has very little tolerance for "hatred" of the police, regardless of whether it is of the traditional variety, the ghetto Jew's antagonism to police, or the New Left version, the one that equates policemen with the establishment.

Like retired Israeli General Avraham Jaffe, who was once described as "the only Israeli general who looks like one," Rosolio, even out of uniform attending a concert of the Israeli Philharmonic Orchestra, looks the part of a law-and-order man. His handsome face has a determined expression and his manner of speaking is taciturn, although in a circle of friends he is a relaxed, charming story teller.

In September, 1972, when Chief Inspector Aharon Sela died after serving only fifty-two days as head of the Israeli police force, there was no doubt that Rosolio would be appointed to replace him. Although he had served as a police officer since the establishment of the State and was by no means "a new face" in the ranks of Israel's law enforcers, Rosolio's appointment nevertheless heralded a new era for the police.

Until the appointment of Rosolio, the chief inspectors of the Israeli police were senior officers of the Haganah, men who had experience in military fields, in administration or even law. Rosolio is Israel's first number-one policeman whose education, in-service training and career are associated entirely with the Israeli police. Many of the officers around him and those who will succeed him have a similar background; they belong to a new breed of "all Israeli" law-enforcement officers, bent on modernizing the force and its techniques of operation.

Shaul Rosolio was born in Tel Aviv in 1923. His German-born father, David Rosolio, was Civil Service Commissioner and at the same time wrote music reviews for the daily press. His mother was the sister of the late Zionist leader Haim Arlosorov, who was murdered in 1934.

Rosolio served in the Jewish Settlement Police and became one of the few Jewish officers in the force organized by the British Mandate authorities. After Army service in 1948, he became one of the founders of the Israeli police. His formal education both in Israel, in business administration and law, and abroad, mainly at the British Police Academy, was undertaken while serving as a police officer.

Unlike many of Israel's top bureaucrats, Rosolio does not mix his private and professional life. At home he enjoys listening to records from his extensive music library. Yet, in his office, he is a hard-driving administrator, faced not only with a rising crime rate and juvenile delinquency but also with maintaining security under the special conditions prevailing in Israel.

12
The Generals

In the summer of 1967, shortly after the Six-Day War, the Israel defense forces' top commanders paid a courtesy call on the President of the State. The picture taken on that occasion shows the faces of twenty-three men in uniform. Six years later, only five of them were still on active duty. The rest had retired to civilian life.

Early retirement is typical of the Israel military elite. Although the time has passed when an officer could become Chief of Staff at the age of thirty, as did Generals Yigael Yadin and Mordecai Makleff— the present Chief of Staff, David ("Dado") Elazar was appointed at the age of forty-seven—nevertheless the average age of Israel's full generals on active service is forty-five. Israel's high command is still the youngest in the world.

The rule that officers leave the Army while still young makes the Israel defense forces an important source of recruitment for the elites of various sectors of civilian life in the country. Among the seventeen generals who were in that 1967 picture but are out of uniform today, six are now in government or public service, five hold positions in the economic sector, two are in politics and one has become a university professor. At least seven of the fourteen hold top positions in civilian life, underscoring again the amount of influence that Army commanders have on Israel's life even after their retirement from military service.

As a result of the departure of old-timers from command, changes have occurred in the characteristics of Israel's top officers. It is still possible to divide the high command into those who came from the Haganah (the Jewish underground army during the period of the British Mandate) and those who learned their profession as officers in the British Army during World War II. However, twenty-five years of service in the Israel Army have blended the qualities and experience of the two groups. Some insiders claim that those who came from the Haganah are better improvisers and are ready to take bigger chances, while those who were educated by the British put greater stress on discipline and meticulously detailed planning. Now, however, the top ranks are beginning to fill up with officers whose pre-Statehood experience was very short and who served as privates or noncommissioned officers during the War of Independence: people like Shmuel Gorodish, Mordecai Gur and Eliahu Zeira are the up-and-coming men whose personalities were formed in independent Israel.

The old-timers are represented on the General Staff by its chief, General David Elazar (a Haganah veteran), and by the head of the General Branch (who is considered next in line for the job of Chief of Staff), General Israel Tal (a former British Army officer). The differences in their upbringing and early experiences never affected the close cooperation between the two during twenty-five years of service together.

David Elazar, who comes from Bosnia in Yugoslavia, came to Palestine in 1940 with Youth Aliyah and was a member of Kibbutz Ein Shemer. In 1946 he enlisted in the Palmach—the elite corps of the Haganah—and, at the start of the 1948 war, commanded its Fourth Battalion. Elazar was wounded in the fighting in Jerusalem but commanded the effort to break the siege of the Jewish Quarter of the Old City. Later, he directed the units which occupied the southern part of the corridor connecting Jerusalem with the coastal plain. After the war, he studied economics and Near Eastern affairs at the Hebrew University. After obtaining his first degree, he went back to the Army, but in the 1960's, as a high-ranking officer, returned to the University, getting his second degree in history. In the 1956 Sinai Campaign, Elazar commanded a brigade that fought in and occupied the Gaza Strip.

The great turning point in his professional career occurred in 1957, when he was transferred to the Armored Corps. Within four years, he became commander of the Corps. His service with the tanks ended in 1964, when he was appointed to head the Northern Command, one of Israel's three regional military commands. At that time the Syrians were the most active supporters of the Arab terrorists and the northern frontier was the only "hot" one. Tension in the area was heightened by Syrian attempts to divert the headwaters of the Jordan in order to prevent their utilization further downriver for Israeli irrigation schemes. General Elazar stayed in the Northern Command until 1967, the year of the Six-Day War.

Full supremacy of civilian authority over the military is one of the basic tenets of the Israel defense forces. Adherence to it was greatly strained in the waiting period before the Six-Day War. In the top echelons of the military, there was a growing feeling that any further delay would heighten the danger and increase the number of casualties that would result. A critical point was reached in a particularly unfortunate speech over the radio by the late Prime Minister Eshkol, who stumbled several times in reading his prepared text, thus increasing the national sense of frustration, both among those in uniform and those who were still in civilian life. Yet, at a press conference the next day, General Elazar reiterated his firm adherence to the principle of civilian authority by stating that the political leadership must be given sufficient time to deliberate on crucial decisions and that the duty of officers was to keep up the soldiers' morale.

Several days later, General Elazar faced what was possibly the severest test of his career. When, in the third day of the Six-Day War, he finally received the green light to attack the Syrian positions that had been shelling Israeli settlements in the north, the skies were overcast and there was doubt that the Air Force would be able to soften up the Syrian positions. Therefore, Elazar asked permission to delay the attack by twenty-four hours. However, on the next day, the decision to attack was canceled out of political considerations. The go-ahead signal came again one day later, but in the intervening hours General Elazar was haunted by the fear that his hesitation had lost Israel a historic opportunity.

After the war, Elazar remained as head of the Northern Command. During the War of Attrition, when the Arabs tried to regain in small-scale hostilities what they had lost in June, 1967, Elazar described the task of the Army as "making life bearable for us and unbearable for them."

When General Ezer Weizman retired from active service, "Dado" Elazar was called upon to become head of the General Branch at GHQ, second in command to General Haim Bar-Lev (also of Yugoslav origin, and a friend from Zionist youth-movement days in Zagreb), who had been Elazar's instructor in the Haganah.

It was Elazar who, as commander of the Tank Corps, initiated the custom that new recruits take their oath at Masada, the ancient Jewish fortress which was the last to fall to the Romans in the twilight of Jewish independence nineteen hundred years ago. When Elazar became Chief of Staff in January, 1972, his first order of the day warned the Arabs: "If the enemy reopens fire, we and not they will decide the nature and the extent of the next war." At the end of February, 1973, Elazar took upon himself the responsibility for giving the order to shoot down the civilian Libyan airliner that had blundered over Sinai.

Simultaneously with Elazar's appointment as Chief of Staff, General Israel Tal was appointed as head of the General Branch. While General Elazar, both in pictures and in real life looks like a dashing officer, younger than his years, General Tal ("Talik" to his friends) looks more like a teacher or scholar. His approach to military matters is completely professional. His attitude toward those under his command resembles that of an educator who does not have much patience with foolishness or incompetence. David Elazar is a man for field operations; Israel Tal is a man for planning and works at his desk into the late hours of the night. General Elazar is a gifted improviser; General Tal has a feeling for the complexities of a situation.

Israel Tal was born in 1924 in the northern village of Mahanayim and grew up on a farm. At the age of eighteen, he joined the British Army and served in the Western Desert. He gained his first Armored Corps experience as a machine gunner in a personnel carrier. Because of this experience, he was sent at the beginning of the 1948 War of Independence as a member of Israel's first arms-purchase mission to Czechoslovakia. Upon his return, he was appointed executive officer to General (later Chief of Staff) Haim Laskov, who commanded the units that took Nazareth. Later, Tal studied military tactics at British staff colleges and during the 1956 Sinai Campaign commanded the units that fought in the center of Sinai.

After this campaign, it was decided that the Armored Corps would play a larger role in the future and Tal was transferred to the tanks. With his usual thoroughness, he went first to tank-mechanics school and only after completing his technical training accepted his first armored command. For two years he was deputy commander of the Corps and then was transferred to GHQ as Deputy Chief of Operations. Like many other Israeli officers who reached the top without any higher education, General Tal took a leave of absence to become a university student. After taking his degree in philosophy and political science, he returned to serve as Deputy Commander of the Tank Corps. In 1961 he was awarded the Defense Prize, the top annual award for a contribution to national security in the form of an invention or technical innovation. In 1964, Tal became the Commander in Chief of the Armored Corps.

Talik's thoroughness and meticulousness are almost legendary. He studies every single part of each new weapon and demands the same care from those under his command. On the one hand, he can give one of the most biting tongue lashings in the army and yet, on the other hand, he is always ready to assist his officers and soldiers not only in official but private problems.

No economic or social organism can operate without discipline, says General Tal, who maintains that there can be no separation between discipline and performance in any technical or organizational sphere. A soldier who dresses sloppily will not take proper care of his tank. He hates what he calls "approximate people"— people who know things approximately but not exactly. He has great powers of persuasion, using them in the mid-1960's to convince his superiors to expand the Armored Corps, which subsequently became a key factor in Israel's quick victory in the Six-Day War. Tal is widely credited with being one of the main contributors to that victory because of his plans for the deployment of tanks in desert fighting, utilizing tactics that led to the speedy demolition of numerically superior Egyptian forces.

His theory of armed warfare is based first on the concept of taking the fight to the enemy's territory at the very beginning of battle. Second, he advocates using armor in large numbers to make the best use of open terrain in the areas separating Israel from its main enemy, Egypt. Third, he believes in making the tank a decisive weapon in the fighting, not a supporting weapon, and fourth, he believes in adapting the types of tanks obtained by Israel to the special conditions of desert warfare.

Tal's doctrine has four operative conclusions: (a) the tank is an attack weapon; (b) the tank is the main vehicle of attack under *all* topographical conditions; (c) tanks should operate in depth without waiting for or expecting support from other units; and (d) in tank attacks, all effort must be concentrated against one main target, even at the expense of neglecting secondary targets.

The success of this doctrine in the Six-Day War made Tal one of Israel's most celebrated commanders. Yet, after the war, Tal decided to quit the Army. At that time the Israel Defense Forces were debating whether to hold the Suez line with a string of fixed fortifications or to base it on mobile armored units. This became a public issue during the War of Attrition, with the rise in the number of casualties among soldiers in the fixed fortifications and in the cost of bombing the Egyptians across the canal. It was one of the few occasions when a technical strategic matter became the subject of public debate. With the end of the War of Attrition in 1970, the debate subsided, but it showed the interaction that can occur between military and political considerations even on a technical level.

In 1968, when General Tal was about to complete his tour of duty as Armored Corps commander, it was generally assumed that he would be appointed head of the General Branch at GHQ. However, the post did not become vacant, and a brief official communiqué in March, 1968, announced the General's retirement from active service and his appointment to a "senior post in the Ministry of Defense." In March, 1970, Tal was offered the post of director-general of one of Israel's largest industrial concerns but at the last moment changed his mind. Defense Minister Dayan, in one of the most unusual moves in Israel's military history, canceled General Tal's resignation from active service and reappointed him to his Defense Ministry post. In June 1973, Tal became Deputy Chief of Staff, in addition to head of the General Branch. The man whose military career had seemed over is now in line to become Israel's number-one soldier.

Another general who returned to the defense establishment is Zvi Zur, who had retired from active service in the early 1960's after serving as Chief of Staff. He now serves as special assistant to the Minister of Defense, Moshe Dayan. Officially, he is in charge of about half of the Defense Ministry's business—primarily those aspects that deal with matériel and research. Yet, at the same time, he is one of the main channels through which the military elite influence life in Israel in general and its economic life in particular.

Zvi Zur ("Chera" to practically everybody who knows him) was born in Russia in 1923 and came to Palestine at the age of two. When he was sixteen, he joined the Haganah. After graduation from high school, he spent a year at the Tel Aviv School of Law and Economics and, in 1942, joined the Haganah full time and attended its clandestine officers' course.

In the War of Independence, Zvi Zur fought in the Tel Aviv

region; later he was sent to the south and organized a special jeep-borne commando unit which helped break the Egyptian siege of several Jewish settlements in the Negev. After the war, he became Chief of Operations of the Southern Command, headed at that time by General Dayan. In 1951 he went back to school, taking graduate courses in business administration in the United States at Syracuse University. When he became head of the Manpower Division at GHQ in 1953, he modernized methods for calling up recruits and reservists, standardized officers' promotion procedures, and published the first unified military code for the Army.

At the age of thirty, he was appointed general and, during the Sinai Campaign, was Military Governor of the Gaza Strip. In 1958 he became Deputy Chief of Staff, but shortly thereafter went to study political science at the Sorbonne in Paris. During vacation periods, he joined French Staff College courses and made several study trips to French Africa. Returning home at the end of 1960, he became Chief of Staff in January, 1961. His term of office was marked by improved military cooperation with France, especially in weapons procurement. The great efforts he devoted during that time to the absorption and utilization of French equipment paid off in 1967 when French planes and weapons played a crucial role in the Six-Day War.

After serving for three years as Chief of Staff, General Zur retired from the Army and became a civilian businessman: he was appointed director-general of Mekorot Water Development and Supply Company. He negotiated in Washington for the supply of scientific know-how for the desalination of water by nuclear energy and for financial assistance for the construction of the required reactor in Israel. However, the protracted negotiations never were concluded. Zur's dynamic nature was also reflected in the constant expansion of Vered, a subsidiary of Mekorot engaged in development work overseas. When Vered encountered severe economic difficulties in the early 1970's, Zur, who by then had left Mekorot, was among those criticized for the uncontrolled growth of its activities.

Prior to his becoming de facto Deputy Minister of Defense, Zvi Zur joined David Ben-Gurion, Moshe Dayan, Shimon Peres and Teddy Kollek in 1965 on the Rafi list of ex-Mapai candidates for the Knesset. Zur was elected but never sat in the House: he resigned before even taking the parliamentary oath in order to continue his efforts on behalf of Israel's water-desalination project. Not being a Knesset member, however, made his position difficult when Moshe Dayan became Minister of Defense and appointed Zvi Zur as his deputy. Since, under Israeli law, deputy ministers are required to be members of the Knesset, Zur could be given only the title of Assistant Minister and not the more significant title of Deputy Minister.

With his big Cuban cigars, his love of art and music and the good things in life, Zur appears more of a *bon vivant* than an Army general. He is a confirmed optimist and for a long time after June, 1967, refused to believe that France would maintain the arms embargo imposed by General de Gaulle. It was his duty to try to find ways to overcome the embargo's effects, and many credit him with success in this.

As the man in charge of weapons procurement for the defense establishment, Zvi Zur exercises an extraordinary influence on the economic, particularly the industrial, development of Israel. The channeling of defense funds has been a prime factor in the establishment of highly sophisticated industries and the rapid expansion of others. Zvi Zur is the man who often initiates and almost always has to give the final approval for such projects.

Another area in which the generals have significant influence is that of the military government of the territories occupied by Israel in the 1967 war. Whatever happens in the Gaza Strip and on the West Bank affects not only the political atmosphere among the Arab population but also their economic situation. This also has repercussions on the economic life of Israel proper, which both sells and buys goods and services from the occupied territories.

Yet another sphere of influence is the direct one: a general with persuasiveness and prestige can convince the Minister of Finance and the Finance Committee of the Knesset to allocate funds for new military projects. He also can have considerable impact on public opinion in general through interviews in the press and on radio and television. Some of the generals have created for themselves the image of "doers" who get things moving in civilian life.

But the most important influence by far of the defense establishment on the country's civilian authorities is exerted by the head of the Intelligence Branch of the defense establishment. His evaluation and reports are a basic element in the government's assessment of possible or probable reactions of the enemy to any proposed course of action. His reports carry great weight in determining the size of the armed forces, the level of armaments, the optimum division between domestic production and overseas procurement of weapons, and on the concomitant budgetary implications. On the political level, the defense concepts developed by the military elite are translated directly into government policy, such as the policy of retaliation of the 1950's or the 1968 concept of static defense along the Suez Canal, and thereby have impact on Israel's international relations.

Last but not least, members of the military elite, by their very prestige, influence public opinion on fundamental matters such as national self-confidence, the kind of borders that are needed for defense or the share of the GNP that should be devoted to security expenditures. By and large, these influences are predictably hawkish, but there are some notable exceptions, such as General Matityahu Peled, who has become a leading spokesman of the doves since he retired from the Army and joined the faculty of the Hebrew University.

The considerable influence of generals out of uniform on Israel's civilian life is due to the fairly large number of top officers who have assumed executive jobs in business and public service after retiring. They have introduced organizational methods customary in the Army, leading to more rational and efficient procedures in banks, business enterprises and factories throughout the country. They have also pioneered the use of up-to-date technology and larger expenditure on research in industrial enterprises. Such trends, of course, have had an indirect impact on other enterprises in the economy.

When a senior officer reaches the age of forty, a kind of red light goes on: he begins to wonder what he will do in civilian life. The Army has helped him to learn a profession useful in civilian life and thus has a considerable share in promoting the entry of top officers into the civilian elite. Civilian employers believe that by "acquiring a general" they can assure their companies not only an aura of efficiency but also a smoothness of operation which is still lacking in many sectors of the economy. Yet there are some disappointments too, when it develops that being an ex-general does not automatically make one an efficiency expert, especially because civilian decision making is so different from the analogous process in a military framework.

The tendency of the Israeli military elite not to question the absolute primacy of civilian authority in making all decisions of a political nature goes back to pre-State days. The Haganah was an ideological and political entity. When Israel came into being, the question was how to assure that politics would not be mixed with military affairs, in addition to preventing the military from mixing in politics. The latter possibility, in a way, was never even considered to be a real danger. The firm hand wielded by Ben-Gurion in depoliticizing the military in 1948 established the concept of separation, according to which the civilian authority decides and the military implements its decisions.

The only significant occasion when the military elite emerged as a pressure group upon civilian leadership occurred on the eve of the Six-Day War in 1967. The officers of the General Staff called upon the late Prime Minister Eshkol and warned him in no uncertain terms of the consequences of any further hesitation on his part in giving the order to attack the Egyptian forces massed on Israel's border.

Naturally, not every retired general has an equal influence on the civilian leadership of the country. To some extent, this depends on his former position in the military hierarchy; but mainly it depends on his personality. The same two factors also determine the importance of a general in the Army itself. The Commander of the Air Force is considered more important than the Commander of the Navy, whoever the two officers may be. Yet, in each case, the respective officer's personal caliber carries much weight. Furthermore, there are pressure groups in the Army, too, and he who represents a stronger pressure group has greater personal influence.

In a reverse way, an officer's influence within the defense establishment is also determined by the weight he carries in civilian public opinion. This is not only a question of popularity but also of personal contacts with the civilian elite. Although the Army will probably not admit it, the limits of what a top officer may or may not say in public are also influenced by his public image.

Each of the generals has a long military career behind him during the course of which his recommendations—or lack of recommendations—influence the promotion of junior officers under his command. Personal acquaintanceships inevitably play a role in the promotion policies of every organization, including the military, and one may occasionally discern the reflection of this on the emergence of groups of supporters of one general or another.

There are not many outward indications of a general's belonging to the innermost circle of the military elite. One of the few signs is his being included among those invited from time to time to informal consultations, usually held in the evening or on Saturday at the home of Defense Minister Dayan. The fact that the Minister of Defense values an officer's judgment sufficiently to ask for his opinion outside of formal channels obviously carries much prestige. When this happens to a colonel or a lieutenant colonel (who may be invited to Dayan's office for a talk but practically never to his home), it is a sign that the man is definitely on the way up.

The Chief of Staff is, of course, among those who attend such private consultations at Dayan's villa in Tel Aviv's suburb of Zahala. Among the regulars is also the Commander of the Air Force, General Mordecai Hod; the head of the General Branch, General Tal; the former head of Military Intelligence, General Aharon Yariv, who retired in October, 1972; as well as the head of the Central Command, General Rehavam Ze'evi ("Gandhi").Rehavam Ze'evi was born in Jerusalem in 1926, a fifth-generation sabra on his mother's side. Young Rehavam went to agricultural school and joined the Palmach. In Israel's War of Liberation, he served as an intelligence officer. He was among the first graduates of the Army's battalion commanders' course and his chief instructor (subsequently Chief of Staff and Ambassador to Washington) General Yitzhak Rabin, wrote in his personal file: "An individualist, a sharp and fast thinker, suitable for any assignment."

After two years of field service, he began fifteen years at various desk jobs in 1953. While in the Operations Division of GHQ, he was planning officer for the raids of the 101st Unit, the commando force that went behind Arab lines in retaliation for terrorist attacks. Ze'evi was sent to Staff College in the United States, but on the eve of the Sinai Campaign was urgently recalled by General Dayan and made his executive officer. Subsequently, he became deputy head of the General Branch at GHQ under General Bar-Lev and later under General Ezer Weizman. He achieved the rather unusual distinction of being able to make friends with such diverse personalities as Moshe Dayan and Haim Laskov, Ezer Weizman and Haim Bar-Lev.

On the eve of the Six-Day War, Ze'evi was raised to the rank of general but continued as a desk-bound staff officer. In 1968, he finally attained his long-time desire and received a field command: he was appointed head of the Central Command—at that time the most sensitive regional command, since it included most of the occupied West Bank, which was then the main target of Arab terrorist efforts. In his new command, General Ze'evi used to participate personally in ambushes and shoot-outs with terrorist bands along the Jordan and was even accused—but fully exonerated—of charges that he shot five captured terrorists. His quickness on the trigger served him well in the spring of 1969, when he was first to open fire on Arab terrorists about to throw a hand grenade at visiting officials in the Arab town of Hebron. With the same firmness, he removed from Hebron a group of Jewish nationalists who wanted to settle there contrary to government policy.

General Ze'evi can take a large measure of credit for ending terrorist activity on the West Bank, although this required harsh measures, such as the demolition of houses where terrorists were permitted to hide. Ze'evi is also credited with organizing the combination of static and mobile antiterrorist defense along the Jordan River. His success in restoring tranquillity along the Israel-Jordan frontier was given an indirect but clear compliment in the spring of 1971 when Arab farmers on the Jordanian side of the border returned to lands abandoned by them two years earlier because of the terrorists' presence along the river.

Though head of a regional command, most of his duties are administrative. He makes it a rule to spend half of the week outside his office visiting camps, outposts and depots to check every detail of their day-to-day work. The moment he receives a report about any incident or clash, he drops whatever he is doing to rush to the scene by car or helicopter. There have been occasions when he left meetings with cabinet ministers for that reason. General Ze'evi was also the first who reached the scene when a Sabena airliner, hijacked by Arab terrorists, landed at Lydda Airport, and he was in charge of the commandos who shot their way into the plane and captured the terrorists. Again, he was the first at Lydda after the Japanese suicide attack at the passenger terminal there in May, 1972.

He came out of this last operation with somewhat mixed glory. The surviving Japanese terrorist testified in court that he made his full confession after General Ze'evi promised to give him a loaded revolver so that he could commit suicide. Ze'evi's image was not improved by his own testimony that he never really intended to keep his promise to the Japanese terrorist.

The very fact that he commands the Israel Air Force automatically makes General Mordecai Hod a member of the military inner elite. The Air Force plays a central role in Israeli strategic doctrine: hence the Commander of the Air Force is high on the list not only of the military elite but also among the top policy makers of the country. When the Israeli General Staff adopted and the Cabinet approved the daring plan of General Mordecai ("Motti") Hod to make an all-out attempt to destroy the Egyptian Air Force on the ground in the very first hours of the June, 1967, war, this was much more than a purely military decision. For one thing, the plan was central to the basic concept of conducting a brief, striking war which would establish the results of the fighting before the built-in hostile majority at the UN could try to prevent an Egyptian defeat. For another, this fast-strike strategy was the chief means of deterring air attacks against Israel's densely populated coastal plain, relatively easily accessible to hostile planes from the sea.

In a broader sense, the Commander of the Air Force shapes Israel policy making by the weight of his opinion in two crucial fields: first, estimates of what the Air Force can or cannot do in an all-out effort; second, formulation of plans for constant strengthening and modernizing of the Air Force. For a long time, Israel Air Force commanders were wary of ideas to establish a domestic aircraft industry. Not only was there a subconscious inclination to trust foreign planes more but (and perhaps primarily), it was felt that, dollar for dollar, the Air Force could get more numerous and more modern planes for the same budget by purchasing foreign-made planes.

This attitude had effects beyond military policy making: it prolonged Israel's extensive dependence on French aircraft and material, and postponed the development of Israel's own aircraft industry and of other highly sophisticated industries which act as subcontractors to any aviation manufacturer. A dent on overseas dependence was made in the 1960s with the assembly in Israel of the Fouga-Magister jet trainers and light fighters from parts manufactured in France. But the big boost to the Israel aircraft industry was given by the sudden embargo imposed by General de Gaulle three days before the outbreak of the Six-Day War, in an effort to impose his will on the June, 1967, Middle East crisis.

It is thus probably no coincidence that General Hod, who played a key role not only in the lightning destruction of the Egyptian Air Force but also in the smooth and speedy absorption of the American jet fighters that succeeded the French ones, was followed in the top post by an officer who is also an aeronautical engineer.

General Benjamin ("Benny") Peled started his military career as a maintenance mechanic in the first squadron of the nascent Israel Air Force in the 1948 War of Independence. To this very day, he knows the insides of war planes as well as he knows how to fly them. In 1947 Peled began his engineering studies at the Haifa Institute of Technology. The war interrupted his studies; he was sent, with a small group of engineers and mechanics, to the air strip of Ekron, to put together the Air Force's first Messerschmitts, brought in semi-knocked-down from Czechoslovakia. "I painted the first Star of David on the first fighter plane of the Israel Air Force," he recalls proudly. In December, 1948, Peled was among the seventy-seven men admitted to the first basic flying training course of the Air Force. Of the thirteen who completed it and received their wings, Benny Peled is the last one still in uniform.

Peled is thus entirely the product of the Israel Air Force, the first to reach the top command. He is a descendant of one of the oldest Jewish farming families in the Galilee: his great-grandfather was one of a group of East European Hassidic faithful who in 1860 emigrated to Palestine but, unlike most of the pious of those days, did not settle in one of the towns to devote their time mostly to study and prayer. They purchased one thousand dunams of land near Mt. Canaan, near Safed, and started farming. The family moved several times: Benny's father grew up in the village of Rosh Pinah near the Lebanese border, where he was so impressed by the motorized vehicles of the British Army in World War I that he decided to become a mechanic. As such, he later moved to Tel Aviv, where his son was born in 1928. Benny graduated from Herzlia High School, one of the top three of its kind in Palestine, and volunteered for the Haganah. He was assigned as a driver to Zvi Zur, who later became Chief of Staff and is now Special Assistant to the Minister of Defense.

In 1952 Peled was among the Israeli pilots sent to England to learn to fly jets and was appointed Deputy Commander of Israel's first Meteor jet squadron. Two years later he was among the officers who went aircraft shopping to France. His insistence influenced the decision to limit the orders for available aircraft and wait for the new series of Mystère planes, which later played a crucial role in Israel's victory in the 1956 Sinai Campaign.

Peled was flying at the head of a Mystère squadron attacking the Egyptian coastal cannons that blockaded Israel shipping to Elath at Sham-el-Sheikh when he was hit by anti-aircraft fire and forced to bail out, landing with a broken ankle a few hundred yards from an Egyptian gun position. While the Egyptians chased his discarded parachute, Benny ran in the other direction. He was picked up by a small Piper that landed and took off on the rough desert, amidst a hail of Egyptian bullets.

In the late 1950's, Benny Peled finally made it again to school: after eleven years of absence, he returned to the Haifa Institute of Technology and graduated in aeronautics. Later he pursued postgraduate studies in the United States. Since then Peled has worked in both planning and weapons-developments projects and in field commands, rising through the ranks to the number-two post under General Hod, whom he succeeded in May, 1973.

There are not many officers in Israel who can be described as "controversial." General Ariel ("Arik") Sharon, Commander of the Southern Command, is one of the few. Of medium height, stockily built, General Sharon evokes strong positive as well as negative reactions in public opinion because of his sharp military and political views. In the eyes of many Israelis he personifies the hawks of the military establishment.

Sharon was born in 1928 in Kfar Malal, a farming village in Palestine, and joined the Haganah in his youth. In 1947 he joined the British-officered Settlement Police, and in the War of Independence was wounded during the unsuccessful attempt to capture a Latrun police fortress controlling the Jerusalem highway. While many of his colleagues rose slowly in the ranks, Sharon was appointed at the age of twenty-two to head the commando units which developed the technique of behind-the-lines raids and other unconventional methods of fighting.

After a two-year leave of absence from the Army, during which he studied history and Oriental studies at the Hebrew University, Sharon was appointed to organize the 101st Unit, which operated behind Jordanian and Syrian lines. Sharon was wounded in one of its operations, but what he learned during those commando years had a decisive influence on his views of the nature of the Arab-Israel confrontation. These views were decisive in formulating the kind of counterattacks planned and executed by Sharon against Egyptian-controlled terrorist units on the eve of the Sinai War in 1956. He participated personally in some of the paratroop raids, and when the war broke out, he was in charge of a paratroop brigade. After the war, he was sent to Staff College in England, and upon his return home became one of the heads of the Training Command of the Israel Army. In the early 1960's, he, too, was shifted to the Armored Corps and became commander of a tank brigade. Subsequently he returned to GHQ and became head of the Training Command. In the Six-Day War, Sharon was in charge of the Tank Corps which breached the Egyptian lines in Northern and Central Sinai.

During the War of Attrition, Sharon was opposed to the concept of fixed defense lines and, like many other Armored Corps veterans, advocated the concept of flexible defense based on mobile units, combined with deep penetration commando raids behind enemy lines. While his concept of mobile defense was not adopted, the idea of deep strikes was taken up, and he personally commanded some of the raids.

Ariel Sharon's military career came to an abrupt end in July 1973. When he resigned his post as head of the Southern Command, he hinted that the move was made "against his will." On earlier occasions it had been rumored that Sharon was at odds with the country's political leadership, who did not consider him a potential Chief of Staff. Sharon, whose political views are close to those of the Liberal faction in Gahal, is expected to assume an active role in the party, which lacks popular new leaders.

Among the younger officers, the fastest career advancement into the top ranks is predicted for General Mordecai ("Motta") Gur, the

Israeli-born youngest general in the Army. He was only eighteen when the War of Independence began and he is the first Israeli general who was an ordinary private in that war.

His military career began as a jeep platoon commander and his formal education includes a B.A. in Middle Eastern studies from the Hebrew University and studies at the Ecole du Guerre in Paris. In the early stages of his career, he served with a paratroop unit and received one of Israel's highest military decorations for his performance in a commando raid before the Sinai Campaign.

The road to the elite of the Army opened to Gur when he was appointed to the faculty of the Israel Army Staff College. Shortly before the Six-Day War, he received a field command as head of the Parachute Brigade, and his soldiers were the first Jews to reach the Wailing Wall after twenty years of Arab rule.

Shortly after the 1967 war, he was sent as special military advisor to the Israel Delegation at the United Nations. This was his first experience as a "military diplomat." Upon his return, he was appointed commander of the Gaza Strip, one of the most unrewarding tasks of that period; the teeming refugee camps of the Strip were a hotbed of unrest and terrorist activity. It was his task to maintain a balance between repressing terror and obtaining the cooperation of the local Arab population. It was at this time, too, that Gur developed a smooth working relationship with Defense Minister Moshe Dayan.

In November, 1969, Gur was appointed Commander of the Northern Command. This was an opportunity for him to gain varied military and political experience: he had to cope with terrorist attacks originating in Syria and at the same time assure the continuation of relations with the Lebanese, through whose territory most of the terrorists passed on their way to Israel. In June, 1972, Gur was sent to Washington as Israel's military attaché in the United States and Canada. That post, too, traditionally has been a stepping stone to the innermost circle of the Israeli military establishment.

Gur's predecessor in Washington, General Eliahu Zeira, is now head of Military Intelligence. His appointment was part of the trend to put younger officers into top positions in the Army. Today, Zeira is the youngest of the generals on active service and his appointment to the General Staff began a process of reducing the average age of that level of command, an age which had slowly but steadily been rising during Israel's twenty-five years of statehood.

Zeira is of the generation which barely made it to fight in the War of Independence, and his military education is entirely made-in-Israel. He was born in 1929 in Haifa and graduated from the Reali high school, where many of the Israeli civilian and military elite have studied. At the age of seventeen he enlisted in the Palmach and later studied economics and statistics at the Hebrew University. During the period of anti-Egyptian retaliation attacks in 1954–55, he was Dayan's chef de cabinet. After the Sinai Campaign, he attended officers' courses in the United States; back in Israel, he commanded a paratroop brigade and was moved to GHQ as head of the Operations Branch. He joined Military Intelligence in 1963.

In 1968 Zeira became deputy head of the Intelligence Branch and in 1970 went to Washington, where his job of military attaché made him the liaison between the Israel Army and the Pentagon. The importance of the job was underscored when his rank was raised to general. When General Aharon Yariv retired from active service in late 1972, General Zeira was recalled from Washington and appointed head of the Intelligence Branch.

While many of his colleagues owe their positions in the military elite both to personality and to official status, General Amos Horev belongs to that circle primarily on the strength of his personal qualities. He is now head of the Logistics Command at GHQ, a post which is not usually considered among the most important in the inner circles of the military. However, Horev is very active on various committees and study groups dealing with technological problems both in the Army and in civilian life, and this is one of the avenues through which his views and decisions have an influence exceeding his narrow official task.

Born in 1924, freckle-faced Amos Horev has always looked younger than his years. (One story has it that while he was nervously awaiting the birth of his first child the nurse came out of the delivery room and told him, "Go tell your father that you have another brother.") Horev has mechanical engineering degrees from MIT, where he was sent to study by the Israel Defense Forces from 1950 to 1952. He returned in 1962 for additional graduate work.

During the Palmach period Amos Horev became involved with arms maintenance and matériel problems. After serving in the War of Independence, rising to Chief of Operations of the Southern Command and completing his studies in the United States, he was appointed to the General Staff, at a time when the Israeli Defense Forces were entering the electronic age.

After the Sinai Campaign, Horev was in charge of reconditioning and adapting for Israeli use the tons of Soviet equipment, including dozens of tanks, captured from the Egyptians. This experience led him to conclude that the Israel Defense Forces were capable of building and supplying most of their needs in heavy vehicles. In 1961 he submitted a plan for the design and manufacture of armored vehicles within the framework of the military establishment.

In the spring of 1964, Horev was appointed again as Chief of the Ordnance Corps and was given the rank of major general with greatly expanded responsibility. The Ordnance Corps was then engaged in a massive rebuilding of most of the tanks in the Army's possession. The aim was to make them into highly sophisticated vehicles equipped with the newest electronic devices, capable of confronting the latest-model Soviet tanks in Egyptian hands. But the role and status of the Ordnance Corps was, at that time, the subject of discussions and changes. Soon another reorganization occurred, again reducing the Corps' scope of responsibility and that of its commander. Amos Horev quit, becoming Deputy Chief Scientist of the defense establishment. (The post of Chief Scientist was held by Professor Ephraim Katchalski of the Weizmann Institute.)

Amos Horev frequently stresses the close connection between Israel's qualitative military superiority over the Arabs and the availability of technically qualified personnel in the country. In his view, the much higher efficiency of Israeli weapons compared to those in

Arab hands is due not to their inherent qualities but to the greater ability of the Israelis to make the best use of whatever equipment they have.

In the summer of 1968 General Horev was appointed head of the Logistics Command in GHQ, which is the largest technical and economic organization in Israel. In his new job he supervised construction of the Bar-Lev Line along the Suez Canal under the fire of the Egyptian guns during the War of Attrition; he directed the further modernization of the armored units while installing diesel engines and new guns; he also directed the absorption of American arms and equipment which were replacing obsolescent French weapons. In October 1972, he was appointed Chief Scientist of the defense establishment. However, when the board of governors of the Haifa Institute of Technology selected him to be its next president, Horev decided to accept. He will take up the post at the end of 1973.

It is generally assumed by those studying the Israel Defense Forces that its present high command is a cohesive group, despite the varied experience of its members. The main factor promoting this cohesiveness was their common service as young officers in the War of Independence and in the early years of Statehood. In those days the Army was small and practically all the officers knew each other personally. In addition, there was a high degree of mobility among the services. An officer of the Tank Corps would be shifted to the Air Force, or a naval officer moved to the paratroopers; thus, most officers had a good knowledge of several branches of the Armed Forces. In addition, many of the young officers in those days had a distinctly ideological background: they came either from kibbutzim or from youth movements affiliated with ideological organizations.

In all these areas, considerable changes have occurred in recent years. The officers who are now reaching the top were youngsters, if not children, in the pre-independence days. They achieved their promotions in a larger Army where no one could know all his peers personally and where one specialized as much as possible.

One of these younger men now nearing the top is General Shmuel Gorodish-Gonen, whose appointment as head of the Training Command at GHQ was among the first official acts of the new Chief of Staff, General Elazar, upon taking office in 1972. A year and a half later Gonen took over the vital Southern command, where Israelis face Egyptians across the Suez Canal. This appointment marked a further step in his meteoric rise in the Israel Defense Forces hierarchy.

Shmuel Gorodish was born in 1929 in Jerusalem and in his youth was a rabbinical student. At the age of fourteen he joined the Haganah and fought in Jerusalem in the War of Liberation. When Israel's first "secret weapons"—two old military flame throwers brought from America—arrived in Jerusalem, Gorodish volunteered to operate one of the weapons in a vain effort to break into the Old City through the Zion Gate. Kerosene from the flame thrower burned his left hand but he volunteered a few days later to operate it again in an attack to recapture Ramat Rachel east of Jerusalem—and this time his right arm was burned. Before he was evacuated, shrapnel wounded his back. His bad luck did not end there: the pouch in which the commanding officer sent the recommendation for his decoration was lost and never reached the office of the Chief of Staff.

In 1949, Gorodish was among the first young officers in the Tank Corps just being organized. He was still a tank officer in 1956, when his units were the first to get within sight of the Suez Canal. Decorated for his role in that campaign, Gorodish and his tanks fought in Sinai again in the Six-Day War. His command tank always drove at the head of the attacking column, with Gorodish himself standing in the open turret.

In an interview after the war, he summed up his philosophy as follows: "The Israel Army's task is not to fight but to win. If you can win without a fight, so much the better. But, if you have to fight, the duty of a soldier is to kill and not to be killed." As a pupil of General Tal's doctrines and ideas, Shmuel Gorodish insists on scrupulous performance of every order. He attaches utmost importance to the professional and technical side of soldiering and to stern discipline. Discipline prevents those who are too daring from rushing ahead and those who are frightened from lagging behind. Without motivation, discipline is useless, but motivation without discipline is insufficient. A good officer is always suspicious of the enemy and expects the worst, Gorodish maintains; he was the first after the Six-Day War—months before terrorist activities made it standard procedure—to oblige all soldiers in the occupied territories to carry arms at all times, forbade them to take lifts in other than military vehicles and restricted the use of non-asphalted roads to armored vehicles, as a precaution against hidden mines.

"The most important motivating force in my life is the memory of the Nazi Holocaust," Gorodish once declared, explaining that one cannot rest from an all-out effort to assure that no such catastrophe will happen again to the Jewish people.

When Shlomo Gazit was given the rank of general in January, 1973, the number of general officers on active duty with the Israel Army rose to fifteen. Gazit is the "most civilian" among them, not only because of his appearance, which reminds one of a typical Jewish intellectual rather than a military officer, but also because of his official duties. His full title is Coordinator of Activities in the Occupied Territories and he is also head of the Military Government Division at GHQ. In fact, since August, 1967, Shlomo Gazit has been both the planner and chief implementer of Israel's policies in all the areas taken from the Arabs in the Six-Day War.

Formally, his rise to the rank of general served to end a bureaucratic anomaly: until then, he had held the same rank as the military governors of the various Arab territories, who were actually his subordinates. In fact, however, the appointment was an expression of the great appreciation Defense Minister Dayan had for Gazit's work, both as an administrator and as advisor to him on all matters concerning the Arab territories. The acquaintance between Dayan and Gazit goes back to the early 1950's when Dayan was Deputy Chief of Staff and Gazit was in charge of his office.

Shlomo Gazit, the younger brother of Mordecai Gazit, the Director-General of the Prime Minister's Office, was born in Turkey in 1926 and came to Palestine in 1933. In 1944 he joined the Palmach and remained in fighting units until the end of the War of Independence. After the war he was transferred to the editorial board of *Ma'arachot,* the journal of the armed services. His later training at the French Staff College equipped him for his role as liaison officer with the French military mission in Israel during the 1956 Sinai Campaign. In 1964, he transferred to the Intelligence Branch at GHQ and drafted political-military evaluations on the eve of the Six-Day War.

Social and personal relations among members of the top military elite are not always the friendliest. There is a keen sense of competition among them for the uppermost rungs of the ladder: this is particularly evident among the generals heading regional commands. The Six-Day War provided some of them with the aura of heroes and projected some of this competition into the civilian realm. Nor is there a very intimate social life among the families of the military elite, although many of them live in two "army suburbs" of Tel Aviv, Zahala and Neve Magen.

The private lives of the generals are as different as their personalities. General Gur, for example, is a family man, not interested in social activities, and devotes his free time to writing children's books. General Ze'evi is an extrovert and likes to attend private and official parties. General Sharon tries to use social life to promote his interest in public affairs. General Tal is always interested in tanks, in his office and at home, and young officers tend to see him as their military mentor.

Many of the generals have their own faithful admirers inside the Army and out of it. While on active service, many of them "take along" in their career young officers who often become known as this or that general's man. When these admirers move to civilian life, and assume positions in private business or government service, they continue to maintain contacts with each other and their former bosses. This creates at times an ad hoc employment service:

the general can always phone one of his friends and try to get a job for a noncommissioned officer—or even a senior officer—who is leaving the service.

Children of top-ranking officers, almost without exception, volunteer for officers' courses and for service in fighting units—possibly to prove that they are not inferior to their fathers. Some of the more "dangerous" special units have a particularly high percentage of soldiers who come from officer families. However, unlike their fathers, the sons of top officers tend to quit the service as soon as their military service ends and go on to university studies.

There has been a considerable increase in the prestige and influence of the military elite in Israeli public life since 1967. In part, this is due to their role in the Six-Day War. But it is also due to the role they played in the days before the war when it became evident that the country's civilian heads depended to a great extent on the military elite for their strategic thinking.

One of the results of this situation is that members of the military elite do not hesitate at times to take the initiative in conveying their views to Cabinet members—something that was quite unthinkable during Ben-Gurion's time. Some generals have developed friendships with influential ministers. The Finance Minister, Pinhas Sapir, has been known to confer with the generals after receiving the Defense Ministry's draft of the coming year's budget.

It was inevitable that this new intimacy should heighten the interest of some of the generals in political careers after retirement from the service, as well as whet the interest of the political parties in acquiring ex-generals as their candidates. However, the first examples of generals entering politics have not been too successful.

The new elite, which is steadily replacing the retiring generals, will obviously differ from them. Each of its members has a university degree and each of them is a specialist in a specific military field, rather than knowing about many branches of the service. The new elite will probably be a much more homogeneous group—but a much less colorful one. The crucial experience of having participated in the establishment of Israel will be a thing of the past.

13

The Big Families
of Business

WHEN the Middle East was cut off from its sources of supply in World War II and the British authorities preferred to allocate shipping space to cargoes destined for the allied forces fighting the German and Italian armies, a group of fourteen of the largest importers of building materials in Palestine came together in 1944 and established the Central Israel Trade and Investment Company, Ltd. They realized that together they would be able to obtain larger import licenses than they would have received by acting separately. They soon became aware that in the field of financing as well, their combined effort would be more successful. In May, 1945, Central Trade (as the company became known as), together with Solel Boneh, the Histadrut-owned contracting company, purchased the Nesher cement plant from its founder, Michael Pollak.

The joint venture, undertaken by a company belonging to the private sector of the economy, together with a Histadrut-owned enterprise, drew severe criticism at the time from some labor-movement ideologists. Today it can be said that this deal—which was very successful from the point of view of the buyers—as well as the establishment of Central Trade, marked a turning point in the development of the Israeli economy. The novelty of the move was three-fold: (a) Private merchants found it necessary to organize a stock company, realizing that as the intervention of the government in business increases it is more advantageous to be a large unit. (b) Merchants who until then had been involved only in importing decided to invest together in industry. (c) This was the first time that a "model" for partnership between private and Histadrut capital in an industrial concern was created.

In later years these three trends became more and more wide-spread. In an economy split into tiny units of direct ownership, one of small stores, thousands and thousands of industrial workshops and private agricultural enterprises, there began to develop a tendency to concentrate the ownership of the means of production. New forms of partnership between private, government and public capital came into being in Israel, creating a unique economic structure which is not paralleled in any other country in the world, capitalist or socialist.

In 1934, when there were fewer than half a million Jews in Palestine, there were seventy-three commercial banks and fifty cooperative loan associations serving the Jewish community. In 1944, there were only twenty-six banks and sixty-six loan associations. In recent years there again has been a decrease in the number of banks, as a result of collapses of smaller banks, mergers and takeovers: by 1973 there were only eight banks or banking groups in Israel.

In the early 1950's, soon after Israel's establishment, hundreds of new family-owned enterprises were established. However, soon afterward, when the main effort of the government's development drive shifted from agriculture to industry, it became clear that the family firm was no longer suited for new conditions. Modern technology required the establishment of plants much larger than those that were built by individual manufacturers. The new plants required entrepreneurship, managerial ability and investments of a size that were until then unknown in Israel. It was also soon realized that the increasing influence of the government on the running of the economy required a different kind of management than that to which private industry was accustomed. There was a need for managers who could succeed in contacts with government officials, no less than in their relations with their employees.

Since the mid-1950's, therefore, a gradual process of transfer of ownership of industrial enterprises, shipping companies, insurance companies and even real-estate and building companies from private hands to financial concerns has taken place in Israel. Large company groupings or business "families" have begun to emerge in consequence.

The first to have anticipated this process were the founders of Central Trade: Israel Taiber, Aharon Netanel, Gershon Gurwitz, Joseph Gluckman and others, who by now have either died or retired from active management of the company. In recent years Central Trade has been managed by Abraham Friedmann.

It is most likely not mere chance that Abraham Friedmann, who was born in Haifa in 1905, is an appointed manager who came to the company in 1951, after it was founded. He differs in personality from the importers and construction-materials merchants who established the first large private concern. As one who was born to a well-to-do family (his father, the founder of the Friedmann Wine Cellars, was one of the pioneers of Israel's wine industry), he had no difficulties in developing an understanding with his employers— the Peker, Taiber, Swirsky, Perlman, Gurwitz, Natanel and Zimmermann families—but he also showed special talent in finding ways to the hearts of the pilots of the economy, such as Levi Eshkol and Pinhas Sapir, despite the obvious differences in background and political beliefs.

Abraham Friedmann, a friendly and easygoing person, soon became one of the frequent guests of Pinhas Sapir in his Kfar Saba home on Saturday mornings. Sapir pushed Central Trade into investments in various industrial firms. Urdan Foundries, Kitan Dimona, Israel Chemical Fiber, Telrad, Samson Tires (which was sold in 1971 at a considerable profit to the other tire factory, Alliance) are only some of the industrial firms which Central Trade bought into.

Levi Eshkol and Pinhas Sapir saw in Abraham Friedmann an ideal representative of Israeli nonsocialist big business. He fraternized with Diaspora Jewish businessmen and played a prominent part in the establishment of investment companies initiated by the government, such as Clal and the Israel Corporation. He is a member of the Ports Authority and serves on a number of public committees. His big white car has a reserved parking place on Nahlat Benjamin Street in the heart of Tel Aviv's business district. This privilege is given to him as the Honorary Consul of Finland in Tel Aviv.

The connections of Abraham Friedmann and others in Central Trade with Minister of Finance Pinhas Sapir were of assistance in the spring of 1970, when the company was forced to sell at a loss its shares in the Swiss-Israel Trade Bank, a Geneva-based bank in which the Israeli government had invested in the early 1950's. When Central Trade sold shares in the bank to a financier from Chile, the Israeli government agreed to forgo the debt balance of fourteen million Swiss francs which Central Trade had owed it from the time the company bought the Swiss-Israel shares in 1954. Despite the generosity of the government, Central Trade suffered a disclosed loss of 15 million Israeli pounds as a result of the Swiss-Israel deal.

Central Trade never recovered from this deal and from other difficulties which confronted it during the economic recession in Israel in the mid-1960's. In December, 1970, the company was swallowed up by a younger and more aggressive conglomerate, Clal, which Central Trade itself had helped to establish ten years earlier. Clal's biggest asset in the struggle to gain control of Central Trade was its dynamic management, active stockholders and, above all, good relations with the government—advantages which earlier had worked in Central Trade's favor.

Abraham Friedmann remained as joint general manager of Clal, but most of his colleagues on the board of directors of Central Trade turned to their own affairs.

Central Trade was not the only Israeli concern to go into the banking business at a certain point in its development. Almost every group of companies in Israel became the proud owner of a bank of its own in the early 1960's. During the same period there was also a development in the opposite direction: banks which had started their operations in conventional fashion, taking deposits and offering loans, became active in other fields as well, investing in industry, shipping, real estate and even in the import of computers.

The large and small banks which went into business in those years in the name of diversification did so to a large extent in imitation of the Israel Discount Bank, which already by the early 1960's was a multinational company based in Israel, active in many fields in various countries. The story of the Discount Bank, established in 1935 by Leon Recanati, who started as a teacher in Salonika and after immigrating to Israel, invested 60,000 Palestine pounds in his Tel Aviv bank, which in less than thirty years developed into a formidable economic empire, is a success story of international scale.

Of the four sons of Leon Recanati—who succeeded in mobilizing the support of old Sephardi families living in Palestine—two, Daniel and Raphael, today share control over the firm's banking activities. A third brother, Jacob, manages the company's shipping business, Cargo Ships El Yam, and the oldest brother, Harry, who lives in Europe, recently left the family business. Like the Rothschild brothers before them, Daniel, who lives in Tel Aviv, and Raphael, who for many years has lived in New York, utilize the distance between them to act separately, but in carefully coordinated fashion, in order to effect a constant expansion of the family empire. Daniel and Raphael Recanati divide between themselves a management fee of 5 percent of the profits of the bank—a sum that is equal to an annual salary of hundreds of thousands of Israel pounds for each of them.

In Israel the influence of Daniel Recanati, who is respectfully called "Mr. Dani" by employees of the bank, is obviously stronger. He was born in Salonika in 1921. After graduating from high school in Tel Aviv he studied at the London School of Economics, but returned soon after the outbreak of World War II, and later joined the British Army, serving in Egypt and Italy. He also served in the

Israeli Army in 1948 but at that time was already involved in the activities of the Discount Bank, whose general manager he became in 1954.

Daniel Recanati is thin, his face narrow and his hair graying. He is always elegantly dressed, mostly in dark suits. When he receives someone in his office he is relaxed and never looks at his watch, the telephone does not ring, and the secretary never interrupts to bring letters for his signature. His behavior is conservative to the nth degree. The bank has no public-relations consultant, and Mr. Recanati personally signs the invitations to the yearly press conference (invariably held on a Tuesday), on the occasion of the publication of the bank's financial report. He once told a journalist, "My aspirations are the aspirations of the bank. I grew up in the Israel Discount Bank, and I identify with it."

Daniel Recanati knows that in order to live by his conservative, capitalist beliefs, he must compromise with the unique reality of Israel, and with the people who grew up with a different background. The Discount group has learned through the years to walk a tightrope suspended over the difficult reality of doing business in Israel. When asked how he, as a private businessman, adjusts himself to government intervention in business, Daniel Recanati reportedly replied: "When you are in a vineyard, you have to decide if you want to eat the grapes or antagonize the watchman."

The representative of the South American group in the Discount Bank family is Benno Gitter, who joined the group in 1958, after a group of investors from Argentina sold its holding in the Accadia Hotel and established a mortgage bank, together with the Discount Bank, with the sums that were realized.

Gitter, born in Holland in 1919 to a family involved in the tanning business, escaped in 1942 from Holland to Argentina, where he rejoined his relatives, whose business had already begun to flourish on the new continent. Young Gitter, who in his youth had planned to immigrate to Palestine, after 1948 began to devote his energies to developing business connections with the young State of Israel. In Argentina he founded an Argentine-Israel trading company and headed a group of investors in a number of Israeli enterprises.

In the Discount Bank group, his influence grew fast. He was appointed vicechairman of its holding company and of its industrial-investment company, as well as to the board of half a dozen other companies. He is an ideal board member, a type almost unknown on the Israeli scene. He is quick, thoroughly at home with complicated financial reports. He speaks many languages (with a Dutch accent), and makes friends easily. Like someone who has always been well-to-do, money to him is not an object in itself. He gladly undertakes public responsibilities, and serves on the board of governors of the Hebrew University of Jerusalem, as well as of the Tel Aviv University, the Israel Philharmonic Orchestra and the Cameri Theater.

Gitter served for two and a half years as Clal's first managing director (a job for which he earned one dollar for the whole period). In December, 1970, he went so far as to resign from all his functions in the Discount Bank and accept an economic mission abroad. However, when his expectations did not materialize, he returned a year later to business in Israel. Despite his close relations with the government and especially with Finance Minister Sapir, he did not hesitate to write a letter to the editor of the *Ha'aretz* daily newspaper in May, 1972, bitterly condemning some well-publicized early-morning raids by income-tax inspectors at homes of private citizens.

In recent years the management of the Discount Bank group absorbed a number of retiring senior Army officers, who play a growing role, especially in running the company's industrial enterprises. The first and senior member of this group is General (Res.) Dan Tolkowsky, a one-time Commander of the Israeli Air Force, whose influence on the thinking behind Israel's industrial development goes beyond his specific position in the Israel Discount Bank industrial complex. He is today one of the ideologists of Israel's technological progress.

Dan Tolkowsky, short, thin, with light hair, does not look at all like a sabra who was born in Tel Aviv in 1921. His blond mustache, mannerisms and even his accent in Hebrew show the clear impact of four years of studying mechanical engineering in London and four years of service in the Royal Air Force during World War II. He was trained as a pilot in South Africa and served as a fighter pilot in Italy and France and later in Crete and Greece. For ten years he served in the Israel Air Force and was its commander in the 1956 Sinai Campaign, which was one its finest hours. It was during his service as Air Force Commander that it became an all-jet Air Force, and the foundations were laid for this technological transition.

As managing director of the Israel Discount Bank Investment Company, Dan Tolkowsky is loyal to the conservative line of the firm. However, as an industrialist, more than a financier, he does not hesitate to recommend investing relatively large sums in fields which he thinks have a future in Israel, such as electronics and chemicals—although the final decision, as is usual in the Discount concern, is not made by him alone.

Dan Tolkowsky initiated the investment of his firm in Elron when the company, now a leading electronics complex, was still a struggling workshop founded by a number of instructors from the Haifa Technion. Some of Tolkowsky's efforts are directed to increasing cooperation between Israel's private industry and the defense effort. He is convinced that industry must participate in the application of the new technologies needed by Israel's defense; at the same time, he thinks industry will benefit from the spin-off of the huge investments in the country's defense.

Tolkowsky seems to be trying consciously to stay out of politics. Even when he undertakes a national assignment, it is usually associated with technical or aeronautical subjects, such as the public committee that investigated the Lod airport fire in 1970.

It is interesting to note that the Discount Bank family of companies, despite its patriarchal and conservative nature, was the first of the large Israeli business concerns to hand over key positions to younger people. Other groups, especially the Histadrut-owned enterprises, were run by relatively old people until very recently. Likewise, only in 1970, in an almost revolutionary sweep, the two other large Israeli banking groups, Bank Leumi LeIsrael and Bank Hapoalim acquired young managers: Ernst Japhet and Ya'acov Levinson.

It should be emphasized, however, that Ernst Japhet, who in 1970 became the chief executive officer of Israel's largest commercial bank, is by no means a revolutionary. As a banker and scion of an old established banking family, he meticulously maintains the conservative tradition of his profession. Even the German language, in which many conversations are still held in the bank (where a branch manager is often still called *Prokurist*), is Japhet's mother tongue. Still, Japhet reflects the start of a new era in this large and awkward banking institution, which is controlled by a publicly-owned holding company called Jewish Colonial Trust. He is more "Israeli" than any of his predecessors—less involved in politics and public affairs and more a professional banker, who is determined to keep Bank Leumi out of the fields of industry, real estate and commerce to which other banking groups were attracted, especially in the 1960's. It was probably not just coincidence that in 1964, when Ernst Japhet was still one of the deputy managing directors of Bank Leumi, he was vehemently opposed to the idea advocated by its head at that time, the late Dr. Yeshayahu Foerder, that Bank Leumi buy the government's shares in the Swiss-Israel Trade Bank.

Although Japhet, who was born in Germany in 1922 and brought to Palestine by his parents at the age of twelve, is related to the owners of the financial empire of the Japhet Bank (which had branches in Frankfurt, Berlin, Munich and London—where the branch was established by the brother of Ernst Japhet's grandfather) young Ernst made his career in the banking world outside the family business. He served as a sergeant in the British Army in World War II, studied banking in England and later became manager of the Haifa branch of the Israel Union Bank, which was later bought up by Bank Leumi.

In 1963, Dr. Foerder, who was a powerful figure in the Israeli business world (he was the founder and managing director of the Rassco investment company, served as chairman of the board of the Industrial Development Bank of Israel, and was a member of the Economic Ministerial Committee, where he represented the Independent Liberal party), persuaded Japhet to join Bank Leumi. In

1965 he became joint managing director, and in 1970, when Dr. Foerder was ill, the decision to appoint Japhet as sole managing director, thus forcing into retirement or "kicking upstairs" other senior directors, was tantamount to a revolution.

The decision was even more surprising in view of the fact that unlike the late Dr. Foerder, who was a close associate and admirer of Pinhas Sapir, despite their different political backgrounds, Japhet considers himself first and foremost a banker and not a financial agent of the government. It should be noted that although the Jewish Colonial Trust was formed by the Zionist movement more than seventy-five years ago, and is today controlled through a somewhat awkward mechanism by the Jewish Agency, it has succeeded in maintaining its independence throughout the years. Yet, despite the fact that Japhet considers his loyalty to be first and foremost to the bank and its many private stockholders, who provided it with new capital in recent years, he too sees his role through "public" spectacles and tries to avoid clashing with the government over economic policy as much as possible. The appointment in May, 1973, of Mendes Sachs as chairman of the board of Bank Leumi was a boost to Japhet's independent line. Sachs, a private businessman, is by no means a blind supporter of Mr. Sapir's policy of government intervention in the private sector of the economy.

A more independent, aggressive spirit in recent years has also characterized the third of the Big Three of Israeli banking—Bank Hapoalim, the financial arm of the Histadrut. The revolution there was spearheaded by the child prodigy of the Israeli banking world, Ya'akov Levinson. Levinson, born in 1934, differs from many of his contemporaries and colleagues in the Israeli power elite in that he shuns publicity. He does not like to be interviewed by journalists, and resents having his picture taken, and his name is not listed in the telephone directory. Although Levinson's background seems to have prepared him for his present position in Bank Hapoalim (he is a sabra whose father, Gershon Levinson, was for many years treasurer of the Histadrut), his meteoric rise in the conservative banking institution of the labor movement, whose progress was slowed by bureaucratic deadweight for many years, surprised everybody.

Levinson was a member of Kibbutz Rosh Hanikra, near the Lebanese border, and had become treasurer of the kibbutz before he had to return to Tel Aviv after the death of his father. He took up economics at the Hebrew University and at the same time began to work in the Economic Division of Hevrat Ha'ovdim—the holding company of the Histadrut enterprises. In 1964 he became the director of the economic division, turning it into a powerful instrument. This became the body in which the economic thinking and information of the whole Histadrut economy was concentrated; soon Levinson and his economists held a virtual veto power over all the economic decisions made by Hevrat Ha'ovdim and its affiliates.

Since Levinson took over Bank Hapoalim, the bank, which for many years was considered a "sleeping beauty," has begun to flex its muscles. It has since taken over the position of Israel's second-largest bank from the Israel Discount Bank, and through its control over employees' provident funds, has become number one as Israel's supplier of credit. In the private sector of the economy, Ya'akov Levinson is considered the "wise man" of the Histadrut economy. It is said of him that he is tough and inconsiderate, that he likes to pull strings behind the scenes and is a "natural" candidate for a cabinet post. Yet if he has any political ambitions, he does not reveal them, he rarely speaks in public.

Parallel to its phenomenal growth in the early 1970's, Bank Hapoalim underwent another important change. It began to retreat from intervention in branches of the economy other than banking and even sold some of its holdings in Clal. One of the reasons why Bank Hapoalim followed the example of other banking groups, in the early 1960's, and went into direct investment in business, was the pressure of Pinhas Sapir, who, in constructing new investment enterprises, tried to balance Histadrut firms against firms of the private sector in each new venture. Thus the number of the Histadrut company groupings (which already included Solel Boneh and Koor) had to be increased. Another reason why several families of

Histadrut firms developed was the competition between them. Even after the all-powerful manager of Solel Boneh, the late Hillel Dan, was removed from office in 1958, other Histadrut concerns continued his tradition of competing with each other—each one trying to establish its own financial arm, its own industrial concerns and even trading firms.

The streamlining of the Histadrut enterprises, with each group of companies limiting its activities to one sector of the economy, in fact had begun before Levinson took over Bank Hapoalim in 1970. It started in 1966 when Asher Yadlin became secretary-general of Hevrat Ha'ovdim, the holding company which until then was just a loose framework for virtually independent, self-reliant Histadrut bodies. Yadlin, short and stocky, has since become one of the strong men of the Histadrut economy, enjoying the support of Pinhas Sapir, yet at the same time accumulating his own sources of power. He seems to be unshaken even when he is in direct confrontation with the secretary-general of the Histadrut, Yitzhak Ben-Aharon, or even the directors of Kupat Holim (the Histadrut health services), who unsuccessfully objected to Yadlin's takeover as secretary-general late in 1972, in addition to his position in Hevrat Ha'ovdim.

Asher Yadlin, who was born in Jerusalem in 1923 and grew up in Rishon Le-Zion and Tel Aviv, was a member of Kibbutz Hamadiya between the years of 1943 and 1956. Yet his membership in the kibbutz did not prevent him from accepting a number of assignments in Israel and the United States, where he also received an M.A. degree from the College of the City of New York, in economics and labor relations.

In 1958 he became the secretary of the Civil Service Workers Union. His appointment in 1966 to Hevrat Ha'ovdim with the strong backing of Pinhas Sapir initiated a new era in the Histadrut-owned enterprise. It is said that, when Yadlin met Pinhas Sapir before his appointment, the Minister showed him a notation in his famous little book, in which he had marked down the names of twenty-five top managers of Histadrut enterprises whose ages at that time ranged between sixty-five and seventy. Sapir told Yadlin that he was determined to change the situation and, in fact, three years later, seventeen of the old managers had been pensioned or moved to other assignments.

In the central committee of the Histadrut, Yadlin is considered the "capitalist" in the group. He defends the right of the manager of a Histadrut company to get a bonus, demands higher remuneration for managerial competence and warns that a law against wildcat strikes which does not include sanctions is meaningless. Yadlin was one of the first who negated the accepted idea in the Histadrut economy that, since this sector is not profit motivated, it may decide on investments even if it is known in advance that no profits can be expected.

Yadlin is by no means a deep thinker. He believes that drive, efficiency and the basic principles of management can do more for the Histadrut enterprises than many of its traditional "ideologists." At first, after taking on the Kupat Holim responsibility in 1972, it seemed as though he would have to give up the Hevrat Ha'ovdim secretaryship, but Yadlin showed little inclination to relinquish either of his two important power bases.

Zvi Rechter, manager of the huge Histadrut-owned contracting concern, Solel Boneh, was one of those who followed Asher Yadlin in the managerial revolution that took place in the Histadrut economy in the late 1960's. Solel Boneh, which was established in the 1920's initially in order to provide work for unemployed Histadrut members, had its ups and downs until it became one of the giants of the Israeli economy in the 1940's and 1950's.

When Zvi Rechter took over the company, Solel Boneh was close to bankruptcy. The recession of the mid-1960's hit Solel Boneh in the same way that it hit other basically undercapitalized construction companies which were left with large stocks of unsold apartments. After succeeding in saving Solel Boneh from the fate of Rassco, which nearly collapsed in 1967, Zvi Rechter had to hold back his colleagues, who were tempted, in the boom years that ensued, to drift again into unrestricted expansion along the line of the early 1960's.

Being first and foremost a financial expert rather than a "man of vision" for whom growth is an end in itself, Zvi Rechter belongs to the new generation of Histadrut business executives who are no longer ashamed of the profit motive and claim that often the "public spirit" of a manager and his managerial ability do not go hand in hand.

Born in Vienna in 1921, Zvi Rechter, who arrived in Palestine in 1940, was a member of a kibbutz until 1968. In fact, since 1953 he has been almost continuously away from his collective settlement, Ma'aleh Hahamisha, near Jerusalem. He specialized in financial assignments within the kibbutz movement and the Histadrut economy before becoming the treasurer of Solel Boneh and later its managing director.

Aside from his professional responsibility in Solel Boneh (which in 1972 reached a turnover of over twenty million Israeli pounds), Rechter is the elected treasurer of the Labor party, a position which, although demanding much of his time since the party is always short of funds, provides him with an important power base influencing Israel's ruling party.

The revolution introduced by Zvi Rechter in Solel Boneh was relatively limited as compared with the changes introduced by another of the new managers of the Histadrut economy, General (Res.) Meir Amit, who in 1968 took over Koor, the conglomerate of industrial companies in the labor realm. Amit, who had won considerable popularity as one of Israel's top military leaders, came to an unwieldly group of companies run by a peculiar coalition of representatives of the various interest groups within the Histadrut.

Meir Amit (Slutzky), who comes from Kfar Yehoshua, a moshav in the valley of Jezreel near Nahalal, where Moshe Dayan grew up, studied business administration at Columbia University in New York, but he basically is an Israeli Army officer. His thinking may be slow but is thorough and he believes that if you are on the right track you will definitely reach your objective. Amit's many years in the Army, and especially the years that he served in Intelligence, make him object to what he calls "management by functionaries," meaning opportunistic interference in the way various companies are managed, or the exploitation of clashes within a workers committee in a plant. He believes that within a large unit like Koor, there must be a hierarchy and even a somewhat formal relationship.

The almost naïve belief of Amit in the principles of management were somewhat shaken at the end of 1971 when Israel's large automobile-production concern, Autocars, Ltd., collapsed. Koor, which had at one time been a partner in Autocars, with Meir Amit as the chairman of its board, had sold its shares in Autocars a year earlier. Amit was blamed for withdrawing from the company when he felt things were going wrong rather than pulling his weight to correct matters and avoid disaster. Amit himself revealed his own opinion in a conversation with a journalist: "Let's talk for a minute in simple, colloquial Hebrew: we flunked in Autocars."

But Amit was given another chance. His big challenge is the seventy companies and fifty-two industrial plants of Koor. Like others of his generation of managers, Amit disagrees with the notion that the profits of some companies should be used in order to cover the losses of others which were established for "pioneering" purposes, rather than for the accumulation of profits. He has not hesitated to close down some plants and clash with their workers. On the other hand, he introduced a system of profit sharing, which in itself was a revolutionary act in the Histadrut economy, where increases in salary until then were expected automatically by the workers regardless of the success or failure of their plants.

The biggest worry of Amit is the relatively low profitability of Israeli industry in general and of Koor in particular. He is determined to invest hundreds of millions of Israeli pounds in each of the next few years, not only because the country needs more industry, but because, as he sees it, only economic advantage resulting from large production units will enable each of the plants in his concern to become competitive in terms of world industry. Amit is luckier than other Israeli industrialists, since he is not dependent only on internal capital accumulation for financing expansion, or even on government loans alone, but can obtain long-term loans from the

Histadrut-managed pension and provident funds. Although private industrialists also contribute to these funds as employers, the Histadrut economy traditionally has priority in the use of the hundreds of millions of pounds which accumulate each year in these funds. In addition to these sources of finance, Amit has his eyes on Wall Street and hopes to float an issue of Koor stocks there.

In his manner and way of doing things, Amit has helped to change the image of the typical Histadrut manager. He was preceded in this role by Benjamin Gibli, now the managing director of Shemen, also known as "the manager who brought cigars to the labor economy." Gibli, a tall, good-looking man, brought to Koor not only cigars, cocktail glasses and long hair, but also a new style of management.

When he took over Shemen in 1967, the company, one of Israel's first factories for soap, detergents, cosmetics and edible oil, was in serious financial trouble. Since then the profits of Shemen and its volume of sales have risen steadily. In September, 1971, when Gibli became chairman of the Israel Export Institute, he made use of his new platform to express his often unorthodox ideas on production and export. Benjamin Gibli, born in 1919 in Petach Tikva to a farming family, was forty-five years old before he went into business. His first career was in the Israeli Army, where he was a member of the staff of the Haganah even before the establishment of the State, and later alternated between being a combat officer and being in Intelligence. In 1950 he became chief of the Army Intelligence Branch, and in this capacity was involved in the Lavon Affair, a security flap, which brought about the dismissal of the Minister of Defense, Pinhas Lavon, in 1955, and ten years later caused one of the most serious crises in Israel's power elite.

When the storm over the affair broke, Gibli (who, because of the futile attempts at censorship that prevailed at the time, could not be officially mentioned, but was called "the senior officer"), was military attaché at the Israeli Embassy in London. He had to resign from the Army but soon found that the business world could provide him with equally interesting adventures.

Gibli, who looks happy kissing beauties in an advertising campaign for the Mary Quant cosmetics produced by his firm, does not deny that someday he may decide that he has had enough of selling soap and toothpaste and may look again into the areas of defense and diplomacy.

The Histadrut-owned families of companies thus entered the 1970's after having gone through an extensive process of reorganization and "face lifting." Some other conglomerates of the 1960's, like Rassco, which were badly shaken during the recession, lost their positions and sank to minor importance. Other groups of companies, such as Clal and the Israel Corporation, emerged as economic giants only in the early 1970's.

One of the few families of companies which continued to operate in the early 1970's almost along their original lines was the Mayer brothers group. The headquarters of all their companies, including industrial firms, financial groups, real-estate-development organizations and foreign-investment units, is in the Shalom Tower, Tel Aviv's thirty-story skyscraper, which when completed in 1966 was "the tallest building between Europe and Japan."

While many tourists believe that the Shalom Tower is called after the popular Israeli greeting "Shalom" (which means "peace"), it is really named after Shalom Mayer, the father of the energetic Mayer brothers, who built one of Tel Aviv's most formidable financial empires. The group is still dominated by Moshe Mayer, born in 1909, who is in charge of financial connections abroad; Mordecai Mayer, born in 1911 and once a star of Tel Aviv's soccer team, who is the manager of the Israel Financial Enterprises, and Benjamin Mayer, the eldest, born in 1906, who manages the industrial companies of the group.

Shalom Mayer, with his wife, three sons and a daughter, came to Palestine in 1921 from Rumania. The brothers started in the 1930's by managing orange groves and other agriculture enterprises and only later went into industry, establishing textile and plastic plants. Their financial activities were concentrated in the family bank—the Export Bank, which in recent years was managed by Zalman Shuval, Moshe Mayer's son-in-law, who is also a Knesset member (running on the State list). In October, 1972, the Export Bank merged with the First International Bank of Israel, and the financial activities of the Mayer group were channeled to a new company called Comprehensive Financial Corporation.

Like other Israeli conglomerates which became dependent on foreign sources of finance, the Mayer brothers succeeded in mobilizing the resources of overseas financiers, especially the British Jewish millionaires Sir Isaac Wolfson and Sir Charles Clore. With them, they established the Wolfson, Clore, Mayer Investment Company and went into partnership in a number of enterprises, including Kol-Bo Shalom, Israel's largest department store, situated in the Shalom Tower.

The Mayer brothers, under the leadership of Moshe Mayer, began spreading their empire into other countries. At first they began operations in Liberia, where they built the first luxury hotel as well as a number of prominent buildings in Monrovia, including the presidential palace. From there they turned to the Ivory Coast, where they built the luxury Hôtel Ivoire, which has become a tourist attraction in that part of the world, as well as an entire Riviera (financed mainly with German capital), which is a resort suburb of the Ivory Coast capital, Abidjan. Moshe Mayer also has an interest in a Catskill hotel in New York State.

Like Moshe Mayer, for whom the scope of activities in Israel became too limited, Maritime Fruit Carriers, another Israeli conglomerate, has in recent years given the impression that it has "outgrown" Israel. Although its headquarters is still in Haifa, it has become a true multinational company different from other multinational groups only in that its two top executives are Israeli: Ya'acov Meridor and Mila Brener.

Although many of the managers of the companies are Israelis—some of whom had held senior positions in other Israeli organizations—the present connection of Maritime Fruit Carriers with Israel is relatively limited: only some of the ships still fly the Israeli flag. Most of the company's ships are registered outside of Israel and only a limited amount of business is done with Israel (transport of meat from South America and fishing off the coasts of South Africa). The company mobilizes its finances outside of Israel and most of its stocks are held by non-Israelis. In less than ten years the growth of Maritime Fruit Carriers became a fascinating success story of global proportions. The aggressive company run by this team of two unusual Israelis captured the imagination of the world early in 1973 when it placed orders with British shipyards for oil tankers totaling more than £500 million. Earlier the company had ordered tankers from American shipyards for amounts totaling hundreds of millions of dollars.

These stupendous orders for oil tankers came in addition to the company's virtual control (together with a Swedish and an American firm) of a large part of the world's refrigerated-cargo business, huge investments in gas tanker ships, beef cattle in Australia, oil prospecting in the North Sea and the production of aircraft parts in Israel.

When two large Buicks were unloaded in Haifa for Mila Brener and Ya'acov Meridor and brought to the company's headquarters, Brener was unhappy. "Someone who sees me driving this car might think that I am a manager of a Histadrut enterprise or a contractor working for the Ministry of Defense," he said almost seriously. In fact, the two partners may have accumulated larger personal fortunes in a shorter time than anybody else in Israel. Yet, interestingly enough, their position in Israel's power elite has not grown accordingly. They may now be less dependent on Israeli bureaucracy— being able to transact business without requiring any assistance from the Israeli government—but their political power or even their financial influence, which at one time was considerable, has not grown along with the company's expansion abroad.

Ya'acov Meridor, who until 1969 was a member of the Knesset and for many years served as its Deputy Speaker, was the number-two leader (after Menahem Begin), of Israel's second-largest party, Herut. He had been a heroic figure in the underground struggle against the British before the establishment of the State. Mila Brener was one of Israel's first sea captains, who fought in the Battle of the Atlantic in World War II as well as in the Israel Navy. They are different both in background and in personality. Yet in MFC they work together as a team, with Meridor contributing the financial vision and growth ideas and Brener supplying the professional shipping know-how.

Meridor, born in Poland in 1913, immigrated to Palestine in 1932, after already having joined Betar, the Revisionist Zionist youth movement. In Palestine he became the deputy of David Raziel, the commander of the Irgun Zvai Le'umi, the right-wing underground organization which broke off from the Haganah, after accusing it of being too restrained in its reactions to Arab attacks on Jews. In 1940 Meridor joined Raziel on a secret mission on behalf of the British, who at that time were trying to put down a pro-Nazi Iraqi revolt. When David Raziel was killed by a German plane during that mission, Meridor returned to Palestine and took over the command of the Irgun Zvai Le'umi. He was later arrested by the British and sent to detention camps. His book of memoirs on that period, *The Long Way to Freedom,* which describe his imaginative and daring escape attempts from camps in Sudan, Eritrea, Ethiopia, and Kenya (the last one just before the establishment of the State), reads like a first-rate thriller.

Although Meridor was one of the founders of Herut and represented the party in the Knesset for more than twenty years, he finally realized that he was not a political man; long meetings bored him and factional clashes annoyed him. He looked for interest elsewhere and turned to business in East Africa—an area he had known since the time of the detention camps. He established a meat-packing plant, Incode, in Eritrea, and later joined with Brener in supplying Israel with fish from the Red Sea.

Mila Brener, who was born in 1921 in Russia, also longed for a business of his own. He left the command of one of the ships of ZIM Israel Navigation Company, and joined Meridor. Soon after they abandoned the idea of shipping in the Red Sea, they conceived the idea of refrigerated cargo ships. Their simple idea was executed at the right moment and brought them almost immediate success.

Until the early 1960's, most refrigerated cargoes were transported in regular cargo ships which had small refrigerators. Brener and Meridor believed that, as a result of the rapid rise in the standard of living of many nations in the Northern Hemisphere, larger and faster refrigerated ships would be needed to transport fresh fruit and meat from the Southern to the Northern Hemisphere.

The first refrigerated ships (whose names all end with the word "Core"), built by the Akers shipyard in Norway, were the most expensive of their kind at the time of building. However, their prices soon rose, leaving MFC with a large capital gain. The president of the Akers Company at that time, Martin Siem, a hero of the Norwegian underground during World War II, proved to be of great help to Israel.

Some believe that the development of MFC has been too rapid and that the company lacks the reserves needed for its huge investment plans. They say that if Brener and Meridor had only waited a few years to consolidate their gains the company would have been one of the most successful ventures in the world. However, Meridor has no time for waiting. His active mind teems with new ideas and complicated financial deals.

While in their international activities Meridor and Brener in the early 1970's seemed to be steering away from the center of action in the Israeli power elite, they nevertheless continued their ties with the Israeli establishment by continuously hiring senior Israelis for management positions in their group. Ezer Weizman (whose cousin Michal is Mila Brener's wife) became an official of an MFC subsidiary when he resigned his post as Minister of Transport. Two former generals, Moshe Goren and Shlomo Erel (formerly Commander of the Israeli Navy), are MFC executives, and David Hacohen, a veteran Labor party leader and former chairman of the Foreign Affairs Committee of the Knesset, is chairman of the board of Atlantic— an MFC-owned fishing company.

While Maritime Fruit Carriers pays little tax in Israel, it makes considerable contributions to various Israeli causes. Its managers often admit to a dilemma, new for Israeli conglomerates: how to grow big and still not sever the ties with the small land.

14

The Rise of the Technocrats

DAVID GOLAN spent twenty-one years in government service. He was born in Jerusalem in 1926 and was one of the large group who joined the Civil Service after completing his studies in economics shortly after the War of Independence. He once said about his first years in the Ministry of Finance, "I was not a senior official then, yet I had enormous practical responsibilities. In that period our foreign currency situation was so bad that each week we had to decide who would get an allocation and who would not."

Golan then served for four years in the Foreign Service (as commercial attaché in Turkey and Minister in the Philippines). He returned to the Ministry of Finance, served in the Bank of Israel, went abroad again for the Foreign Ministry, and in 1966, when he was forty years old, became Director-General of the Ministry of Commerce and Industry. Almost four years later, in December, 1969, he left his post and went into private banking.

The transit from an important government power base to the management of a medium-sized bank was interpreted by some as desertion of the government service in preference for material benefits. David Golan was aware of this problem and felt the need to explain his motives to journalists. His words reflect not only his personal views but also those of many Army officers and senior officials who left their careers to manage companies and banks, becoming the "generation of technocrats," whose part in managing various branches of the economy is growing from year to year.

"I had reached the end of the road," Golan said. "Where can you go once you have been Director-General? I thought it was not healthy to hold on too long to the position of Director-General. I did not want to go into politics—since my student days I had not been active in political parties. Private business became more or less my only alternative. It seemed to be an observation post from which I could view the government service. I looked for a position which would force me to compete. The material consideration was not the least one to make me decide in favor of private business. My government salary was not low in terms of the public service, but now I do not have to make calculations and count every pound. Today I manage to save. On the average, I work less now than when I was in government service and go abroad less. I spend more time with my family and I think that my wife and children are pleased with this change. My loss in status does not bother me or my family. Even the fact that I an not 'in the know' does not disturb me. In the meantime I have a number of public activities."

The young technocrats liked the government service and valued the feeling that they had the power to decide on crucial issues, but they also were perturbed about their future: "What will happen when I get to the end of the road?" They did not look forward to ending their careers as government pensioners.

The private market, with its demand for managers who are versed in the problems of the economy, men who have proved themselves in handling executive responsibilities, attracted the senior civil servants. A large salary, a generous expense account and freedom in making decisions in the private sector as against the unavoidably rigid "official channels" and petty rivalries of the government service were a temptation that many officials were unable to resist.

The private economy did not always justify the expectations of those who transferred from public service. Many division directors, former ambassadors and even managing directors of government units were swallowed in "jobs" in companies and small enterprises, positions that may provide them with adequate salaries, but with very little influence or prestige. In North Tel Aviv, in Herzliya Pituah and Savyon—Israel's fashionable residential neighborhoods —one can find dozens of frustrated has-beens who have disappeared from the public arena. For others like David Golan, Michael Tsour, Moshe Kashti, Aharon Dovrat, Avigdor Bartel, Dov Ben-Dror, Issachar Haimowitz, Ya'akov Ben-Yehudah, Shimon Horn and Baruch Barak, the jump from the government ministry to private business was accompanied by distinct advantages.

In many cases the retiring civil servants did not change employers; they left a government unit and entered a commercial company owned by the government, or a public unit in which the cabinet ministers, especially Pinhas Sapir, have more than a minimal influence. They also found out that life in private enterprise is not always boring as they were warned, and even not always devoted to profit making. The desire to build an empire, to expand constantly with or without justification, has spread in Israel from the public sector into private business. In Israel the number of a company's workers and the volume of its operations are often more impressive than its profit-and-loss statement.

When David Golan planned the establishment of "The First International Bank of Israel," which was expected to take its place alongside the Big Three of Israeli banking (and also strengthen the influence of the government on banking, since the government was to be a shareholder in the bank), he did so out of a combination of ambition to become involved in private banking and yet, at the same time, continue, albeit indirectly, in government service, as well as out of a desire to re-create some of the influence he had when he was Director-General of the Ministry of Commerce and Industry.

A dual loyalty like this—to the firm for which he works and to the government which he left—also can be noticed in Michael Tsour, David Golan's predecessor in the Ministry of Commerce and Industry. It was because of his affinity for public service that he acceded in 1969 to Pinhas Sapir's request to take over the problematic management of the recently-established Israel Corporation in addition to duties as chairman of the board of ZIM Israel Navigation Company and chairman of the board of the Haifa Oil Refineries.

When he left in 1966 after sixteen years of government service, ten of them in the top post of the Ministry of Commerce and Industry, Michael Tsour went into areas which interested him most: shipping, oil, petrochemicals and later finance and investments. Yet, despite his many activities and the fact that all ministers' doors are open to him, Michael Tsour often looks impatient in his present assignment. From time to time he makes newspaper headlines with critical remarks on government policy. He looks as if he misses his direct influence on policy making.

Tsour, born in Germany in 1923, came with his family to Palestine in 1934. He received a religious education and was active in the Mizrachi youth movement. He entered government service at the time when Hermann Hollander, who was active in Orthodox politics, was for a short time Director-General of the Ministry of Commerce and Industry. Tsour soon impressed both Levi Eshkol and Pinhas Sapir with his sharp mind and original thinking. His rise in government service was rapid and by 1956 he was a very young Director-General.

Tsour is given to unconventional thinking. "He has a tongue like a razor blade," Sapir once said of him. However, his talents also antagonized people who worked with him, both in government services and outside.

Tsour once said that he was proud of his many years of work in close association with Pinhas Sapir in the Ministry of Commerce and Industry. He may have hoped that this association would result in a political career similar to that of another of Sapir's close associates, Zevi Dinstein, and at one time he was even mooted for the post of Minister of Commerce and Industry. But Tsour today apparently has given up any political ambitions.

In the Israel Corporation, where Tsour was successful in mobilizing $50 million in capital from 270 stockholders as well as obtaining another $35 million in debentures, Tsour sees a power base whose importance will grow gradually. Unlike many of the technocrats of the government school, Tsour is not a believer in expansion at all costs. He has proved himself to be a cautious executive.

Tsour's colleague in the management of ZIM—Israel's largest shipping company—Moshe Kashti, the managing director of the company, shares with him the frustration of being excluded from decision making concerning some of the country's most crucial issues. Kashti, who came to ZIM in 1970, left behind him an even larger empire, that of the Ministry of Defense. He served there for fourteen years, first—while in uniform as a colonel—as manager of the Financial Division, and then, in the last five years, as Director-General of the Ministry, which controls the largest budget of any government unit.

Kashti, born in Poland in 1918, arrived in Palestine in 1935. He went to work early, first as an agricultural worker, and later went into defense activities. His financial background, his understanding of electronics, a subject to which he devoted most of his time during the last years at the Ministry of Defense, and his knowledge of a number of languages were acquired by Kashti while working in the Ministry of Defense. He used to spend hours in the early mornings and late at night studying to make up for the deficiencies in his formal education.

Moshe Kashti can be aggressive and even bitter when he is fighting for an idea in which he believes. When he left the Ministry of Defense he made serious accusations against a number of people, including Dr. Zevi Dinstein, one-time Deputy Minister of Defense, and Yitzhak Rabin, one-time Chief of Staff, for having held back the development of Israel's Defense Ministry. When he came to ZIM, Kashti had a chance to put his strong feelings about modernization and the need for technology to use. The company, which at one time was a joint venture of the government, the Histadrut and the Jewish Agency, but is now jointly owned by the government and the Israel Corporation in equal parts, was burdened with an obsolete fleet.

Kashti soon involved himself not only in the complicated finances of the company, but also in speeding up its program of containerization, making it into a company with a world-wide container service.

Despite his involvement in ZIM, Kashti succeeds in maintaining his public position by willingly accepting assignments such as heading the committee that studied the problems of the Tel Aviv bus cooperative, or participating in the committee which investigated the security bungling at the 1972 Munich Olympic games. He is also often seen at the office of Pinhas Sapir, where he has participated in many informal discussions.

One of the companies of Israel's Defense Ministry to which Kashti devoted much of his time before going to ZIM was Tadiran, an electronics concern which started out as an almost private company of the defense establishment and grew into one of Israel's largest electronics concerns. It is now half owned by General Telephone and Electronics.

Moshe Kashti's protégé in Tadiran, its manager, Eklana Caspi, was able to utilize the Ministry of Defense umbrella to insure the progress of the company during its first years. At the same time he was far-sighted enough to realize that this backing could become burdensome and therefore sought to integrate the company into the world-wide electronics industry.

Caspi, born in 1921 in Lithuania, arrived in Palestine when he was a year old. Like his friend and former boss, Moshe Kashti, Elkana Caspi began his career in the Ministry of Defense and served twice in the Ministry of Defense supply mission in New York. During his second tour of duty, which ended in 1959, Caspi and his superiors at that time, Moshe Kashti and Shimon Peres, the Director-General of the Ministry, developed the idea of a defense industry that would serve Israel's defense needs.

At first, objections came even from within the Ministry of Defense itself, which already had a nucleus of an electronics plant (today called Elta) within its Aircraft Industries. Objections came also from private industry, which felt that unless local industry were to receive defense contracts it would never develop sufficiently to face world market competition. Kashti and Caspi argued that unless the Ministry of Defense demonstrated industrial initiative it could never expect to supply its needs at the right price and quality.

Strangely enough, Caspi was among the first to admit indirectly that private industry's argument was correct. Tadiran's great success came when defense orders constituted an ever-declining proportion of the total volume and when the company gradually entered the fields of professional electronics and entertainment electronics as well as developing export markets for its defense products. General Telephone took over the ownership of Tadiran gradually, beginning with 37 percent in 1969, utilizing its option for another 13 percent in 1972. The other half of the company is owned by Koor (Histadrut). By increasing its holdings in Tadiran, the giant American company—which also supplies Tadiran with know-how on marketing outlets—expressed its satisfaction with its Israeli venture. At the same time Tadiran gained access to both know-how and markets it never would have reached as just an Israeli company.

Elkana Caspi seems to be determined that Tadiran will not be just another Israeli company. With sales already exceeding 250 million Israeli pounds a year, Tadiran was among the first to introduce a five-day work week in Israel as well as a scheme to distribute shares in the company to its workers.

Like many other top Israeli technocrats, Caspi succeeded in turning his position in Tadiran into an important power base in the Israeli establishment. In fact, although Tadiran has been half American-owned since 1972, it is attached to the Israeli economy by many threads, one of them being the personality of Elkana Caspi.

The period of Moshe Kashti in the Ministry of Defense also marked the rising influence of another technocrat, Adolph William ("Al") Schwimmer, the director-general of Israel Aircraft Industries —Israel's largest industry.

Al Schwimmer, who has lived in Israel off and on since the establishment of the State, still does not speak Hebrew. He approached David Ben-Gurion in 1952 and later Shimon Peres (when the latter was director of the supply mission in New York) with the idea of establishing an aircraft industry (at first called Bedek) devoted mainly to servicing Israel Air Force planes.

Schwimmer, an American Jew without a Zionist background, who had turned to a field which was closed to Jews until then, that of flying and flight engineering, soon found a common language with his Israeli bosses. He had the idea of establishing an aircraft industry in Israel and believed in realizing it without paying attention to objective obstacles, bureaucracy or skeptical public opinion. His enemies claim that in Schwimmer it is difficult to distinguish between vision and promotional skill.

Schwimmer, born in 1917 in Bridgeport, Connecticut, had dreamed of aeronautics since his early childhood. Because of the Depression, he had to realize this dream not through academic studies but by starting to work as an aircraft mechanic. Only later he succeeded in obtaining the certificate of an aircraft engineer as well as a pilot's license.

He served as a pilot in World War II, flying bombers and transport planes. In 1947, when he was a TWA pilot flying transatlantic runs, he came in contact with Haganah people in New York. Soon he was involved in obtaining bombers and transport planes for the nucleus of the Israel Air Force. Within months he organized crews of pilots, engineers and navigators, all of them Jews who had served in the American Air Force in World War II. He established dummy companies, rented air strips and later bought ten twin-engined C-46 cargo planes at $5,000 each and a number of Constellations at $50,000 each. The planes, purchased from American Army scrap depots, were flown through Panama, Dakar, Casablanca and Sicily to an airport near Prague, there were loaded with arms and immediately sent to Israel, where they were used to supply the besieged Negev settlements.

One of the most daring exploits of Al Schwimmer was in the spring of 1948 when he purchased three Flying Fortresses (B-17's) in Miami. The purchase of the planes and their transport to Israel, despite the U.S. embargo on arms shipments to the combatants at that time, led to legal proceedings against Schwimmer.

The achievement of Israel Aircraft Industries, in supplying the needs of the Israel Air Force, building its Fouga-Magister jet trainers, servicing its planes and constructing sophisticated equipment, as well as its success in developing and expanding export markets for its products, amazed even the professionals in the field. It seemed almost a miracle that a small country like Israel could compete in such a specialized market.

However, beginning in 1972, Schwimmer came under growing criticism for his way of running the government-owned company, and especially for three projects to build civilian aircraft in which the company became involved. In one of these projects, the Arava commuter plane, designed as a STOL (short take-off and landing plane), the company incurred heavy losses when no markets were found. There have been recurrent demands to break up Israel Aircraft Industries into a number of companies, and even to dismiss Schwimmer.

Extreme identification with a company, seeing in it a base of power rather than a source of revenue and profits, is one of the characteristics of Israeli technocrats. Mordecai Ben-Ari, the director-general of El Al Israel Airlines, is a striking example of this trait. It is possible that even if he were asked to continue in his present position at half salary he would not refuse, since he enjoys every moment of his work, despite the continuous strains, the long hours and nerve-racking negotiations with air crews, cabin crews and technicians, as well as the serious security problems that El Al has faced in recent years.

El Al under Ben-Ari has an annual volume of operations reaching hundreds of millions of pounds. Ministers, Knesset members of all parties and senior officials try to keep on good terms with Ben-Ari. Even if they are not invited to inaugural flights, they may obtain VIP treatment (the "Shalom Service"), which El Al extends to special clients. Director-generals of ministries quarrel over the chance to serve on the El Al board of directors, which provides its members with special privileges. Ben-Ari knows that more than he is dependent on his board the members of the board are dependent on him.

Even the Histadrut seems to have a special attitude toward El Al: when Ben-Ari asks for its assistance in settling a labor dispute he can expect a sympathetic reply.

In IATA and other international air transport bodies, El Al was hailed as the initiator of group flights. At a time when large airlines established subsidiaries to run charter flights, Ben-Ari vehemently opposed this trend and fought for a multi-fare system using scheduled flights. He convinced the Israeli government to ban charter flights and introduced a number of group flights instead. At one time El Al was the only airline to use this system, but soon other companies reluctantly followed suit, and today the varied-fare system prevails in all IATA companies.

Marketing has always been Ben-Ari's strong point. Like the other El Al chief executives who preceded him, Aryeh Pincus and Ephraim Ben-Artzi, Ben-Ari did not have a background in aeronautics. Yet the company succeeded in developing high professional standards which gained it an international reputation. Mordecai Ben-Ari (Leibowitz), born in 1920 in Transylvania (his speech still reveals a slight Hungarian accent in any language), came to Palestine in 1940, was a member of a kibbutz and in 1943 began to study at the Hebrew University in Jerusalem. He received his master's degree in history and sociology, joined the staff of the Haganah and in 1948 was sent to Austria to help with the organization of immigration from Eastern Europe. Upon his return he joined Israel's young commercial airline and worked his way up until he became director-general in 1967.

While the late 1960's were very good years for El Al—which was one of the few government companies to make considerable profits —the company's difficulties began to accumulate in the early 1970's. Costs increased; it was plagued by strikes as well as threats by Arab terrorists; tourism to Israel, which rose sharply after the Six-Day War, began to level off. Yet Ben-Ari did not lose his confidence. He cut expenses, found ways to make better use of equipment and showed firmness, unusual for executives of Israeli government companies, in his confrontations with striking workers. It was thanks to his efforts that the company did not slide into the red.

Ben-Ari's efforts to balance his profit-and-loss accounts took the form of not showing excessively high profits even when the company had its fat years. There were two reasons for this: one was the justifiable caution of an executive who knows that lean years will follow the fat ones, and that he must build up internal reserves; the other was typical of Israeli government companies, where traditionally high disclosed profits become a target for wage demands, and arouse the jealousy of other technocrats. Similarly, when Ya'akov Ben-Yehudah became the director-general of the Timna copper mines in 1964, at the time when world market prices for copper began to rise, his first task was to plough back these profits into the company to make up for hidden losses of previous years, and to build up reserves for a possible drop in the price of copper on the London Metal Exchange.

In 1970 Ben-Yehudah felt that the Timna copper works, near Israel's Red Sea port of Elath, had succeeded in developing its own strong management so that he could leave and take over the management of all Israeli government-owned chemical industries. As director-general of Israel Chemicals, Ltd., the holding company of concerns such as the Dead Sea Works, producing potash and bromine; Chemicals and Phosphates, which extracts phosphates in the Negev and produces compound fertilizers and other chemicals; the Timna copper mines; and the ill-fated Arad Chemicals, Ben-Yehudah holds the keys of some of Israel's most promising and at the same time problematic firms.

The companies which were designed to exploit Israel's natural resources have required investments totaling hundreds of millions of pounds since the establishment of the State. Israel encountered some of its most bitter disappointments in the potash plant at Sodom, on the Dead Sea, at the Negev phosphates deposits and even at the Haifa industrial plant of Chemicals and Phosphates. In recent years many of these plants finally turned the profit corner. The potash industry, for example, has already covered most of its past losses and economists are prophesying that Israel's heavy chemical industry has reached the "takeoff" point.

Yet Ben-Yehudah has scarcely been able to enjoy the prospect of a new era since taking over Israel Chemicals, with its heartbreaking problem of the plant of Arad. Over $50 million were invested in Arad Chemicals, which was planned to produce 150,000 tons of phosphoric acid a year. However, the new production process which was introduced by the former American partner of Arad Chemicals, Allied Chemicals, did not succeed, and Israeli engineers had to try to salvage the huge investment by improving the process.

Although most of the damage at Arad Chemicals was done before Ben-Yehudah took over Israel Chemicals, he did not give up hope or blame his predecessors. He has linked his career with the effort to save the plant. Ben-Yehudah, a stocky dark man, polite and firm at the same time, is one of the lesser-known Israeli technocrats. Although he immediately wins the admiration of the people who work with him (they call him by his Polish nickname, Yanek), he has not mastered the art of public relations. It seems as if he does not mind that the managers of the individual companies, rather than he himself, are frequently in the limelight.

In 1970, when Ben-Yehudah became the director-general of Israel Chemicals, the holding company of the Israel-government-owned chemical industry was the subject of bitter controversy. While its first director, the American millionaire and chemical engineer Jerry Sudarski, believed in turning the company into a large complex like Montecatini in Italy or ICI in Britain, its second manager, the late Meir Ilan, had a different approach. He believed in direct management of all companies as if they were small stores. Ben-Yehudah restored the independence of the various companies, enabling each of them to have its own finances and development programs. Yet he gradually tightened his control over the companies, assuming a central role in the development of one of Israel's largest industrial branches.

The government-owned chemical industry provided the training ground for another senior technocrat, Avigdor Bartel, who since 1966 has been the manager of the Haifa Refineries. The company, which also has a plant in Ashdod, has a refining capacity which will soon reach ten million tons a year, and is one of Israel's largest industrial plants. Bartel's influence is felt far beyond his immediate field of activities. Since leaving government service in 1959 (where he was manager of the Public Works Division in the Ministry of Labor), Bartel has been almost a permanent advisor of the economic ministers whenever they are plagued by serious problems.

He seems to be the most eligible person to serve on committees studying such issues as the National Water Carrier, which brings irrigation water from the north to the south; the advisability of assembling automobiles in Israel; the organization of oil exploration in Israel; or even the lack of security arrangements which enabled the Arab terrorists to carry out the Munich massacre.

When he serves on government committees, as when he handles the affairs of his own company, Bartel is a typical public servant— devoted, thorough and modest about his own share in the decision-making process. Therefore, it was unusual for him to warn early in 1972 of the negative effects of ignoring his recommendations on the subject of automobile assembling in Israel. Avigdor Bartel (Berger), born in Russia in 1914, came to Palestine as a boy, yet his slight Russian accent, his graying blondish hair, thin mustache and horn-rimmed glasses give an appearance of a Russian intellectual. His tendency to understatement reflects his British education.

The oil economy, which became a big business in Israel in the 1970's, has attracted a growing number of government administrators. One of them is Dov ("Dovale") Ben-Dror, a former Accountant-General in the Ministry of Finance, who in 1968 became the manager of Trans-Asiatic Oil Company and other firms that control the forty-two-inch pipeline that transfers oil from the Red Sea port of Elath to Ashkelon on Israel's Mediterranean coast.

The challenge of the oil world was only one of the reasons that pressed Dov Ben-Dror to leave his powerful position in the government hierarchy for the relatively modest suite of offices in Hachashmonaim Street in Tel Aviv. Like others, he felt that he had reached the end of the road in government service and looked for an arena of activities where the salary is high and the possibilities many.

Dov Ben-Dror, born in Moscow in 1928, reached Palestine at the age of five. In 1952, after graduating from the Hebrew University, he became one of a group of young economists in the Budget Division of the Ministry of Finance known as the "Arnon boys," trained by the Director of the Division, Dr. Ya'akov Arnon. Although Ben-Dror was one of the youngest of the group, he was appointed Director of the Division in 1956 when Arnon became Director-General of the Ministry. Although he filled a key post at a relatively young age, Ben-Dror did not hesitate to give it up two years later in order to go into the Foreign Service, first as Economic Counselor in Paris and then as Economic Minister accredited to several West African states. When he returned to Israel in 1961 and became Accountant-General, he was given the additional assignment of being in charge of the government oil economy.

Dov Ben-Dror is a capable, self-confident man who never looks as if he is exerting himself. He does not hide his tendency to enjoy the pleasant things of life, which ministers with whom he worked for many years pretend to ignore. While in Paris he learned to appreciate French cooking; he enjoys a good cigar, and at times when Levi Eshkol and Pinhas Sapir would insist on long meetings into the night, he was not ready to give up seeing his friends or taking his wife to the movies.

Ben-Dror has a quick grasp of problems and is articulate in expressing his opinions. In the Ministry of Finance as well as in the management of the pipeline he sometimes clashed with Deputy Finance Minister, Dr. Zevi Dinstein. Yet he succeeds in avoiding open rifts with his opponents and critics, of whom there are quite a few.

Like other Israeli technocrats with whom he grew up, one can hardly discern in Dov Ben-Dror ambitions beyond a nice house in Ramat Hasharon, a comfortable car and frequent trips abroad. He apparently has no political aspirations.

Aharon Dovrat (Sagitman), the general manager of Israel's growing conglomerate Clal, was also a senior civil servant before he took over management of the large investment company. Yet he differs from his fellow technocrats in that he is neither a sabra nor one of "Patinkin's boys." He is a comparatively new immigrant, born in Argentina in 1931, who arrived in Israel in 1959 after marrying Dalia, the daughter of Ya'akov Tsur, then Minister of Israel in Buenos Aires.

Young Dovrat, who already spoke fluent Hebrew upon arrival, had previous business experience and also had directed the Israel-Argentina Cultural Center in Buenos Aires. He soon made his way up the hierarchy in the Ministry of Commerce and Industry. At first he was only a liaison officer with investors from South America, but soon after he became Director of the Industrial Division of the Ministry. Pinhas Sapir, then Minister of Commerce and Industry, took a liking to the "Argentinian." He accompanied Sapir on his trips to South America and took part in the preparations for the establishment of Clal, many of whose original investors were from South America.

Benno Gitter, on loan from the Israel Discount Bank, which owns a large slice of Clal, was the first managing director of the company. However, Dovrat seemed the natural choice for manager of the young conglomerate, which in its first years failed to have an independent policy of its own. Dovrat steered the company safely through the dangerous recession years of the mid-1960's, but in 1969 his position in Clal was endangered as a result of a controversy between the major shareholders of the company. When it was discovered that the Discount Bank group had picked up Clal shares and accumulated 40 percent of the holdings of the company, other large banks, namely Bank Leumi and Bank Hapoalim, felt that these takeover attempts might upset the delicate balance between the large families of companies in the Israeli economy.

As usual in such cases in Israel, a compromise was reached in which each of the large banks agreed to limit its holdings in Clal. Dovrat's own position was strengthened. The new chairman of the board, "Don" Israel Pollak, a businessman originally from Chile, who owns Polgat, one of Israel's large textile concerns, allows Dovrat a free hand in the management of the company. Unlike other technocrats who left the government service to go into private companies, Dovrat has not moved away from Jerusalem. His company provides him with a suite at the Sharon Towers in Herzliya.

Pinhas Sapir and other cabinet ministers assisted in the sale of the first shares of Clal. South American Jews who had had bitter disappointments in stock investments in Israeli companies were often hesitant; Sapir used to confer with Clal directors each year in order to help them find ways to provide their stockholders with a minimal annual dividend. Today most Clal stocks are owned by private groups—other Israeli investment companies and individuals. The company has grown to such proportions that it hardly needs the Minister's advice on its investment policies or distribution of profits. Aharon Dovrat, however, is careful, walking the narrow path between independent decision making and following the hints given by Sapir. Thus, when Sapir wanted Clal to acquire one of the plants of the failing Autocars company, Aharon Dovrat agreed despite his better judgment and in the face of vehement opposition by his partner in Clal's automotive enterprises, Mr. Joseph Buxenbaum, who was not interested in the Autocars deal. Dovrat realized that by acceding to the wish of Sapir Clal would acquire important good will which the company could benefit from at a later date.

The swallow-up of the Israel Central Trade and Investment Company by Clal in December, 1972, was carefully engineered by Aharon Dovrat, who proved again that good business sense and a flair for human relations go hand in hand.

When Mordecai "Motke" Makleff resigned his post as managing director of the Citrus Marketing Board in May, 1973, Israel's largest economic unit, with an annual volume of over $120 millions, was left without a chief executive. (The Citrus Marketing Board is a unique semipublic body which has legal powers and encompasses all Israeli citrus growers.) For Makleff himself, his leaving the Citrus Marketing Board was yet another move in the versatile career of an Israeli technocrat who had already managed to serve as Chief of Staff of the Israeli Army, deputy-director general of the Israel Electric Corporation and general manager of the Dead Sea Works, one of Israel's largest industrial concerns.

Although Makleff's hair has already become gray, he has not lost the boyish expression, which was especially noticeable when, in 1952, he became Israel's third Chief of Staff at the age of thirty-two, and later, at the age of thirty-five, took over the management of a large industrial plant. Yet Makleff knew tragedy early in life, for in 1929, when he was just nine and a half years old, he survived an Arab massacre in which his parents, two sisters and a brother died, at Motza, on the outskirts of Jerusalem.

Makleff studied in Jerusalem and Haifa and in 1939 joined the special night squads under the command of Captain Orde Wingate. In 1942 he joined the British Army and reached the rank of major. Upon his release he planned to engage in agriculture, but then was called to join the staff of the Haganah and did not take off his uniform until thirteen years later.

There are conflicting views on his success as Chief of Staff. Some believe that he was too young for the job. Others say that Makleff's direct approach just did not pay enough attention to public relations. In fact, even in his later assignments at the Dead Sea Works and in the Citrus Marketing Board, he sometimes was at the center of controversies.

Even his critics agree that Makleff is a capable administrator, a man with a natural charm, executive ability and fairness in human relations. His biggest problem perhaps is his willingness to undertake assignments that a cautious person would try to avoid. The potash plant in Sodom, for example, was in serious trouble when Makleff took over. He managed to solve not only the knotty technical problems but also the human difficulties as well. His breakthrough came when he moved the workers from Sodom itself to the more bearable climatic conditions of Dimona and Arad. In the Citrus Marketing Board as well, Makleff was faced with an impossible situation of an antiquated marketing system, bad methods of sorting fruit and a decline in the quality of the famous Jaffa orange, just when European market demands were changing in the early 1970's. Confronted with these obstacles, and plagued by his own hesitations, Makleff on several occasions handed in his resignation to the members of the Citrus Marketing Board. Several times he was convinced to stay on, but then in May, 1973, his departure became final.

At the time when Makleff's resignation seemed final and other candidates were approached for the job, the management of the Citrus Marketing Board—a unique organization which has legal powers and encompasses all Israel citrus growers—was offered to Joseph Tulipman, himself the son of a citrus-growing family, a chemical engineer who is the manager of Israel's nuclear research complex in Dimona.

Although Tulipman is in charge of one of Israel's most important scientific units, he is not widely known. The nature of his present assignment, as well as his previous posts, have kept him out of the limelight, but perhaps also as a result of his own character his name rarely appears in the newspapers.

Joseph Tulipman was born in Jerusalem in 1925, to a family which was among the founders of Rishon Le-Zion. He was a battalion commander in the War of Independence, studied chemical engineering at the Haifa Technion and held a number of government positions, including that of Deputy Director-General of the Ministry of Development.

Tulipman is known as a tough administrator, a first-rate professional and a man who many Israelis believe will fulfill many major assignments in the future.

15
The Captains
of Economic Branches

In March, 1972, when Haim Bar-Lev became Minister of Commerce and Industry, Mark Mosevics, the president of the Manufacturers' Association, remarked approvingly: "Finally, industry has a minister of its own!" He expressed a sentiment shared by many Israeli indusrialists, who felt that their branch, which had already become the most prominent component of Israel's national product, was being slighted by the country's political leadership. In fact, in the four years that preceded Bar-Lev's appointment, there was no cabinet member whose sole responsibility was to represent the interests of Israeli industry.

Although Mosevics was wrong in his basic assumption when he viewed Bar-Lev as "representing" industry, since a minister is not supposed to be a partisan of any single interest group, his confusion was typical of the situation prevailing in Israel. Various personalities are considered "representatives" of different branches of the economy, and yet no one bothers to measure their real strength. It seems that closeness to a minister and to foreign investors, or the ability to get things done in government offices and in the Industrial Development Bank, determines who is a "captain of industry" to a much larger extent than the volume of business he controls.

Even the position of Mark Mosevics as industry's representative in collective bargaining with the Histadrut on cost-of-living allowances, as in the package deal of 1970, which determined the country's economic policy, is fortuitous. The Manufacturers' Association represents only private industry and not even all private manufacturers. Government-owned industry and Histadrut industry, the volume of which exceeds private industry by far, are not represented in the Manufacturers' Association.

The captains of Israel's economic branches are thus not members of a definite economic class. They are a group composed of the heads of large economic concerns, the technocrats of the public sector and those who head other groups representing the various sectors of the economy.

In the past, some leaders of the Manufacturers' Association were simply owners of large workshops; Mark Mosevics is different. He is one of the managers and main stockholders of Elite, a concern composed of eight factories employing over 2,200 workers. Elite's annual sales exceed a hundred million Israeli pounds. The secretary-general of the Histadrut, Yitzhak Ben-Aharon, attacks "the millionaire" Mosevics. In fact the industrialists' president, even when criticizing the government, calling on it "to tighten its belt" and, declaring that industry cannot afford to pay higher wages, talks from a position of strength. Mark Mosevics is always elegantly dressed, wears monogrammed shirts and exudes self-confidence. He has a chauffeur-driven Jaguar and for an extensive period lived in a suite at the Tel Aviv Hilton.

Mosevics was born in Russia in 1920 and moved with his family to Palestine when he was twenty. He studied for a short time at Cambridge and at the Hebrew University in Jerusalem, but soon went into business, becoming one of the managers of Elite, where his father was one of the founders. He likes public activites: although he devotes much of his time to the Export Institute and, in recent years, to the Manufacturers' Association, Elite apparently does not suffer. It has become a monopoly, controlling most of

Israel's chocolate, candy and instant-coffee industry.

Despite his tough statements, Mosevics is really not a fighter but a believer in compromises. When he talks of a "new deal for industry" or of a "basic change," he readily agrees to a slight increase in export premiums or to palliative loans for industry.

Mosevics does not hide his great admiration of Pinhas Sapir. Like previous leaders of private industry, he has learned from experience that manufacturers gain more from cooperating than by confronting the Labor-led government.

The driving force behind the efforts of the Manufacturers' Association to project a new image, that of a body representing the economy's most important branch and not a mere trade union of industrialists, is a group of young manufacturers, together with the director-general of the association, Peleg Tamir. The most outstanding of those young manufacturers is Avraham ("Booma") Shavit.

Shavit, a tall, good-looking man with a graying head of hair, was born in Tel Aviv in 1927. He inherited his father's electric-appliances business and expanded the manufacture of gas stoves. The factory is now one of the largest in Israel. Shavit, an articulate go-getter, who has become the voice of private industry in debates with the government and organized labor, likes to feel that he represents the new breed of Israeli industrialists. In fact his "extremism" is well balanced by the soft-spoken, diplomatic approach of the president of the association, Mark Mosevics.

Peleg Tamir, who is a contemporary of Shavit, grew up in Haifa. But, while Shavit and his friends were in the Palmach, Peleg Tamir was arrested in 1945 as a member of the Irgun. This seemed to be only natural, since his grandmother on his father's side was the sister of Ze'ev Jabotinsky, the founder of the Revisionist Zionist Organization. After the War of Independence in 1948 he remained in the Israeli Air Force and ended his career as a full colonel. During the course of his Air Force service he obtained a master's degree in business administration from George Washington University in Washington, D.C. When he decided to leave the Air Force in 1968 he was offered a number of positions, but decided to accept the offer of the Manufacturers' Association, believing that he could wake up the sleepy group of Israel's private industrialists.

He succeeded in giving a new look to the administration of the industrialists' organization and in becoming the spokesman of many of its young members. Although he is an official and not a lay leader of the manufacturers, his present position provides him with a springboard for future activities.

One possible avenue for advance is politics. Tamir seems to be one of the few qualified young people to be interested in Gahal politics. In fact he was the "architect" of the 1969 appointment of Ezer Weizman as Minister of Transport, representing Gahal. His association with Weizman began during their long years of service together in the Israeli Air Force. The setback suffered by Weizman in Gahal politics in December, 1972, served as a warning to Tamir, who is determined to be more careful before leaving his present safe base in the Manufacturers' Association.

The coalition Mosevics-Shavit (with the cooperation of Tamir) in the leadership of the Israeli Manufacturers' Association alienated many of the old guard of this body. But it did not weaken the position of the past president, Zalman Suzayeff, whose standing as one of the captains of the economic branch is assured even without the Manufacturers' Association title or even the control of his own plant (manufacturing corrugated cardboard).

Suzayeff was Deputy Minister of Commerce and Industry in the years 1952–1954, when his party, the General Zionists, participated in the government coalition. Since the early 1960's he no longer has been active in party politics and in 1972 even resigned as chairman of the labor relations committee of the Manufacturers' Association. Yet Suzayeff seems to be a favorite representative of the private business sector on such bodies as the advisory committee of the Bank of Israel or the Public Council for the Defense Loan.

Suzayeff is a typical public servant, with no personal axe to grind, representing a sector of the economy rather than a special-interest group. He has served on various public committees, which drafted the first Israeli antitrust law in 1955, suggested an income-tax reform in 1964 and studied the problem of the bus cooperatives on various occasions.

While Mosevics and the Manufacturers' Association today constitute the voice of Israeli industry even beyond the actual proportion of manufacturers they represent, the Israeli insurance industry finds it difficult to speak in one voice. Whenever the question arises who should represent the insurance companies in negotiations with the Minister of Finance concerning investments of insurance funds, or whenever the industry finds itself at loggerheads with the Controller of Insurance over maximum premiums and other details, the companies find it difficult to appoint one or two "captains of industry" to represent them.

Aharon Saharov, president of the Sahar Insurance Company, is often considered the spokesman of the industry. Saharov, one of four brothers, the son of a timber merchant, attempted in the early 1960's to build his insurance company into a financial empire, but has been only partially successful. Today he is concentrating again on insurance. The Saharovs are typical of the old-time families (Aharon Saharov was born in Jerusalem in 1916), who always mixed private business with public affairs. One of the brothers, Eliahu, was involved in cloak-and-dagger activities of purchasing arms for the Haganah at the time of the British Mandate. Another brother, Yechezkel (who changed his name to Sahar), was the first Chief Inspector of the Israeli Police.

The rising power in Israel's insurance industry is no doubt Abraham ("Rami") Taiber—the director-general of the Zion and Yehuda insurance companies. In 1971, Taiber was elected president of the Association of Insurance Companies, which is composed of life-insurance companies. He hoped to amalgamate this body with the Union of Insurance Companies, representing the general-insurance branch, by becoming chairman of both bodies, but he could not obtain agreement among other leaders of the industry.

Some insurance people complain that Taiber cannot represent the industry since he is "Sapir's man"; others feel, however, that his close association with the Minister of Finance is an advantage to private industry.

Rami Taiber did in fact work in close association with Pinhas Sapir for many years. It was even rumored that when he took control of the family group of insurance companies in 1965 and made it the most important factor in the Israeli insurance industry he did so reluctantly.

Tall, lanky, scholarly-looking, Rami Taiber was born in Tel Aviv to a wealthy family. He was recruited into public service in 1946 when he was a student of economics and international law at the University of Geneva. Pinhas Sapir, who arrived in Geneva to purchase arms for the Haganah, picked two young Israeli students as his assistants—Rami Taiber and Zevi Dinstein, who later became Deputy Minister of Finance.

After completing his work in Europe, Taiber returned to Israel, served in the Israeli Air Force and returned to Switzerland to complete his studies. In 1952 he replaced Dinstein as the head of the Arms Purchasing Mission in France, at a time when France was becoming Israel's largest arms supplier. When he returned to Israel in 1965, Taiber was torn between his desire to continue in public service and the temptation to go into private business. For a short time he went to work for Israel's Central Trade and Investments Company, in which his family had large holdings. He also served for a number of years as Director of the Industry Division in the Ministry of Commerce and Industry, and as the representative of the Israeli Government Investment Authority in New York.

Talking to a journalist about his New York experience, Taiber once said: "I think that I am the only one who was sent to direct the Investment Authority in New York who did not come back as the representative of some American investor." He was referring to Shimon Horn, who returned to Israel as vice-president of the Israel Investors' Corporation headed by Samuel Rothberg, and Baruch Barak, who upon his return home became the representative of Victor Carter, whose personal investments in Israel already reach nearly $5 million. These representatives, who also include Mordecai

("Moka") Limon, at one time Israeli military attaché in Paris, who became the Israeli representative of Baron Edmond de Rothschild, now constitute a class in themselves among the captains of the various economic branches. Their source of power is the fact that they speak and act in the name of many millions. These millions entitle them to seats on boards of directors of large corporations, to voices in hiring and firing managers of these companies and to close contact with ministers and other captains of industry. General Haim Herzog, who represents some of the interests of the British millionaire Sir Isaac Wolfson in Israel, also belongs to this group.

The most prominent among the representatives is no doubt Shimon Horn, not only because the company on whose behalf he acts has invested over $30 million in Israel, but also because of his personality—he can insist on his point of view and antagonize his opponents—and his record as economic advisor of the late Levi Eshkol, when he was Minister of Finance.

Horn, who was born in Vienna in 1919 and arrived in Palestine in 1937, spent several years as a student in the United States before he was appointed as advisor to Eshkol in 1953. He became involved in controversies over economic policies and set precedents in the government's policy of subsidies for essential goods and services and indirect price control. Many of Horn's ideas about the involvement of the government in the economy persisted long after he left government service and in some cases even after he adopted new ideas about the role of private initiative.

When he returned to Israel in 1961 from his service in the Investment Authority in New York, Horn had to overcome widespread public criticism of his sudden switch from government service to public industry. Since then, however, his name rarely appears in the press and his influence is mostly felt in meetings of boards of directors and in companies in which Israel Investors' Corporation holds a large interest. Yet he seems to miss the excitement of formulating economic policy. Horn can often be seen in Kfar Saba on Saturday mornings elaborating his ideas on the economy to Pinhas Sapir. Sapir is said not to be one of Horn's greatest admirers but enjoys listening to his sharp analysis and pointed barbs.

It is not surprising that relations between Shimon Horn and Baruch Barak, who represents Victor Carter in Israel, are far from cordial. The two are different in their personalities and recently clashed over the control of the Israel Central Trade and Investment Company. Although the Israel Investors' Corporation was the largest single group of investors in Central Trade, Barak joined other partners in 1971 in ousting Horn from the board of directors of the company. Late in 1972, Barak assisted Victor Carter in arranging the takeover of Central Trade by the Clal Investment Company, an act which was vehemently opposed by Horn and Sam Rothberg.

Unlike Horn, Barak is not an officer of an American-based corporation, but a personal representative of the investor. He also was an official of the Ministry of Finance before he headed the Investment Authority in New York, and was particularly close to the Deputy Minister of Finance, Zevi Dinstein. During the years Dinstein served as Deputy Minister of Defense, Barak served with him in that ministry. He was born in Germany in 1927, arrived in Israel when he was ten years old and joined the Civil Service soon after finishing school.

Barak is a capable administrator and good at personal relations. He is well acquainted with Israel's power elite and in this respect is a prominent member of the establishment. Yet, on the personal level, he may find it hard to compete with the representatives of Baron Edmond de Rothschild. Mordecai Limon, balding and muscular, left a military and diplomatic career when he went into business early in 1970. The high point of his career was December, 1969, when as head of the Defense Ministry's mission in Paris he planned the secret sailing of five Israeli missile boats from Cherbourg harbor. Because of his involvement in this action, the French government requested his recall.

Limon spent seven years in France heading arms purchases in Western Europe. These were years of close relations between France and Israel and years of deteriorating relations, from June, 1967, when De Gaulle objected to Israel's role in the Six-Day War, to January, 1969, when France declared a total arms embargo on

Israel. Limon, who was born in Poland in 1924, joined the British merchant navy at the age of seventeen. He participated in the Battle of the Atlantic on the Murmansk run. His naval training enabled him to take command of three Haganah ships bringing "illegal" immigrants to Palestine during the years before Israel's establishment. When the Israeli Navy was founded, he became commander of a frigate and was wounded on the bridge when Egyptian planes bombed his ship off the coast of Gaza.

In 1950, at the age of twenty-seven, he was the youngest high-ranking officer in the Israel Army, when he was appointed Commander of the Navy. After completing this assignment he studied in the United States, and served as Deputy Director of the Ministry of Defense before going to France.

Unlike Horn's and Barak's relationships to their employers, Mordecai Limon does not have to deal with the daily business affairs of Baron de Rothschild. Not only are his investments of a limited nature, but they are concentrated in a few projects like the General Bank, which is managed by an experienced and able banker, David Shoham, and in real estate, which also has its separate manager. Thus, Limon's activities are confined to representing Baron de Rothschild's general interests in Israel, such as the Trusteeship for the Rehabilitation of Arab Refugees, in which other prominent Israeli personalities including the governor of the Bank of Israel, Moshe Sanbar, are involved. The Limons are prominent in Tel Aviv society and are part of the military and economic establishment.

Another retired general who performs a similar function is Haim (Vivian) Herzog, representing the British Jewish financier, Sir Isaac Wolfson, in Israel. His role in the economic field is only part of Herzog's public image, which also is composed of his military past and his phenomenal success as a military commentator during the Six-Day War and after, which has made him a sought-after speaker for Israel abroad.

In 1972 Herzog limited his activities as Wolfson's representative. He never was a businessman in the normal sense of the word and even after he opened a law firm, he maintained his outside activities.

Herzog is an asset to any company which would like to decorate its list of directors with his name. Thus, when Keter Publishing Company presented the sixteen volumes of the *Encyclopaedia Judaica* to the Pope in Rome early in 1972, it was fortunate to have Herzog perform the function. His association with Keter is indirect: Keter is a subsidiary of Clal, which at one time absorbed a company called GUS-Rassco in which Sir Isaac Wolfson has an interest.

For a man active in business, Herzog's work output is astounding. Apart from regular participation on the Army Broadcasting Station programs, he writes frequently for *Ma'ariv, Ha'aretz* and numerous foreign papers. He often undertakes lecture trips abroad on behalf of the United Jewish Appeal, the Israeli Foreign Office and other groups.

Despite his many activities, Haim Herzog is a relaxed conversationalist, who always gives the impression of a person who has considerable time on his hands. His appearance is that of a typical British gentleman: with his slightly graying mustache and his conservative business suits he scarcely looks like a retired Israeli general and even less like the son of a former Israeli Chief Rabbi. He also does not look like a politician, although he was a candidate in the Knesset election of 1969 and almost made it.

Haim Herzog was born in Dublin, where his father, Rabbi Yitzhak Halevi Herzog was Chief Rabbi. In 1935 he came to Palestine and studied in two Jerusalem yeshivot—rabbinical schools. In 1939 he went to England to study law at Cambridge. When the war broke out in 1939, he volunteered for the British Army and graduated from the famous Sandhurst Officers' School. He served in the Infantry and Armored Corps and took part in the invasion of Europe and the liberation of France and Germany. After his release from the British Army in 1947 with the rank of major, he hoped to practice law in Jerusalem. However, he soon became involved in another war, the Israeli War of Independence. He was operations officer in a brigade on the Negev front and later was moved to Intelligence. When he was sent to Washington as Israeli military attaché in 1950, his success seemed assured. Pentagon officers appreciated his faintly Irish brogue, while the Jewish community was happy to welcome the son of the Chief Rabbi.

Upon his return to Israel in 1954 he held a number of senior military assignments and in 1959 was appointed Chief of Army Intelligence. When he doffed his uniform in 1961, he agreed to serve as Sir Isaac Wolfson's representative in Israel.

When Herzog returned in May, 1967, from a business trip to London, as the clouds of war gathered, he was irritated when the Army refused to call him to active duty. He was then approached by the director of Israeli Radio, Hanoch Givton, and his commentaries during the tense days before the war and in the height of battle had a tremendous impact. Herzog was considered a "secret weapon" that maintained Israeli morale in those trying days.

Sir Isaac Wolfson has another representative in Israel, Moshe Bitan, the director-general of the Paz Oil Company. Although Sir Isaac controls only a third of the ownership of Israel's largest oil-distribution company, whose volume of operations reached 400 million Israeli pounds in 1972, it was he who chose the successor to the late manager, Meir Sherman, from a number of candidates who offered themselves for the job.

It is difficult to say what made the British millionaire choose the former kibbutz member and diplomat, whose only business experience was within the framework of the Histadrut economy. Yet it seems that the choice was successful. Bitan, who assumed his position in October, 1970, succeeded in turning his listening post in Paz into an important position influencing economic policy decisions.

Bitan's strength lies in his talent for analysis and creative thinking. He is known for his independent actions and allows himself to express his opinions freely. Thus, although he was considered to be close to Prime Minister Golda Meir and was appointed member of the Broadcasting Authority on the quota allotted to public servants, he nevertheless voted to allow television broadcasts on Friday nights, despite the fact that he knew that Mrs. Meir had agreed with the religious parties not to permit them on the Sabbath eve.

Bitan was born in Czechoslovakia in 1918 and, upon his arrival in Palestine in 1939, joined Kibbutz Kfar Ruppin in the Bet Sh'ean Valley. On behalf of the kibbutz and Histadrut, he fulfilled numerous missions, including the establishment of a Histadrut office in the United States in 1952. The main function of this office is to mobilize support for Israel in the American labor movement. He joined the Foreign Ministry in 1960 at the request of the Foreign Minister at the time, Golda Meir. In his ten years in the Ministry he served as Ambassador in Ghana and later in Sweden and rose to the rank of Deputy Director-General. Israel's oil economy offers a new challenge to Bitan and he seems determined to develop it into a lever of power.

Issachar Haimowitz, the director-general of the American-Israeli Paper Mills in Hadera, reached the rank of captain of industry by virtue of the fact that the firm he manages not only is one of the largest industrial plants in Israel, but also indirectly affects other branches of the economy. He was selected for this job by Dr. Astorre Mayer, a Milan-based industrialist and a man of learning, who is one of the large stockholders in the Paper Mills. Mayer came to know Haimowitz when he was in Italy on a mission and recommended him as one who could save the plant after its American management brought it to the threshold of disaster.

Haimowitz is more than just a successful manager who has succeeded in turning an ailing paper plant into one of Israel's most profitable industries. He is a man of wide connections, who likes to represent industry as a whole. At one time he agreed to serve as chairman of the board of directors of a government company which was established in order to finance industrial firms which are basically sound but lack equity capital.

Haimowitz is short, wiry and a mass of nervous energy; he often astounds his younger assistants with his capacity for work. He was born in Bessarabia in 1919 and on his arrival in Palestine became involved in "illegal" immigration, undertaking numerous secret missions to various Mediterranean countries.

Realizing that the viability of Israel's paper industry is dependent to a large extent on high government tariff protection, Haimowitz is determined to diversify the investments of the American Israeli Paper Mills. Therefore he acquired, together with another Israeli firm, the local production rights for the revolutionary Wankel engine developed in Germany. This firm, Sav-kal, in which the Paper Mills have an interest, is working on various types of Wankel engines. News about this interest of American Israeli Paper Mills resulted in a considerable rise in its share price quoted on the American Stock Exchange.

Israeli family firms are mostly small and their individual impact on the economy is marginal. When these firms expand beyond a certain size, they frequently are forced to sell out to one of the large concerns. One of the few Israeli captains of industry to be in full control of his own firm is Dr. Reuben Hecht, owner and manager of the Dagon Grain Silos.

If Israel were to unload imported wheat and fodder grain by filling individual sacks and taking them out from the ship's holds as was done until 1954 when Dagon went into operation, the country would have had to spend at least an additional 25 million Israeli pounds, of which $5 million are in foreign currency. The Dagon Silos made possible this saving and at the same time set world records in the unloading of grain. Although the project benefits from government loans, it is the result of the ideas (and their execution) of one man, namely Dr. Reuben Hecht.

Hecht, who looks like a turn-of-the-century aristocrat, is a gray-haired man with a sharp, pointed goatee and a spare figure. He wears conservative suits and horn-rimmed glasses. Usually relaxed, he nevertheless gets excited when he talks about his two hobbies—archaeology and art—or when he expresses his political opinions, which follow a traditional right-wing revisionist line.

The entrance hall of the Dagon office building in Haifa port is a museum of Israeli grain farming. It contains a rare collection of millstones, clay jugs, figurines and coins starting from the period of the Stone Age up to the period of the Second Temple. Unlike so many personalities of his position, Dr. Reuben Hecht rarely attends the social functions of the Israeli establishment. He spends most of his evenings in his home on Mount Carmel, painting or listening to records. His public activities are devoted mainly to preserving the Carmel's scenery against high-rise buildings. Although he lives in Haifa most of the year, Dr. Hecht remains a Swiss citizen; he still controls the family business, the grain silos, storage dumps and Rhine shipping concern Neptune-Renania founded by his late father. The Dagon Silos will revert to the Israeli government in the year 2000, according to the 1950 concession granted to Hecht.

The idea to build a grain silo in Haifa had occurred to Dr. Hecht during his first visit in 1931. His influence on the economy is not limited only to the saving made possible by Dagon, but by virtue of the exemplary labor relations which the somewhat authoritarian investor, who has never completely mastered the Hebrew language, introduced in the plant. He invites all his workers to an annual symphony concert, pays them relatively high wages and at the same time demands of them international standards of efficiency.

As in most modern technocratic societies, lawyers occupy a place of special prominence in the Israeli establishment. They not only help their clients with the phrasing of complicated contracts, "save" them from paying excessive taxes and represent them in the courts of law—they very often afford them contacts and position in the Israeli elite.

The activities of lawyers in the political parties, their personal relations with ministers and their assistants, and their position in the government and the Knesset are often an important asset to their clients. Certain lawyers, it is often claimed in Israel, have a better chance of obtaining lucrative assignments as legal advisors of large government corporations. Yet many Israelis also feel that the record of lawyers in public life has been positive on the whole.

The most influential among Israeli lawyer-politicians is no doubt Haim Zadok, the chairman of the Foreign Relations Committee of the Knesset. The law firm headed by Zadok is composed of fifteen lawyers and handles the legal matters of some of Israel's largest corporations, including Koor, the Histadrut-owned industrial concern; Tefachot, its largest mortgage bank; Shikun Upituach, the housing firm; and Mekorot, which is in charge of Israel's water supply. Zadok represented the American investors who built the Tel Aviv Hilton and later, when the company was taken over by the government, he represented it until it was sold to German investors.

Yet Zadok makes considerable efforts to separate his law practice and his public life. In 1963, for example, when he headed the committee which was charged with proposing income-tax reform, he took care not to hold its meetings in his office, but in the Tel Aviv office of the Bank of Israel. When he served as Minister of Commerce and Industry, he transferred most of his authority to his partners. Yet, even though he is chairman of the Knesset's most important committee, he often signs documents connected with his law firm and sometimes also travels abroad on behalf of clients.

Haim Zadok has a broad face, with a fleshy nose and bright eyes. His build is stocky with a tendency to become heavy. Despite his many activities, he finds time for unhurried conversations in the Knesset lobby with foreign correspondents and is a frequent visitor and official observer on behalf of Israel at the Council of Europe in Strasbourg.

Zadok has a tendency to delve deeply into matters which are brought to his attention. His thoroughness was perhaps a liability when he served in the government, where fast decision making is often considered not only an unavoidable necessity but a system of operation. When he became Minister of Commerce and Industry in 1965, he introduced a "revolution": the Minister only set policy and refrained from getting involved in current issues. He called for less government intervention and asked industrialists to "work more on your lathes and less on the government."

The trouble with this policy was that it suited other periods but not the particular moment when he was called to lead industry. Israel was at that time in the throes of a recession. Zadok had to cope with unemployment and, for the first time, a decline in industrial production. What was needed then was government initiative to aid individual plants and to establish new industries.

In November, 1966, less than a year and a half after he became Minister of Commerce and Industry, Zadok decided to resign. This decision came after the Prime Minister, Levi Eshkol, indirectly accused him of responsibility for the deteriorating state of affairs in industry. Zadok was bitter and felt he was wrongly accused. Yet, despite the common practice in Israel, where resignation is tantamount to leaving the ring, Zadok did not lose his political position. His position as chairman of the Foreign Affairs Committee is perhaps the second most important parliamentary post, after that of Speaker of the Knesset.

16

The Primacy of Agriculture

AHARON UZZAN is a member of a moshav (cooperative settlement) named Gilat in the northern Negev. He is tall and heavily built. In June, 1949, he arrived on a ship that brought him from his native Tunisia; since May, 1970, he has been one of the two secretaries of the moshav movement and is slated to be Israel's next Minister of Agriculture.

Aharon Uzzan's rise to power marks the change that has been taking place in the early 1970's in Israeli agriculture—the shift in the concentration of power from the veteran settlements established mainly by immigrants from Eastern Europe before the establishment of the State in 1948 to the new settlements established in the early years of Statehood, mainly by immigrants from Asia and Africa.

Yet the candidacy of Aharon Uzzan for the position of Minister of Agriculture nevertheless signifies the continuation of a twenty-five-year-old tradition. Unlike other ministers, who are proposed by their parties or chosen by the Prime Minister in the case of the majority Labor party, the Agriculture post is filled by the nominee of the various settlement movements. These movements, including kibbutz, moshav and private groupings, constitute the Israeli agriculture lobby. In the past twenty-five years this tradition has been broken only once, in 1959, when Moshe Dayan, not a farmer himself, was appointed Minister of Agriculture. Yet Dayan had the distinction of being raised in a moshav, Nahalal, in the Valley of Jezreel, where his father, Shmuel Dayan, was one of its founders.

There is no doubt something peculiar in the phenomenon that Israel's farmers select their representative in the Cabinet, but this characterizes their special position in the elite. During Israel's first years, ministers, party leaders and Knesset members were particularly proud when the word "farmer" was written in their identity card next to "occupation." David Ben-Gurion considered himself an "agricultural worker," an occupation he has not pursued since before World War I; Levi Eshkol, Israel's third Prime Minister, saw his home as Kibbutz Degania B in the Jordan Valley and was buried there.

Not only the labor parties, but also the Orthodox religious parties and, in the past, even a typical bourgeois party like the General Zionists give the farmers in their midst representation in the Knesset and other institutions far beyond their numerical strength, which is relatively small. In 1973 no more than 16 percent of Israel's Jewish population lives in agricultural villages and not even all of them engage in agriculture. Since the process of industrialization in the kibbutzim is intensifying, the proportion of those engaged in agriculture even in these settlements is declining.

Israel, of course, is not the only country in the world where the political power of those who engage in agriculture far exceeds their numerical strength. A similar situation prevails in the United States, in Western Europe and in other countries. But in Israel, where Zionism at first meant "the return to the land," and the early pioneers were first and foremost those who settled the land, agriculture always had a special position.

The kibbutz, or collective settlement where everyone contributes according to his ability and is compensated according to his needs, is an original creation. It was established not by disciples of socialist egalitarian theories, but in response to concrete needs—the hardships of the early pioneers of the Jordan Valley, who were forced to pull together in order to overcome disease, poverty and the harsh climate of their new-old homeland.

Unlike the kolkhoz in Russia, the kibbutz has always been based on voluntary participation. Constant changes in structure and even in the way of life of individual families have always characterized the kibbutz, making it a unique social experiment. Therefore, the kibbutzim could never be organized in a single federation, but are divided into at least four different organizations, each one emphasizing either an ideological or a religious or a structural particularity.

It should be noted, however, that tens of thousands of immigrants who arrived after 1948, lacking Zionist ideological training or the elitist tradition of the kibbutz movement, were absorbed in a different framework, that of the moshav, or smallholders' cooperative settlement. In a moshav, each family lives separately and owns its own farm, with services such as purchasing, marketing, education, and welfare being administered by the village on a cooperative basis. The moshav is a self-governing body that can refuse permission to candidates for admission or to members who wish to sell their land. Private initiative is expressed within this framework by the standard of living of each family.

The earlier moshavim, established in the pre-State period, were marked just as much as the kibbutzim by pioneering and social zeal. The hundreds of new moshavim established subsequently changed the contents of moshav life somewhat. While the cooperative element remains, emphasis is placed increasingly on the private initiative of each family.

Kibbutz life provides the individual member with the utmost security, such as a guaranteed job, housing, health care, education of his children and an old age free from worries. But the life also requires continuous sacrifices: constant accommodation to other members' desires, and abandonment of most personal ambitions, including the natural desire for personal acquisitions. A kibbutz member may lead a carefree life today, but if he decides to leave the kibbutz he may find himself without anything to his name and almost without anything to show for many years of hard work.

The kibbutz, therefore, always attracted a certain elitist group who were ready to make the necessary compromises and to adjust to this form of life. At no time did the kibbutz members constitute more than 4 percent of the population. However, their influence, because of the high personal level of the membership and the special function they performed in the establishment of the State, by far exceeded their numerical strength.

However, since the middle 1950's, when the emphasis shifted from agricultural settlements to immigrant development towns that sprang up in various parts of the country, a gradual decline in the political power of the farmers has occurred. It should be noted that the kibbutzim today are no longer just units of agricultural production as they were in the early days. Industry has become an important branch in almost every kibbutz, and the annual volume of sales of kibbutz industrial production already exceeds the volume of sales of the agricultural yield.

Economists nowadays dare to raise a question that was taboo in the early years of the State: whether a country whose industrial base is still not very strong can really afford to provide lavish assistance to agricultural interests. Yet the priority which the Zionist movement has always given to agriculture since the early days of "practical Zionism" (which, as opposed to political Zionism, believed in "self-realization" or personal application of Zionist theory) still obtains.

Israeli farm interests not only control economic institutions like the Citrus Marketing Board, the Bank for Agriculture, the Agrexco Export Company, but also bodies such as the Farm Center of the Histadrut and the Farmers' Union of the private, nonlabor sector. The most important fortress of Israeli farm interests is no doubt the Ministry of Agriculture itself.

Not only is the Minister selected by the coalition of agricultural interests, but also the positions of Deputy Minister, Director-General, his Deputies and sometimes even department heads are divided among the various agricultural bodies according to their relative strength. During Golda Meir's premiership, the Minister of Agriculture himself was a member of a kibbutz, his Deputy, a member of a moshav. The Director-General was again a kibbutznik, but of a political shade different from the Minister. Among the top officials of the Ministry, religious kibbutzim and moshavim are prominently represented. The moshav movement, which is by far the most numerous among the settlement groups, feeling itself discriminated against in the years 1969–1973, at first demanded that the Minister, Haim Gvati, be replaced by a moshavnik. However, they yielded in return for an unwritten agreement that the next Minister would be a member of a moshav.

In the moshav movement itself there is a delicate balance between its two parts—the older moshavim established mainly before the establishment of the State and the moshavim established by immigrants between 1948 and 1955. The growing strength of the new moshavim led to the appointment of two secretaries-general of the moshav movement in 1970, Aryeh (Arik) Nehamkin of Nahalal and Aharon Uzzan of Gilat.

Uzzan was born in 1924 in Muknin, Tunisia. His family engaged in jewelry making—a traditional Jewish craft; but young Uzzan, who was already active in the Zionist movement in Tunisia, brought together a group of twenty-five, who immigrated to Israel in 1949 and decided to settle in a moshav. Uzzan soon became the leader of all the North African farmers in the area, who found the new reality harsh and often disappointing. For years his official position was "buyer of supplies" for a group of Negev moshavim. But this post also included mediating between quarreling families, finding a job for a son who had finished his Army service or handling requests for enlarged water quotas for various farmers. In those years, his day always started at 5 A.M. He would work two hours on his own farm, drive his son—who was killed at the Suez Canal during his military service—to the regional agricultural school, receive people in his Beersheba office, visit a number of moshavim and upon his return home at 6 P.M. again tend to his chores.

At first Uzzan refused to go into politics or be included in the Labor party list of candidates for the Knesset. "Imagine," he used to say to friends, "me a Knesset member? What shall I do when they discuss their foreign affairs? What do I know about it?" Nevertheless he agreed to be a candidate, and was elected to the Knesset in 1965.

Soon afterward he became Deputy Minister of Agriculture. But four years later he made an unprecedented move and said: "Enough, give somebody else a chance. I am going back to my farm." Uzzan was afraid to lose his identity as a farmer, but his retirement from politics was relatively short. Less than a year later, he agreed to become secretary of the moshav movement. The death of his eldest son on active service in May, 1970, was a severe blow to him. He intensified his involvement in farm politics, and his leadership among the new immigrant moshavim became undisputed.

The other secretary of the moshav movement, Aryeh Nehamkin, is a tall, moustachioed farmer with a permanent suntan. He was born in Nahalal in 1925, where he was a neighbor of Moshe Dayan. Although very different from Uzzan in his upbringing and style of operation, Nehamkin is similar to his colleague in that he insists on keeping up his own farm in Nahalal. Although his eldest daughter and her husband, both of them university graduates, are now doing most of the farmwork, Nehamkin himself often gets to his Tel Aviv office only after putting in several hours with his cows and turkeys in Nahalal.

The outgoing Minister of Agriculture, Haim Gvati, was known for many years as the "wise man" of Israeli agriculture and will probably continue to hold this title even after retiring from political life. Gvati, who was born in Pinsk in 1901 and came to Palestine in 1924 to join one of the early collective settlements in the Valley of Jezreel, is typical of his generation. The formal education of the pioneers had little to do with farming. Their settling on the land was motivated mainly by Zionist, and to a lesser degree, socialist ideals. They became familiar with agriculture only gradually, through a system of trial and error.

It is probably symptomatic of the change in Israeli agriculture that Avraham Katz (Ketzele), the secretary-general of the kibbutz group to which Gvati belongs, is a graduate of the Faculty of Agriculture of the Hebrew University. In recent years the influence of farmers with college degrees has grown in Israel. Agriculture, which still demands preferential treatment in matters of taxation, budgets, and other economic issues, is no longer a profession of self-denying idealists who die of malaria while draining the swamps or making the desert bloom, but an occupation for highly skilled professionals who have acquired the most sophisticated farm methods in the world and even developed many techniques of their own.

While political leadership of Israeli agriculture is firmly in the hands of cooperatives (moshavim) and collective settlements (kibbutzim), the private farmers, who in fact were the first pioneers of Israeli agriculture and established the earliest settlements, mainly during the last quarter of the nineteenth century, are still influential, especially in citrus and grape growing.

The kind of agriculture developed by farmers belonging to the Histadrut was always based on mixed farming. This enabled the individual farmer to do the farmwork himself, since each farm branch has its high season at a different time of the year, while branches like dairy farming and poultry provide the cash which enables the family to subsist during the entire year. Private farming not belonging to the Histadrut, however, at all times centered around those branches that require hired labor, such as citrus groves, vineyards or cotton growing.

The "grand old men" of Israeli private citrus growing, such as Yitzhak Rokach and Zvi Isaacson, who for many years were among the most prominent figures on the Citrus Marketing Board, recently retired from public life. Their places have been inherited to some extent by younger technicians and personalities who are economists as much as farmers. One of them is Mendes Sachs, the manager of Mehadrin, one of the largest companies that invests in citrus and himself a large owner of citrus groves. Sachs, who was born in the United States in 1907, still speaks with a distinct American accent, despite the fact that he has lived in Israel since the 1930's.

For a brief period, Mendes Sachs served as the manager of the Citrus Marketing Board, but when it became obvious to him that he would not succeed in convincing his colleagues, both private citrus growers and farmers belonging to the labor sector of the economy, to introduce far-reaching reforms, he resigned. Sacks believes that the Israeli citrus industry must be based on quality control and modern marketing.

Dr. Eliyakum Ostashinsky, member of the governing board of the Farmers' Union and manager of the Vine-Growers' Association, represents Israel's small private farmers. The "doctor," as he is called in the Rishon Le-Zion Wine Cellars, is one of the first generation of sabras. He was born in Petach Tikvah in 1909 and studied agriculture at the University of Toulouse. His accent in Hebrew is typical of the old-timers of the first settlements. For many years Ostashinsky, a distinguished-looking man with a mop of white hair and a mustache, has been a resident of Rishon Le-Zion and at one time served as mayor of the town. He is representative of a generation whose place at the top of the Israeli establishment is fast vanishing.

17
The Scientists

"**P**ROFESSOR" is still a highly respected title and status in Israel, yet it does not in itself indicate that its bearer belongs to the elite. In the sciences the specific weight one carries in one's own field and the professional esteem of colleagues has an overwhelming role in determining elite status. Social influence or politics are secondary.

In the Israel scientific establishment, evaluation by one's peers is of great importance for the status of a scientist. Yet even more important is his standing in international scientific circles. This fact stems, in no small measure, from the fact that Israeli academicians see themselves as belonging to the first rank of international science. Therefore publication in international professional journals has become one of the most important factors in determining the status of a scientist in Israel.

More than in many other countries, it is the research part of his work that determines the status of a professor in the scientific establishment in Israel. While in other professions engagement in public activities contributes significantly to a person's status, in sciences such engagement, if continued for a long period, often occurs at the expense of research and therefore ultimately reflects on the scientist's stature.

The career of Professor Dan Patinkin can well serve as an example of the ways in which a scientist can influence events in Israel—and also as an example of the limits of his influence.

He can influence the direction of research and studies in his field, as Patinkin did when he shifted the focus of economics at the Hebrew University from a politico-economic and socio-economic emphasis toward modern econometrics.

He can educate a new generation of disciples, who join the Civil Service and private business and implement the conceptual theories learned at the university.

He can advise the government and public institutions. Thus Professor Patinkin participates in various study committees and inquiry commissions on economy-related issues. (Setting up committees is a frequent solution adopted by the government when it gets lost in the maze of its own policy.)

He can always publicize his views in the newspapers—which in Israel eagerly open their columns to letters and statements signed by professors, whether they write on subjects in their own field or in any other. Scientists are also welcome signatories to political declarations and manifestos and honored members of ad hoc groupings which usually form to support political campaigns of parties on the eve of elections.

The largest employer of scientists in Israel is the government, since it channels huge budgets to research via the defense budget. These funds are channeled primarily to applied science, and their use is much more closely controlled than in other academic research. Yet the main problem of Israeli scientists working on defense-related projects is not restriction on research but rather restrictions on publication of their results. Therefore, despite the lure of abundant funds and the chance to have a more direct influence on scientific progress than at a university, the defense establishment has considerable difficulties in keeping top scientists on its staff for any length of time. Some of the top scientists decide, from time to time, to allocate a year or two to defense-related research as a public service; others prefer to do part-time work for defense parallel to civilian research and teaching. Usually it is easier to find scientists to do consulting or actual research for the military than to accept administrative duties in project management. Few are the scientists who are willing to spend most of their time at the peak of their creativity within the defense establishment.

The prestige institution of Israel's scientific elite is the Weizmann Institute at Rehovoth, named after Israel's first President, Professor Chaim Weizmann, who was a chemist. Members of this Institute have probably the highest rate of publication in international scientific publications. Yet there is a conflicting tendency in their influence on the life of the country. On the one hand, many Israeli scientists, like their colleagues abroad, still live in ivory towers, of which the Weizmann Institute is probably the classic example in Israel. Moreover, scientists here too find it difficult to establish a common language with politicians, who do not know how to formulate their questions or interpret the answers, solicited or unsolicited.

On the other hand, this very difficulty of communication contributes to the awe in which politicians often hold whatever is said by scientists. The traditional Jewish esteem for learning reinforces the politicians' respect for scientists' opinions.

Yet the practical impact of the scientists' advice is sometimes most limited. A typical example of this is the failure of the Israel scientific establishment to bring about fundamental changes in the contents of elementary and secondary-school education. For years scientists have been urging basic reforms in order to adapt education to the needs of tomorrow's university students, yet, except for mathematics, very little change has occurred in Israeli school curricula.

As far as politically-related scientific matters are concerned, Israeli scientists who organized themselves into an ad hoc pressure group failed when they tried to influence nuclear research. On the other hand, they were successful as a professional pressure group when they induced the government to continue certain types of research providing jobs for physicists who suffered from "research unemployment."

The most notable example of purely political influence making by Israel scientists occurred in the dispute between David Ben-Gurion and Levi Eshkol over the Lavon Affair: the scientists who lined up behind Eshkol provided intellectual respectability for his position. On the other hand, the most notable public failure of Israeli scientists occurred in the economic field: some of the country's top research economists were among the advocates and planners of the government's policy of retrenchment in the mid-1960's, devised to curb inflation. Yet, instead of curing Israel's economy, the measures devised by economists created a slump from which the country recovered only on the eve of the Six-Day War.

In late 1971, when President Sadat of Egypt threatened to resume the war against Israel unless it agreed to withdraw from Sinai, a number of professors and scientists, including Professor Dan Patinkin, appealed to Prime Minister Meir to "review Israel's position and make proposals which, without hurting Israel's security, could form a realistic basis for negotiations with Egypt." Mrs. Meir angrily rejected the criticism implied in the appeal of the dovish professors and intellectuals and soon afterward gained the support of a counter-group of scientists, which included one of Israel's most noted young physicists, Tel Aviv University president, Professor Yuval Ne'eman.

What has become known as "the affair of the scientists' appeal" indicates several aspects of the relationship between the government power elite and the scientific elite:

The scientific elite, in taking political positions, is not an initiator but rather a spokesman of trends, dovish as well as hawkish, that have emerged in Israel society. The government is very sensitive to this criticism. When scientists organize themselves against government policy, they do not present a unified pressure group: there is always a part of the scientific community which lines up on the government side.

There is no permanent division of roles between critics and supporters of the government among the scientists: Dan Patinkin, who was among the leaders of a group calling itself "Academicians in

Support of Eshkol," subsequently was among the leaders of those who criticized Mrs. Meir; Yuval Ne'eman, who was close to Rafi when it split from the labor party, became a firm defender of Mrs. Meir in the early 1970's.

There is no group in Israel which can create as strong an echo for their views in the mass media as the professors. But they dramatize and perhaps reinforce political trends that already exist—they cannot initiate changes.

The man who has probably had more influence than any other scientist in Israel, and who has been more controversial than any of his colleagues, is Professor E. D. Bergman. If the world today appreciates Israel's nuclear capabilities, it is due first of all to Professor Bergman's stubbornness. If Israel's scientific community had undergone anything approaching a split between those favoring very practical aims for national research and those favoring pure research, this can also be ascribed largely to the personality of Professor Bergman, one of Ben-Gurion's close advisors. In 1969, three years after he resigned from the chairmanship of the Israel Atomic Energy Commission, Professor Bergman explained: "There are no two atomic energies. By developing atomic energy for peaceful uses, one attains a nuclear option." In the same year, the West German magazine *Der Spiegel* claimed that Professor Bergman and the late Professor Yoel Rakah had developed a method of refining uranium from wastes of the Dead Sea potash plant, thus providing about one hundred pounds of uranium a year.

Ernst David Bergman was born in Germany in 1903 and at the age of twenty-six already was a lecturer in mathematics at Berlin University. When he came to Palestine in 1934 he was appointed head of the Sieff Institute in Rehovoth, which he had helped organize in London together with Professor Weizmann. On the eve of World War II he worked in Paris on developing high explosives. Back in Palestine, he became a friend of Ben-Gurion, who appointed him, upon the establishment of the State, head of the Science Branch of the Army. All through his career he combined academic research with work on defense projects. When he was made full professor of organic chemistry at the Hebrew University in 1953, he was also appointed Chairman of the Atomic Energy Commission.

His views on the priorities in research undertaken by the Commission and his authoritarian methods of conducting business ultimately led all other members of the Commission to resign, leaving him a "Commission of One" at the head of Israel's nuclear research. Yet it was Bergman who induced the government to invest enormous sums in research on projects which had no less importance for Israel's security than for civilian research. His main contribution in this respect was his persistent demand for ever-expanding scientific research, in close cooperation with Shimon Peres, who was Deputy Minister of Defense under Ben-Gurion.

When Ben-Gurion was succeeded by Eshkol, the new Prime Minister had different views on the priorities in this field. In 1966 Bergman resigned from his threefold task—as chairman of the Atomic Energy Commission, head of the Research Division of the Ministry of Defense and Scientific Advisor to the Ministry.

Another scholar who plays an influential role in politics and the administration of learning and research is Natan Rotenstreich, professor of philosophy at the Hebrew University in Jerusalem. In July 1973 he assumed a role of major importance as Chairman of the Allocations Committee for Israel's institutions of higher learning. (Their major source of income is government funds.) The "finance commissar" of the country's capital-hungry universities will also supervise the proper implementation of his committee's budgetary allocations.

Born in Poland in 1914 and educated in Israel, Rotenstreich frequently descends from the ivory tower to write on current issues. A man of strong convictions, he was active at the time of the Labor party's cultural split in the 1960's. He formerly served as Rector of the Hebrew University and was mentioned in the past for the post of Minister of Education.

Professor Yuval Ne'eman, at 48 a leading member of the scientific community, shows an interesting similarity to E. D. Bergman in that both manage to combine simultaneously intensive theoretical research and practical defense-related research.

Professor Yuval Ne'eman was born in 1925 in Tel Aviv; his grandfather was one of the founders of the city and one of its first industrialists. Young Ne'eman got his M.A. at the Haifa Institute of Technology at the age of twenty and at the age of twenty-two he was general manager of a hydraulic pump factory belonging to his father. After the War of Independence, in which he fought in the Negev, he remained in the Army and rose to the rank of full colonel. When he was appointed military attaché in London, Ne'eman also studied at the Royal College for Physics and Mathematics, under the Pakistani scientist, Abdul Salem. In 1961 he received his Ph.D. and formulated the foundations of the "eightfold way" theory of unified symmetry—a theory that maintains the existence of a unified system of symmetries in subnuclear particles. Based on this theory, he predicted the existence of a yet unknown subparticle called "Omega-Minus," which was discovered several years later.

This theory was Ne'eman's major scientific advancement. Upon his return to Israel he was appointed scientific director of the Nahal Sorek nuclear reactor research laboratories. With Professor Chaim Goldberg of the Weizmann Institute he formulated a hypothesis that all nuclear subparticles are built of three basic elements which he called "quarks." Joining Professor Murray Gelman at the California Institute of Technology in 1963, he worked on subparticle research, and many feel that he should have shared with Professor Gelman the 1969 Nobel Prize in Physics awarded to his American colleague for that research.

Ne'eman is a hawk in security and foreign-policy matters. He was among the first to demand expansion of Israel's frontiers after the June, 1967, war. In 1969 he was the first non-American to receive the Einstein Prize, and his international scientific status was underscored in 1972 when he was elected a member of the American Academy of Sciences. Lately he has been spending most of his time running Tel Aviv University, of which he was elected president in 1971.

Professor Ne'eman is convinced that Israel is on its way to become one of the major centers for research in physics outside the United States and the Soviet Union. He also has an abiding interest in matters political. "At times I find it very difficult to decide whether to attend a lecture on nuclear physics or on recent developments in Arab society," he says. He solves this problem by "going into hiding" for several days at a time when he devotes all his attention to research. He is also professor of physics at the California Institute of Technology, and his frequent visits to the United States are mostly devoted to research. Lately, however, his foreign trips often have a political purpose as well: he is among the most active scientists in the world-wide campaign against the exit tax imposed by the Soviets on Jews having academic education who want to emigrate to Israel.

Professor Ephraim Katchalski is another leading Israel scientist who, from his early youth, has combined research and defense matters. Born in 1916 in Kiev in the Ukraine, he immigrated to Palestine as a child and joined the Haganah when he was sixteen. As a student of chemistry and zoology at the Hebrew University, he was also commander of the student unit of the Haganah, and produced home-made explosives together with his late brother Aharon Katchalski-Katzir (who was murdered in a Japanese terrorist attack on Lydda airport in May, 1972). He received his Ph.D. at the Hebrew University of Jerusalem for his work in the development of synthetic polypeptides and was among the first researchers at the Weizmann Institute in the field of synthetic proteins. Katchalski contributed to making the Weizmann Institute's Biophysics Department one of the world centers for research in proteins and pseudo-proteins.

In the War of Independence Katchalski was given the rank of colonel and was among those who organized the Science Branch of the Army. In 1956 he, together with the late Professor Shlomo Hestrin, established the monthly *Mada*, which has become Israel's most popular science magazine. In 1966 he was elected nonresident member of the American Academy of Sciences and, after the resignation of Professor Ernst Bergman, became Chief Scientist of the Ministry of Defense. Actually Professor Katchalski inherited only one of Professor Bergman's three defense-related posts: Prime Minister Eshkol personally took over the chairmanship of the Atomic Energy Commission (now held by Prime Minister Golda Meir), and the post of head of the Research Division of the Ministry was left vacant, with some of its duties going to the Chief Scientist—a new title replacing that of Chief Science Advisor to the Defense Minister, held by Professor Bergman.

Professor Katchalski has severely criticized the Israeli defense establishment for its preference for purchasing technological know-how abroad rather than investing in its development in Israel. He charged that this was one of the main reasons why so few scientists were willing to devote all their time to defense research.

In 1969 Professor Katchalski resigned from the Defense Ministry in order to devote his full energies to protein research. He worked primarily on the development of synthetic enzymes as part of extensive research in pseudo-proteins. In this field he has made his main scientific contribution, since synthetic pseudo-proteins built of one or two amino acids (rather than of dozens of amino acids as in the natural proteins), have become an important research tool in the study of living cells.

On March 22, 1973, the central committee of the Labor party nominated Katchalski as its candidate for the presidency of the State of Israel. In his nominating speech Foreign Minister Abba Eban hailed Katchalski as a "man of the people, great scientist and great humanist." Katchalski, who was on a lecture tour in the United States at the time, accepted the nomination, stating he would like to be the "fourth intellectual to serve as President of Israel." On the eve of his election he Hebraized his name to Katzir, and received 66 votes on the first ballot in the Knesset. He took office on May 24, 1973, as the new head of the State of Israel.

Professor Israel Dostrovsky, one of Israel's outstanding physical chemists, is also one of the most "related to" members of Israel's scientific elite. A bald-pated egghead, Professor Dostrovsky is the son of a noted Israeli doctor, the late Aryeh Dostrovsky, former dean of the Faculty of Medicine at the Hebrew University; through his uncle, the late Ya'acov Dostrovsky-Dori, Israel's first Chief of Staff and later president of the Haifa Institute of Technology, Professor Dostrovsky has been closely related both to the defense establishment and to some of the old "first families" of the Israeli elite.

Israel Dostrovsky was born in Odessa in 1918 and was brought to Palestine at the age of one. He was among the first of the young scientists raised in Israel who later constituted the "intermediate group" that reached the top echelons after a long hiatus that followed the arrival of leading Jewish scientists who fled Nazi Europe and were brought to Palestine by the late Professor Chaim Weizmann. In his youth Israel Dostrovsky joined a kibbutz and became active in the Haganah, but later went to study at the University of London, where he became a lecturer. He returned to Palestine in 1947 and set up the Isotope Department of the Weizmann Institute. During the War of Independence, Professor Dostrovsky commanded a special Army unit which was sent to map the Negev. This unit was first to locate the phosphate, copper and uranium ores found in that part of the country.

In 1949, back at the Weizmann Institute, he completed his work on a new method of producing heavy water and became active in the work of the Atomic Energy Commission. In 1960 he was elected chairman of Israel's Scientific and Research Council and was also appointed scientific director of the Atomic Energy Commission. In 1963, after a year at various American universities, he concentrated his research on power and desalination problems and led the scientific side of the negotiations with Washington on a proposed joint American-Israeli nuclear desalination project. In 1966 Dostrovsky became Director-General of the Atomic Energy Agency in Vienna. Though the Soviet delegate threatened to resign if Professor Dostrovsky was appointed to an office at the Agency, he was made scientific advisor to the Director-General of the International Atomic Energy Agency in 1972.

Professor Dostrovsky, who is a very practical-minded man—he is the only nuclear scientist who can fix his own car, his friends say—stresses the importance of increasing the number of scientists in Israel. Since today's research is done in teams, only by enlarging the number of top researchers can Israel remain in science's first rank.

The mathematician in Israel's scientific elite is Professor Aryeh Dworetzky, an internationally-known authority in probability studies. He too is of the "intermediate group," born in 1916 in the Ukraine. He came to Palestine as a child, graduated from the Hebrew University and became professor of mathematics there in 1951. His specialty is applied mathematics and operational research. In 1955 he was elected dean of the Faculty of Mathematics and in 1959 vice-president of the University. Unlike some of his colleagues who jealously guard the primacy of the Jerusalem institution, Professor Dworetzky has been a persistent advocate of establishment of additional universities in Israel. He also warns constantly against the tendency to put too much stress on applied research, at the expense of pure science.

Dworetzky, too, has contributed his share to defense-related research. In 1960 he was appointed head of the Weapons Research and Development Authority of the Ministry of Defense. In 1969 he accepted the post of Chief Scientist of the Defense Ministry, on condition that he handle this task on a part-time basis in order to be able to continue his regular research work. Professor Dworetzky is keenly interested in scientific progress and development in the Arab countries and has repeatedly warned Israelis not to take for granted that the Arabs will never be able to catch up with them in science and technology.

Biology was among the first departments established at the Hebrew University in Jerusalem, and it is still one of the most important branches of Israeli science. An outstanding representative of the younger generation of Israeli biologists is the immunologist Professor Michael Sela. Born in Poland in 1924, he studied at the University of Geneva but interrupted his studies to assist the "illegal" immigration to Palestine of the survivors of the Nazi Holocaust.

After Israel's establishment he served briefly as member of the Israeli mission in Czechoslovakia, which at that time was an important center both of military supplies and immigration from Eastern Europe to Israel.

Sela's research on synthetic polypeptides—which has become one of the major research subjects at the Weizmann Institute—led him to the development of synthetic antigens and to important discoveries in the field of electric charges found in proteins.

From here his research led to the development of methods to establish a patient's sensitivity to penicillin in advance. In 1960 he created a synthetic polymer which behaves as a natural antigen—considered an important step in the advancement of immunological research.

Professor Sela, head of the Immunology Department of the Weizmann Institute since 1963, is advisor on immunology to the World Health Organization. One of his assignments shortly before the Six-Day War, and the rupture of diplomatic relations between Israel and the Soviet Union, was to advise the Soviet government on the improvement of immunological research at Russian research institutions.

It is perhaps no coincidence that the prototype of the Israel scientist who combines a defense role with research is not one belonging to the natural sciences. Professor Yigael Yadin, a former Chief of Staff, is an archaeologist who specializes in the early history of Palestine, and has become famous as the decipherer of the Dead Sea Scrolls.

Yigael Yadin was born in Jerusalem in 1917. His late father, Professor Lipa Sukenik, too was an archaeologist and, on the eve of Israel's War of Independence, it was he who purchased the first Dead Sea scrolls from Bedouin shepherds who found them in the caves of Qumran.

From the age of sixteen Yigael Yadin was active in the Haganah, and before he obtained his Ph.D. at the Hebrew University he became engaged full time in underground activities. During the War of Independence, he became the first head of the Operations Division of the Israel Army General Staff. The familiar story about the unique combination of skills of Yigael Yadin describes how the young scholar put his archaeological knowledge to military use: Yadin knew most of the long-forgotten routes and passes in the Negev and directed his troops and supplies via those old Biblical routes, thus managing to assure complete surprise of the enemy.

At the age of thirty-two he became Israel's second Chief of Staff, and his term of office saw the laying of the foundations of the basic organizational framework of the Israel Defense Forces. The standing Army, the hard core of professional officers, was formed originally to cope with the wave of retirement of officers who wanted to go back to their kibbutzim, businesses or laboratories when the war was over. Yadin also directed the establishment of Israel's unique reserve system, based on instant callup of all former soldiers, as well as the establishment of Nachal, the paramilitary agricultural units.

Yadin left the Army in 1952 to become a full-time academician. He obtained his Ph.D. for his work on deciphering the scroll of *The War of the Children of Light Against the Children of Darkness*, one of the Dead Sea scrolls. He followed in his father's footsteps, becoming Professor of Archaeology, dividing his scientific work between the Dead Sea scrolls and further excavations in the Dead Sea area, at Megiddo and Hatzor. His extensive work at Masada, the last fortress to fall to the Roman legions, made possible the restoration of the site, which is a symbol of Jewish determination and resistance.

Professor Yadin has a rare flair for the dramatic (his brother, Yosef Yadin, is one of the stars of the Tel Aviv Chamber Theater). He manages to evoke for a relatively minor find the interest and publicity that many more important discoveries do not achieve. With his attractive features and deep voice, he would be an excellent vote getter. Yet he stays away from political life and, for this very reason, has been repeatedly mentioned as a compromise candidate. In 1967 General Dayan's opponents urged Eshkol to make him Minister of Defense, to head off pro-Dayan forces on the eve of the Six-Day War. His name has frequently been suggested for the post of Minister of Education and other public offices.

There are few people in science, particularly in the field of Jewish studies, who have shaped an entire branch of it from its inception to full blossoming. Professor Gershon Scholem, president of the Israel Academy of Sciences, and a noted scholar of kabbala and Jewish mysticism, is one of them. His research brought about fundamental changes in the philosophy of Jewish history. Applying a Zionist approach to Jewish mysticism and Jewish messianic movements, Scholem in his studies has also greatly contributed to a deepened understanding of the strength of the Jewish national revival.

Scholem was born in Berlin in 1897, and studied mathematics and philosophy. He immigrated to Palestine in 1923 and became full professor of kabbala in 1935. All his students were men except for one, a young girl named Fania Freud, Sigmund Freud's niece, who later became Scholem's wife.

After World War II, Scholem was sent to Europe to collect and bring back to Palestine whatever remained of the libraries, archives and other cultural artifacts of the rich European Jewish past. Upon his return he established the Institute of Jewish Studies at the Hebrew University, which has become a major center for Jewish philosophical and historical research.

He outlines his basic historiosophic thesis in his major work, *Mitzva Habaa Beavera* (which means "the good that comes in transgression"), in which he analyzed the dialectic process leading from the messianic Shabtaic movement to religious nihilism and from nihilism to the era of Jewish Enlightenment. Scholem pointed out that rabbinical Judaism wanted to obscure the nationalistic aspects of the Shabtaic movement, as it also obscured other irrational elements in the history of Jewish thought. On the other hand, he claimed, the overstressing of the exclusivity of rationalism by thinkers of the Jewish Enlightenment has in fact become a dowry to Jewish "assimilation with pride."

A close friend of Scholem is Professor Ephraim Urbach, Professor of Talmud at the Hebrew University. Born in Poland in 1912, Urbach served as an Army chaplain with the Palestinian units of the

British Army in World War II, and became a lecturer in rabbinical literature at the Hebrew University. His master work, *Ba'alei Hatosafot* is the fruit of almost twenty years of painstaking research. It is considered the definitive work on the history of Jews in northern France, Germany and parts of England between the twelfth and the fourteenth centuries. In 1956 he became full professor and was appointed head of the Institute of Jewish Studies at the Hebrew University. He was among the organizers of the World Congress of Jewish Studies and among the chief editors of the *Encyclopedia Hebraica.*

Urbach, an Orthodox Jew, has often been bitterly critical of Israel's religious establishment and especially of the religious political parties. Again and again he has spearheaded attacks on the religious parties' mixing of belief, business and politics. Yet, in March, 1973, when the Labor party picked Professor Ephraim Katchalski as its presidential candidate, the National Religious party put forward the name of Professor Urbach as its candidate. He accepted, and in the contest between the two, Urbach received 41 votes.

Tall, bespectacled, freckle-faced and youthful-looking Professor Dan Patinkin, who is frequently mentioned as the social scientist with the most influence on public life in Israel, was born in Chicago in 1922. At the age of twenty-six he already was assistant professor of economics at the University of Illinois. He came to Israel in 1948 and agreed to serve as a lecturer at the Hebrew University, where there still prevailed an unbreachable European-style seniority system.

The young Patinkin quickly caused a revolution not only in the teaching of economics but also in the field of economic research in Israel, to which he and his students applied the modern mathematical tools of econometrics for the first time. He organized the establishment of the Falk Foundation, which became the focus of applied economic research in the country. His *Monetary and Economic Policies in Israel,* published in 1953, and *The Israel Economy—the First Decade,* published in 1959, have become basic publications in Israel economic research.

Patinkin, who is active in public life both as a chairman of numerous committees and commissions studying economic problems for the government, and as an avowed opponent of the government's foreign policy, frequently has engaged in public campaigns on purely economic issues.

As Israel's senior teacher of economics, he has had far-reaching influence on senior advisors and top government administrators, many of whom were his students. The first generation of government executives, most of whom joined the Civil Service immediately after university in the early 1950's, even bore the nickname "the Patinkin boys," a title of which they were justifiably proud.

Professor Patinkin's next-door neighbor, at the quiet building of the Israel Academy of Science, is sociology professor Shmuel Eisenstadt, who specializes in problems of social integration of new immigrants and the processes of modernization in new nations.

Born in Warsaw in 1923, he came to Palestine in 1935 and from his early years devoted his attention to problems facing a society with a constant large-scale influx of newcomers. He gained international attention both with his widely-publicized studies of Israel's immigration problems and with his unrelated book, *The Political Systems of Empires,* which earned him the coveted MacIver prize of the American Sociological Association in 1964.

In 1966 Eisenstadt became the dean of the Faculty of Social Sciences at the Hebrew University and, in a sharp debate with then Prime Minister Eshkol, charged that Israel was "eating up its scientific substance," which had been acquired by immigration but not sustained by sufficient "production" of young scientists in the country.

The Israel defense establishment is an important initiator and supporter of research in many fields of the exact sciences. It was also the Army which launched the career of one of Israel's topmost social scientists and, in fact, of an entire new field—that of public opinion research.

Immediately after the War of Independence, David Ben-Gurion appointed Eliahu Louis Gutman, who had arrived a year earlier from the United States, to set up an opinion study in the Israel defense forces. Of interest were not the political or social opinions of the soldiers but their views on conditions of service. Gutman's outfit was also asked to investigate and determine the demonstrable factors for success in officers' courses and advancement in various branches of the service.

When demobilized, Dr. Gutman's outfit became Israel's first public-opinion research center and the basis for the Institute for Applied Social Research.

Professor Gutman's work has had its impact on the life of Israel through two avenues. His studies have become fundamental for determining methods of job classification and promotion in government and public service. The public-opinion polls, conducted regularly by his Institute, are frequently initiated by various Cabinet members to find out what voters think of existing policies and how they would react to proposed changes. However, it is for his work in devising methods for the measurement of personal traits that Professor Gutman is today considered one of the most important contributors to the science of sociometrics in the world.

Eliahu Gutman was born in New York in 1916, studied at the University of Minnesota, and in World War II was psychological advisor to the U. S. Defense Department and was later appointed to the Cornell University faculty. His scale analysis method for determining individual capabilities and talents in specific fields was published in 1952.

Professor Gutman has repeatedly served as a visiting professor at American universities. While his public-opinion studies are mostly financed from Israeli sources, most of his basic research is supported from funds and budgets overseas, including the U.S. Navy and the National Institutes of Health.

In 1971 *Science,* the official publication of the American Association for the Advancement of Science, published an article listing the sixty-two most important pieces of research in the field of social science since the beginning of the twentieth century: Professor Gutman, whose work was among the sixty-two, was the only Israel scientist on the list.

18

The Molders of Public Opinion

For a country which has been in a state of war virtually throughout its twenty-five years of existence, freedom of the press in Israel is observed fairly scrupulously and is considered one of the basic elements of its democratic system. However, there is a certain ambivalence in this: the authorities sometimes infringe on this freedom far more than would be acceptable in countries with a formal constitution or with a centuries-old tradition of press liberty; yet, on the other hand, the government seldom uses any of its wide legal powers to punish or retaliate for violations of numerous censorship, state-secret, and other restrictive laws. Knesset members pay abundant lip service to the principle of freedom of expression—but do not do anything to change the draconian laws on the books which give the government wide authority to control the mass media; editors of many papers, belonging to or connected with government parties or institutions, regularly defend government action—but at the same time, also struggle for their right to criticize the regime and dispute its right to determine what might or might not hurt Israel's political or security interests.

The day-to-day struggle for press freedom is conducted mainly by two organizations: the National Association of Journalists and the Editors' Committee. The first body, which is primarily a professional and trade union, makes declarations and tries to prevent the blocking of sources of information. The Editors' Committee confronts the government directly, both in personal contacts with Cabinet members and through representatives in the Censorship Committee. The Editors' Committee is the successor to the group of editors of Hebrew papers organized during the British Mandate to coordinate the reaction of the Jewish press in Palestine to acts of the foreign ruler. It too reflects to some extent the ambivalence that is symptomatic of the whole spectrum of relationships between the press and the government: on the one hand, it is a pressure group influencing the government; on the other, it is also an instrument used by the government, making the editors privy to information it wishes kept out of the papers.

Two developments in recent years have considerably changed the nature of the influence of the mass media on public opinion and events in Israel: first, there has been great expansion of the role of the broadcasting services and their credibility as a source of information for the public. The Six-Day War was the catalyst in this process: it was the first war which could be followed by transistor radio by soldiers in the Army and the civilian population sitting in bomb shelters. The appearance of newspapers was sharply curtailed, since most of their staffs were mobilized. The radio newscasts kept the population abreast of fast-breaking events, not only during the week of the war, but in the action-filled years that followed. The Six-Day War also marked the beginning of the television era in Israel: until then, the government had postponed introduction of the new medium largely for economic reasons. Today, radio and television, both controlled by the government's Broadcasting Authority, supply most of the initial information about domestic and foreign events that reaches the Israeli public.

Second, and more important, as far as the power of the press is concerned, is the increase in the weight of independent newspapers and decline in the weight of party papers. A few years ago, of the dozen or so Hebrew dailies in the country there were only three independent ones: *Ha'aretz, Ma'ariv* and *Yediot Ahronot.* Nine belonged to political parties. Today, there are only seven Hebrew dailies—four party-affiliated and three independent. Moreover, the circulation of each of the independent papers is considerably larger than that of all the party papers put together.

A third major development has been the diminution of the awe felt by many newsmen, and especially by editors, for security information imparted to them by the government and over their feeling of being part of the establishment. Many editors now feel that they behave just as responsibly as the government even if they do not agree with it on what does or does not endanger national security.

There is an important difference between the newspapers regarding the part of the public which they want to influence. Party papers are addressed almost exclusively to party members and their main task is to reassure the faithful and reinforce their trust. In their editorials, party papers also serve as official spokesmen of the parties on current affairs. Independent papers see their main function as providing information and dispensing commentary to readers.

Davar belongs in the category of party papers, though officially it is owned by a broader, multiparty group—the Histadrut. Repeated disputes in recent years over the role of *Davar* have taken place, initiated mostly by the secretary-general of the Histadrut, Mr. Yitzhak Ben-Aharon, who complains that the paper takes positions contrary to those of the Histadrut. However, Mr. Ben-Aharon's attitude does not necessarily reflect the views of the dominant partner in the Histadrut, the Israel Labor party. In general, *Davar* hews pretty closely to the Labor party line but, in times of intramural disputes, tends to present minority views, too. For example, during the mid-1960's crisis in the Labor party, *Davar* opened it pages to articles reflecting the views of Ben-Gurion's and Dayan's Rafi party, which had split off from the Labor party.

Most independent papers, unlike the party press, want to influence readers of all persuasions. Typical of them is the tabloid *Yediot Ahronot,* one of the two evening papers (both of which actually appear around noon). *Yediot Ahronot* presents its information and commentary in an easy-to-understand form, aimed intentionally at a public that does not go in for deep analysis. Editorially, it supports the government most of the time, except for a few specific subjects on which its editor, Dr. Herzl Rosenblum, holds strong personal views.

His main task is to write the daily editorials of the paper, which frequently represent the most extreme anti-Soviet views in the Israeli press. The chief owner of the paper, Mr. Noah Moses (who also owns the popular women's magazine *Laisha*), inherited the tabloid from his late father, who amassed his fortune from business ventures other than publishing. (This he has in common with his colleague Gershom Schocken, editor and publisher of *Ha'aretz*, whose father owned a department-store chain in pre-Nazi Germany.)

Noah Moses was born in Poland in 1912 and came to Israel in 1934. He steers the paper to avoid controversies with either government or opposition leaders. However, several columnists of the paper do have strong views of their own and the paper permits them to publish them on its pages.

Ma'ariv, too, addresses itself to the man in the street, and its success is attested by its circulation, the largest in the country. The main source of the paper's prestige, by the end of 1972, *Ma'ariv*'s circulation on Friday reached 200,000—an impressive figure by Israel standards. But *Ma'ariv* tries to influence events not only via the man in the street but also by convincing directly those in power. It supports government policies in a more selective way than *Yediot Ahronot*. *Ma'ariv*'s views still reflect the fact that many of its top editors are one-time revisionists and supporters of the former Irgun. This is most clearly felt on such topics as Germany, and its hawkishness when it comes to relations with the Arab countries and policies in the occupied territories. *Ma'ariv*, too, permits free expression of divergent views, mainly by its younger staff members. However, the original group that founded the paper jealously guards its special position as the inner ruling circle of the publication.

The oldest independent daily is *Ha'aretz*, whose origins go back to World War I. It has a smaller circulation than *Ma'ariv* or *Yediot Ahronot* and it does not aim its editorials at the man in the street. Influencing the ruling elite is seen by it only as a secondary aim: the first and most important is to influence the intellectual and opinion-making circles of Israel. Fluctuations in its prestige in the past have reflected changes in the extent of the paper's adherence to this concept. The quality of its columns and other signed articles has also indicated, by and large, how much the editor-in-chief wishes to maintain the image of a highbrow paper.

Ha'aretz is owned by the Schocken family; its editor-in-chief is Gershom (Gustav) Schocken. There are probably people with more influence in the Israeli mass media and on public opinion than Gershom Schocken; there may also be some whose income from the newspaper business is higher; there is no doubt, however, that as an individual Schocken has more power in his paper and possibly more cumulative influence on the Israeli press than any other editor. He alone makes the final decisions on hiring and firing of all *Ha'aretz* employees and his opinion is decisive in determining the paper's policy and the contents of its editorials.

The daily editorial-board meetings at noon in Schocken's office take place under a stern-visaged portrait of his late father, Zalman Schocken, which hangs with some Chagall drawings on the wall. The elder Schocken, a businessman, Zionist leader and patron of the arts, was a domineering personality who had an overwhelming influence on the character of Gershom, his oldest son. Born in Zwickau, Germany, in 1912, Gershom Schocken studied for a year at Heidelberg before Hitler came to power, and then emigrated to Palestine. Zalman Schocken purchased the respected but financially weak *Ha'aretz* in 1936, and Gershom became its editor-in-chief in 1939.

With typical methodicalness, Schocken made *Ha'aretz* into a modern newspaper, serving primarily as a conveyor of information rather than as a forum for ideological disputes. At the same time he raised the standard of editorial material and hired a number of young journalists to whom he gave fairly free rein to express their opinions. In a short time, *Ha'aretz* became the prestige paper of Palestine and was compared by the late Dr. Chaim Weizmann to the Manchester *Guardian*. Not everybody shared this opinion: later, when he was Prime Minister, Ben-Gurion used to refer to *Ha'aretz* ironically as "that decent paper."

In 1948, Schocken went into politics and in 1956 was elected to the Knesset on the Progressive party list. He made an effort to distinguish between the role of party representative and editor of an independent newspaper; this was made easier by the fact that the Progressives took a fairly mild line on practically all political and economic issues. However, his dual role was criticized by many readers and the Knesset took up too much of his time, which formerly had been devoted almost exclusively to the newspaper. Therefore, Schocken did not run again for the Knesset, and in 1959 he also rejected an offer to be the Progressive party candidate in the Tel Aviv mayoral election.

In the early 1960's, there was a sharp confrontation between Schocken and the ruling circles of the Labor party because of the support given by *Ha'aretz* to Ben-Gurion in the Lavon Affair and, later, because of the paper's support of Moshe Dayan and the Rafi faction after its split from the Labor party. At the same time, *Ha'aretz* also spearheaded the fight against attempts to broaden the scope of military censorship of the press, which had begun to encroach on political matters. The latter issue was the background of Schocken's decision in 1959 to quit the Editors' Committee when it decided to abolish the veto power of each editor on all committee decisions affecting publication of problematic items.

In addition to his work as editor of *Ha'aretz*, Schocken is active as a book publisher, heading the Hebrew-language Schocken House, which brings out translations of world classics, topical volumes, books of S. Y. Agnon and European best sellers. In the last two years, Schocken has devoted much of his attention to the construction of a new building for *Ha'aretz* in Tel Aviv. He is also gradually transferring the business management of his paper to his son Amos, who became administrative director in January, 1972.

The editor-in-chief of *Ma'ariv*, Aryeh Dissentchik, recently announced his intention to retire. Perhaps this will slow down his pace of work, although a contemplative life would not seem natural for "Chik," as his friends call him. Dissentchik is *primus inter pares* on the *Ma'ariv* editorial board, successor to the founder of the paper, the late Dr. Azriel Carlebach. Chik got the top post despite the fact that he was not among the "rebels" who one night in 1948 quit *Yediot Ahronot* to found a new evening paper.

Born in Riga in 1907, Dissentchik came to Palestine in 1934 and joined the General Zionist daily *Haboker*. He was chief news editor of this paper when Dr. Carlebach offered him the post of deputy editor of the new paper, to be called *Ma'ariv*, that the "rebels" were planning. He accepted and became the dynamo driving the young reporters who were the backbone of the new paper, while Dr. Carlebach concentrated on his famous editorials and Friday columns.

After Carlebach's death in 1956, it was natural for Dissentchik to take over. Dr. Carlebach once described him as "my complete opposite. If people see me as 'all brains,' Chik is 'all heart.' Behind the gruff façade and commanding voice, there is a very sentimental and romantic person." Tall, bespectacled Aryeh Dissentchik loves to use folksy Yiddish phrases in his sentences, but he also likes to mix with Israeli "high society." Nevertheless he is always at his desk before seven in the morning, checking the front-page stories and deciding on topics for the daily editorial, which he usually writes. Once the presses begin to roll, he starts his twofold administrative chores: as boss of the largest staff of newsmen in the country and as representative of the members of the *Ma'ariv* cooperative vis-à-vis their partner in the paper's ownership, Natanya industrialist and developer Oved Ben-Ami. (When the paper was founded, the late Dr. Carlebach obtained financing from Ben-Ami on a fifty-fifty basis; today Ben-Ami owns half of the paper while the other half is held by the score of veterans who were the original founders.)

Dissentchik is also head of the Modi'in Company, the parent company of *Ma'ariv* and publishers of the glossy women's magazine

At. Until recently, he was also Tel Aviv correspondent of the Associated Press. He is also a member of the executive board of the International Press Institute.

Dissentchik's most likely successor will be Shalom Rosenfeld, *Ma'ariv*'s sharp-penned columnist and present news editor. Born in 1914 in Poland, he came to Palestine in 1934, studied at the Hebrew University, worked with Dissentchik on the staff of *Hayarden* and later was among the editors of *Hamashkif* and *Herut.* He was arrested several times during the British Mandate for his activities in the illegal Irgun group. Rosenfeld was among the top staffers of *Yediot Ahronot* when he joined the "rebels" of Dr. Carlebach, and his first job was to organize and head the Jerusalem bureau of *Ma'ariv.* Now he is also managing director of *Ma'ariv* and clearly the number-two man on the paper.

The weekend supplements of *Ma'ariv* are edited by Moshe Zak, a commentator who specializes in foreign-policy matters. He was born in Bialystok, immigrated to Palestine in the 1930's and studied at the Hebrew University. His phenomenal memory for names and his practically unlimited capacity for work are among the legends of Israeli journalism.

When Hanna Zemer, editor-in-chief of *Davar,* served as the paper's political correspondent in Jerusalem in the mid-1950's, she was the only woman on that beat. Some of her colleagues claimed, only half-jokingly, that she was unfair competition: "Imagine what would happen if I sat down on the arm of the chair of an aging Cabinet member and began to smile at him." Remarks like that are part of the envy that has accompanied Hanna Zemer's fast rise in the ranks of Israel journalism since she arrived in the late 1940's, a new immigrant not knowing a single word of Hebrew. In less than twenty-five years, she has become the boss of the ruling party's newspaper—and, as such, both a spokesman for and an inside critic of the government. Two things helped her on her way: a keen news sense and an acute understanding of the inner workings of the Labor party. Though she used to be among the confidants of the late Prime Minister Moshe Sharett, she managed to keep close and friendly relations with the leaders of other factions in the party. During the premiership of the late Levi Eshkol, she was among the regulars in his house. Today, she is considered close to Justice Minister Ya'akov Shimshon Shapira. Although her relations with Golda Meir seem to be less cordial than with previous Prime Ministers (and this may hurt her political ambitions), her position on *Davar* seems assured.

Hanna Zemer was born in Bratislava in Czechoslovakia. Her first job in Israel was on the staff of *Omer*, the Histadrut's basic Hebrew daily for new immigrants. From there she moved to *Davar*, first as a reporter and then as political correspondent in Jerusalem. In the late 1950's she became the paper's correspondent in Washington. When she returned to Israel, she headed the Jerusalem bureau of *Davar* and in the mid-1960's became deputy editor.

In addition to her editorial work, Hanna Zemer finds time for many additional activities: lecturing in kibbutzim, participating in current-affairs programs on the radio as well as frequent television appearances. She also has served on the Labor party's information committee (headed by Mrs. Meir). She became editor-in-chief of *Davar* in 1970 upon the retirement of her predecessor, Yehuda Gotthelf.

From her very first week as deputy editor, Hanna Zemer conducted a cautious but stubborn campaign to widen the limits of dissent permitted in *Davar*. As editor-in-chief, she finds herself in frequent conflict with Yitzhak Ben-Aharon, the secretary-general of the Histadrut, which nominally owns *Davar*. Their dispute broke into the open in 1971 when Ben-Aharon demanded that she be brought before a Histadrut disciplinary court for publishing an article charging former Achdut Ha'avodah members (of whom Ben-Aharon is one) with attempting to take over all key posts in the Histadrut. However, Hanna Zemer never had to retract the charges, perhaps because so many of the Labor party leaders shared her feelings in this matter. She won again in her next confrontation with Ben-Aharon, when the latter demanded she be fired because of *Davar*'s sharp criticism of the Ashdod port workers' strike, although it had Ben-Aharon's blessing.

There is scarcely a home in Israel without a radio and every two out of three homes has a television set. Shmuel Almog, director of the Broadcasting Authority, should therefore be the man with the greatest influence on public opinion in Israel. In fact, however, his power is limited by the firmly entrenched position enjoyed by the radio broadcasters. This independence is reinforced by bureaucratic procedures dominating the broadcasting service which afford some of the veteran staff members considerable autonomy. The very size of the service and the difficulty of imposing strict rules and procedures prevents its domination by any one person. On the other hand, the absence of firm direction leaves room for pressures and counter-pressures from groups and individuals trying to influence what is being broadcast—mainly what should not be broadcast —by direct appeals to the director of the Broadcasting Authority.

There is no evidence that Shmuel Almog tries to impose his own views on radio and television commentators. His impact is more indirect, in determining the overall programming. Yet there have been instances where he intervened at the last moment to prevent the airing of certain news items or even entire programs. However, most of these interventions were initiated from above; in fact, Almog often acts as an effective brake on efforts of various pressure groups trying to influence the contents of programs. Those in the know claim that the restrictions imposed by him on his staffers reflect only a fraction of what he is asked to do by Cabinet members, Knesset representatives and high government officials.

Shmuel Almog, who was born in Berlin in 1926 and came to Palestine in 1933, joined the Israel Broadcasting Service in 1949 and served as an announcer, head of the news division and UN correspondent of the Israel radio. His rise to the position of director of the Broadcasting Authority (which now includes television) came after the Six-Day War, following an "uprising" unique for Israel, in which some of the newscasters objected to "dictates" of politically-oriented members of the Authority and infringement of their journalistic freedom.

Strangely enough, even after Almog, the candidate of the insurgents, was appointed to be chief executive of Israel's electronic media, complaints of censorship and interference did not cease. Once Almog himself reached the limit of his tolerance for outside interference. In November, 1969, he threatened to resign when Mrs. Meir tried to prevent television broadcasts on Friday nights in response to pressure from the Religious party in the government coalition. However, when the Supreme Court intervened, Mrs. Meir had to back down—and the Religious party did not break up the coalition. Almog remained and there have been television programs on Friday nights ever since.

19
Politics of the Arts

$\mathbf{A}$ politician loses virtually all his power the moment he retires. But a writer whose books are read by every schoolchild continues to influence national values long after he has passed away. In the absence of any major figure, however, it is difficult—and particularly so in Israel—to pick out living artists whose influence on the country is undisputed. The evaluation of artistic creation depends on individual taste. While in all other areas of public life one can find a very high degree of unanimity in the selection of those who belong to the elite, there is scarcely an Israeli artist whose place in the elite is not vehemently challenged by someone else.

In Israel the influence of writers and poets on politicians is greater than the influence of the government or of political parties on individual artists. Very seldom does any government institution try to interfere with the work of an artist or a writer; yet there is a high degree of "self-policing" on the part of those who mount plays, speak before the microphone or go to lecture abroad.

The selection of the establishment's favorites is done mostly through the purse: they secure many of the allocations from cultural budgets, receive scholarships and prizes. In turn, they are asked to produce shows or works of art for government institutions. Naturally they are the first to be chosen when the government wants to send representatives of Israeli art abroad. This does not mean that artists or writers who are not part of the establishment circle never get any share in budgets or prizes. But being "one of us" certainly helps, especially since a former Achdut Ha'avodah member is now the Minister of Education and Culture.

The most conspicuous channel for funneling government funds to the arts is the Public Council for Culture and the Arts, controlled by the Ministry of Education. It has over eighty members, subdivided into committees for each category of cultural and artistic activity. Yet, despite frequent, and at times acrimonious public debates, the entire grant budget of the Council is only about 200,000 Israeli pounds. The main source of government support, the Cultural Department budget of the Ministry of Education, does not even have the nominal control of a public committee. This department channels about 20 million pounds to support artists and cultural institutions. From here comes the money to subsidize theaters, museums and orchestras—without any real public control over their activities. Many artists complain that the Ministry tends to spend the overwhelming share of this budget on major institutions rather than on support for individual creative artists. Among the institutions, theaters receive the lion's share of the funds.

The government is not the only source of support for culture and the arts. The Jewish Agency, for example, joins the government in supplying the budget of Arts for the People, which aims to bring theater and music to new immigrant settlements. The big municipalities have their own cultural budgets and so do civic groups, as well as the Histadrut. In each case there is a public committee which is supposed to direct and supervise expenditures; yet effective control is minimal, with the real power lying in the hands of a few insiders. In effect, a limited number of usually anonymous officials in government and public institutions have a decisive say over the distribution of tens of millions of pounds which have a crucial influence over the fate of some of Israel's most important cultural institutions.

Control over the biggest slice of public funds for the arts is in the hands of a woman who is not anonymous in the least. Not only is she well known to everyone involved in the country's cultural life, her voice is familiar to most Israelis—Leah Porath, Director of the Ministry of Education's Cultural Division, is a former radio announcer. Today, she controls the flow of government funds not only to the arts but also to adult-education projects, to libraries and to Hebrew-language courses for new immigrants.

Leah Porath, now called by some "The Queen of the Theater," or "The Culture Commissar," was born in Czernowitz, Northern Rumania. She came to Palestine in 1935, went to high school in Jerusalem and studied history and French literature at the Hebrew University. While still a student, she participated in radio programs and became news program editor. She joined the broadcasting service on a full-time basis in 1943 as an announcer, but producing became her real specialty. By 1961 she had become director of programming. After serving as Consul for cultural affairs in Boston, she returned to become Director of the Cultural Department of the Ministry of Education when Yigal Allon, a fellow Achdut Ha'avodah member, became Minister.

As are most matters connected with the arts, Leah Porath's contribution is also controversial. Many appreciate her efforts to introduce some system into the confusion which prevails in government policy toward the arts; others charge her with excessive authoritarianism in allocating public funds, without any objective criteria. Nobody disputes, however, that Leah Porath is the number-one figure in the official cultural establishment.

The largest slice of government funds for the arts is taken by Habimah, the national theater; current government support is about two million pounds annually, in addition to special funds given for the recent modernization and renovation of its Tel Aviv building. Habimah obtained much of this money thanks to the persistence and personal contacts of its director-general, Gabriel Zifroni. He is a master fundraiser, who believes in the need to present "spectaculars" from time to time to balance the repertory fare of classic and modern authors. Artistic direction of the Habimah is in the hands of veteran actor Shimon Finkel, but Zifroni has a decisive say on the choice of plays, especially when staging requires great outlay of funds or involves the risks of presenting an unknown playwright. In both cases, Zifroni tends to vote in favor of taking a chance.

Gabriel Zifroni ("Ziff") was born in 1915 in Vilna. He came to Israel in 1919 and became one of its best-known newspaper reporters, then editor-in-chief of *Haboker* (the defunct General Zionist daily), and a popular radio panelist.

His appointment as director of Habimah in 1968 resulted from his friendship with the late Minister of Education, Zalman Aranne. In one of their lengthy kaffee klatsches over the state of the arts in general and of Habimah in particular, the Minister suggested that Zifroni take over the management of the theater. Not everyone has agreed with the choice of plays presented by Habimah under Zifroni's direction, but nobody questions that it was Zifroni who almost single-handedly turned the decrepit gray building of Habimah into Israel's most-modern and best-equipped showplace.

Zifroni's colleague at the Chamber Theater, Israel's second prestige theater, is Yeshayahu Weinberg, considered by many the man with the most influence in the Israeli theater. Unlike Zifroni, Weinberg is not only the general manager but also the artistic director of his theater. He was appointed manager of the Chamber Theater on the strength of his administrative experience in the government, although he had had no previous professional experience in the field of drama.

Weinberg's influence is not restricted to the Chamber Theater. Through joint productions with the Haifa Theater, the third company in the country, Weinberg has a great say in determining what is staged in Israel's legitimate theaters. In addition, he is among the directors of Tzavta, the cultural and theater club of the Hashomer Hatzair kibbutz movement, whose Tel Aviv stage is often made available for experimental productions. Indeed, the Tzavta stage is a better forum for Weinberg's left-of-center views than the Chamber Theater, which in recent years has settled down as an establishment stage, moving away from its original avant-garde position. However, Weinberg tries from time to time, at the Chamber Theater, to present shows with a "progressive social message." The most notable among these was Hanoch Levin's *Bathtub Queen*, a mordantly satirical review aimed at Israel's defense and political establishment, which was staged at the height of the War of Attrition. The play elicited unprecedentedly violent reactions on the part of the public and the theater was obliged to remove it from the boards.

A few years ago, a Tel Aviv theater presented a play entitled *Sammy Will Die at Six*. *Ha'aretz*, Israel's leading morning paper, published a one-sentence review the next day: "As far as I am concerned, he should have died at five." The review was written by Dr. Haim Gamzu, the paper's veteran art and theater critic, whose acid pen is the terror of most Israeli artists. (One of the country's top humorists, Ephraim Kishon, even coined a new word "to gamzu," meaning to subject to withering criticism.) Dr. Gamzu's power in Israel's cultural life is reinforced by his unusual dual capacity. Though he has written theater reviews rather irregularly in recent years, he has become a dominant figure in the plastic arts as director of the Tel Aviv Museum, and as advisor to the government on the plastic arts. Gamzu can make or break any young artist by picking or deleting him from the list of those whose works are to be exhibited abroad or hung at the Tel Aviv Museum. Dr. Gamzu is Israel's representative on the jury of the Italian, French and Brazilian Biennales and his recommendation is the key that opens the door to international galleries for Israeli artists.

Russian-born Gamzu was appointed in 1962 as director of the Tel Aviv Museum and set about raising funds for a new home for the museum. He was extremely successful and the new building has become one of the showpieces of Tel Aviv architecture. It has also become an additional source of controversy involving Dr. Gamzu: many Israeli artists charge him with unwarranted partiality for foreign paintings and sculpture, while Dr. Gamzu maintains that many of the things the Israel artists produce are not worth exhibiting. The dispute has led the Israeli Artists' Union to demand several times that Dr. Gamzu be removed from his post at the museum.

Ephraim Kishon, the humorist who invented the word "to gamzu," after the critic ripped one of his comedies to pieces, is today one of Israel's most influential writers. Most of his income these days derives from his books, plays and films published and produced both in Israel and abroad. But his fame in Israel is assured by his weekly satirical column in *Ma'ariv*. Some of these columns deal with topical domestic and foreign issues but the most popular ones describe the minor frustrations of the average Israeli with the grocery store, the income-tax office, the baby sitter or just his wife.

Ephraim Kishon was born in Budapest in 1927 and arrived in Israel in 1949 after hiding from the Nazis in World War II. His first years as an Israeli were spent in an immigrant camp, and these experiences were the background for the film *Salah Shabbati,* which he wrote, directed and produced. He studied Hebrew after coming to Israel, often memorizing pages from the dictionary. When he began writing, his sketches caught the eye of the late Dr. Carlebach, the editor of *Ma'ariv,* who took him on to national fame.

When Habimah staged his play *His Name Precedes Him,* an autobiographical comedy, presenting a devastating caricature of the bureaucratic manner in which Israel handled immigrant absorption in the 1950's, the late Speaker of the Knesset, Yosef Sprinzak, rose in the middle of the first-night performance and left the hall in protest. The scandal caused the show to be sold out for weeks in advance.

Kishon is probably the only Israeli author who has become rich from writing. His financial success has made him an arch-enemy of the Israel income-tax system. The Minister of Finance ultimately accepted some of his criticisms, and amended the regulations concerning taxes on income from foreign royalties. Kishon's most widely publicized column appeared in Israel on June 6, 1967, the second day of the Six-Day War, when he described how Israel lost the love and admiration of the world by beating the Arabs instead of enabling all humanitarians abroad to write heartbreaking obituaries for the Jewish State. After the war was over, this column was reproduced in almost every newspaper in Western Europe.

The 1948 War of Independence gave rise to a group of young writers, poets, novelists and rhymesters, most of them sabras, who gave fresh, unsentimental and sincere expression to the heroism of a generation which bore the brunt of fighting—and casualties. Their writing was mostly devoid of pathos; it often presented a new, healthy humor and an optimism unusual for a generation which had seen so much death and misery.

This crop of writers, often called the "1948 Generation," included poets such as Haim Guri, novelists like S. Yishar and Nathan Shaham, humorists like Dahn Ben Amotz and rhymesters like Haim Hefer. Many of these talented young men went into journalism in the years that followed the 1948 war. Haim Hefer, for example, has a weekly column in *Yediot Ahronot,* Guri has won popularity for his features in *Davar* and Moshe Shamir is on the staff of *Ma'ariv.*

The writers of the "1948 Generation" had a popular following especially in the years immediately after the War of Independence. Some of them became well-known Bohemians. Yet few have produced works of art since then of a caliber equal to what they produced before or immediately after the 1948 war. Only in recent years, especially after the Six-Day War, has a crop of new writers, such as Amos Oz, Yehuda Amichai, A. B. Yehoshua, Dalia Rabikowich and Natan Zach, emerged.

Since the retirement of Zvi Haftel as general manager of the Israeli Philharmonic Orchestra no other personality has emerged to direct Israel's most important musical ensemble. However, more recently, Zubin Mehta, the orchesta's former guest conductor, has become its guiding figure and musical director. Mehta won the hearts of the Israelis in 1967. When international tension reached its peak on the eve of the Six-Day War, Erich Leinsdorf, who had come to conduct a series of concerts with the orchestra, fled the country. Mehta, who was on a concert tour in Western Europe, received an urgent cable from Tel Aviv, canceled his other concerts, and flew back to Israel, arriving in time to conduct what became the victory concert of the Philharmonic Orchestra.

Mehta has put a younger face both on the composition of the orchestra and on the programs of its concerts. He retired many of the old musicians, some of them refugees from Nazi Germany, replacing them with young artists. Mehta makes a point of inviting young conductors to bring the works of modern composers before Israeli audiences. He also has instituted special series of concerts for children and concerts of contemporary music.

Gary Bertini, the musical director of the Israel Chamber Ensemble, is possibly the most influential musician in the country today. Born in 1927 in Russia, he is active as a conductor, composer and organizer of musical events. After serving in the War of Independence, Bertini took over the Rinat Choir and, within a short time, made this amateur group into a highly polished professional ensemble, which won first prize in the 1956 International Festival of Choirs in Paris.

Bertini is of slight build, narrow-faced and intense. In the past fifteen years he has directed choirs, taught in music conservatories (in two different places in two different cities at the same time), acted as guest conductor with the Israeli Philharmonic Orchestra, made annual guest appearances with some of Europe's top orchestras, visited the Far East, lectured on Israel in the United States, organized European tours of the Rinat Choir, staged several operas and composed music for several theater and radio shows. In 1965 he founded the Chamber Ensemble and within three years made it a first-rank musical group.

Israel has two modern-dance groups, both founded by Baroness Batsheva de Rothschild. First, she helped to organize the Batsheva Theater and obtained the services of some of the best-known choreographers of modern dance in the world, who have educated a whole generation of young Israeli dancers. Subsequently she ended her connection with the Batsheva ensemble and organized a competing group under the name of Bat Dor.

Unlike politicians, businessmen, and generals, who have a strong influence on the lives of most Israelis, the impact of the country's creative artists is considerably diminished as the result of competition from abroad. Because of the polyglot nature of the population and the European background of a large part of it, the average Israeli is more "plugged in" to current trends in secular Western culture than to exclusively Jewish forms of expression or even to original indigenous creations.

The phenomenon of mass culture, propagated by new electronic communications devices, has not prevented the development of original Israeli art forms, but has affected the direction of their development. Thus, popular songs written by Israelis have been "Beatle-ized" just as elsewhere in the world; Martha Graham has taught Israel's leading modern dance company her dance "language"; Israeli painters have gone through "op" and "Pop" and "hard edge" stages just as have those in New York and Paris. The effect has been to make the place of the artist in the Israeli elite much less prominent than that of successful lawyers or industrialists.

In a country where a high percentage of the upper middle class travels to Western Europe, reads *Time, Newsweek, The Economist, L'Expres,* and *Der Spiegel,* and where soloists and conductors, stage directors and painters from all over the world come to present their arts, local writers and artists are not only greatly influenced by external factors but also greatly limited in the amount of influence they exert. This is not necessarily an invidious reflection on the worth of their endeavors but a reflection of the fate of creative artists on the periphery, rather than at the center, of Western cultural developments.

20
The Changing of the Guard

In November, 1972, shortly after becoming Inspector-General of the Israel Police, Rav Nitzav (General) Shaul Rosolio met with the editors of the daily press and disclosed some of his thoughts about the changes that are taking place in Israel's power elite, particularly in the police command. He reminded his audience that the first senior police officers came to the force at the time of the State's establishment straight from the Haganah, the Jewish self-defense underground at the time of the British Mandate. Today this generation of police officers is slowly disappearing.

In fact, the "intimate elite," as it was called by General Rosolio, which ruled Israel during its first twenty-five years of existence, now feels that its days are numbered. In Israel there is, however, no danger that a completely different stratum of society will abruptly take over power, as happened in France at the time of the 1789 revolution, in Russia during the Bolshevik Revolution or even in neighboring Egypt when Nasser and his officers seized power. The Israeli elite, small and concentrated as it is, represents in fact all the sources of power in Israel: any change that it will undergo must come from within.

320

The biological factor to which Rosolio referred is obvious: although Israel's top leaders display amazing vitality and in the eighth decade of their lives are able to perform and withstand a pace of work that would be considered murderous for people half their age, they are nevertheless unable to hold the clock back. One by one each of them reaches an age at which he has no choice but to relinquish his place.

The technological barrier which was also mentioned by Shaul Rosolio in his talk to the editors is of no less grave consequence to Israel's present establishment. What was possible in the early years before administration of government became so complex and ramified can no longer be done today. For example, the first four Ministers of Finance, who served the State of Israel in its first twenty-five years, had no formal academic education and were not economists by profession. One can assume that the fifth Finance Minister, or at most the sixth one, will hold an academic degree. The trend to specialization among Army leaders and those active in the various branches of industry is even more pronounced than among politicians.

The resulting expansion of the Israeli power elite will have two main consequences: First, it will end the extreme centralization of the ruling group. Power will no longer be confined to a group of less than two hundred people, but spread more widely among a larger and more highly educated elite. Second, it will make it more difficult to move from one elite group to the other. It is to be expected, therefore, that the Israeli establishment will gradually lose the flexibility that characterized it during the State's first twenty-five years. The result will be a much higher degree of professionalism, which, however, will be achieved at the price of some of the famous Israeli talent for improvisation.

Yigal Allon and Moshe Dayan left the Army at relatively young ages and could therefore obtain academic educations and also enter politics at the middle level. Thus, they were able to gain experience in politics before they were appointed Cabinet Ministers. Senior officers leaving the Army today at close to the age of fifty—and this now is the average age of the high command of the Israeli Army— will not be willing to begin their climb to the top of the political ladder from the lowest rung.

Haim Bar-Lev jumped straight from his Army post to the Cabinet table in March, 1970. The move encountered surprising opposition not only among old-time Labor party functionaries but also from sectors of the general public. For the first time the difficulties of moving from one elite group to a complementary elite group—as sociologists term it—were felt in Israel. It can be assumed that in the future such lateral or diagonal movements from one elite group to another will become more and more difficult.

An analysis of developments in recent years reveals that the Israeli power elite realizes the dangers that confront it and does the utmost to postpone the date of expansion and loss of the reins of power. In fact, the changing of the guard in Israel so far has taken place not only without the friction that seems to be inevitable in many countries, but also without much ceremony. It is an activity reminiscent of the continuous ticking of a clock.

Senator Edward Kennedy, who visited Israel soon after the Six-Day War, is said to have expressed his disappointment over the advanced age of the Israeli leaders (the late Levi Eshkol was Prime Minister at that time). He is reported to have commented that in Egypt and in Jordan he met with young leaders, whereas young and dynamic Israel was represented by aging statesmen.

Since 1967, the gradual process of changing of the guard that already had marked other facets of Israeli life has reached the top echelons of the government. Toward the end of 1972 it became clear that the process had already affected the Army (where there never had been officers in top positions above the age of fifty), the economy, the senior Civil Service and also the intermediate positions between policy making and administration. In the political elite, as well as in the Histadrut and the government itself, the process of turnover seems to have gained momentum in recent years.

A review of the elite members mentioned in this book shows that

75 percent of them are under fifty-five years of age (although less than 10 percent are below the age of forty), and that a good many of them acquired their present positions in the last five years. This conclusion may cause some surprise since it is generally assumed that "Israel is run by old people." However, these figures represent the current reality despite the fact that the selection of people in this book was done according to a subjective yardstick. It should be noted, however, that all members of the power elite do not have an equal share of power and it can be assumed those above fifty-five have most of the influence, especially in politics.

A closer look will reveal that the coalition Cabinet which was put together by Mrs. Golda Meir after the 1969 elections was of a lower average age than any previous government. Only two members of this Cabinet, Mrs. Meir herself and the Minister of Justice, Ya'akov Shimshon Shapira, are above the age of seventy. It can be safely assumed that the average age of the government to be formed after the 1973 elections will be even lower.

The year 1973, Israel's twenty-fifth anniversary, may mark the end of the period when the country was ruled by its founding fathers. David Ben-Gurion, Moshe Sharett, Levi Eshkol, Zalman Aranne and others were among the leaders in the formative years of the State as well as at the time of its actual establishment. Golda Meir, who for some time was the head of the political department of the Jewish Agency, is the last of this elite still to hold a government position. When she leaves the government, the era of the founding fathers will come to an end. All the "heirs apparent"— Moshe Dayan, Yigal Allon, Abba Eban and Pinhas Sapir—are personalities who began accumulating political influence only in the years following 1948.

The changing character of the Israeli power elite is demonstrated also by the differences in the level of formal education between its old and young members. Of the thirty-nine heads of the political elite mentioned in this book, twenty have an academic education (partial or complete). Two-thirds of those who have a formal education are those political elite members whose age is less than fifty. It also should be noted that some members of this elite, whose age is above fifty, like Moshe Dayan and Yigal Allon, began their university studies only after reaching key positions in the elite.

Among the top administrators only one of the twenty-one mentioned in the book has no formal higher education, and even he studied abroad during his military service.

The number of native-born Israelis is high, especially among the generals: of the twelve members of the Army elite mentioned in this book eight, or two-thirds, are sabras. Among the top Civil Service, however, the proportion of sabras is much smaller, although in their age distribution the top officials do not differ from the Army generals: most of them are between forty and fifty. Of the twenty-one top administrators mentioned in the book, only five, or one-quarter, were born in Israel.

How can the quiet nature of the changing of the guard in Israel be explained? It is very possible that the reason is that no new power elite, with its own characteristics and attributes, has crystallized in Israel. The personnel turnover can be looked upon as a successful attempt of the old elite to retain power as long as possible through heirs it has created in its own image.

The system of promoting younger men, and incorporating them into the ranks of the old guard, is practiced in Israel not only in the political elite but also in the economic elite, including the large business concerns (especially the Histadrut enterprises). The process has occurred in the opposition as well as in the ruling parties. It can be said that all groups of the Israeli establishment have perfected to an art the method of enabling veterans to rule longer by incorporating the young into their regime.

It has been argued that the present system of incorporating young men into the ruling group may prevent the convulsions of the generation gap, but at the same time cause the younger generation to develop without any characteristics of its own, until it becomes just an echo of the former elite generation. At first glance it would seem that this argument is correct: in fact, in those chapters of the book in which the various branches of government are described, the difficulty of finding the right people for the new generation of the Israeli elite emerges clearly. It sometimes appears as though the present method of replacing old-timers is dangerous not only because it passes over young people with independent minds, but also because it attracts careerists who win their way to the top by playing up to the old power elite.

They imitate the older generation without actually having been tested the way the founding fathers were. The young are inheriting what has been built for them without either demonstrating the mental faculties or acquiring the experience that characterized the older generation.

But this is only one side of the coin: the other is more encouraging. It should be realized that even if the power elite were to try to prolong its rule indefinitely by choosing "approved" successors, new leaders without principles or ambitions of their own could not succeed. Moreover, the control of the power elite has never been so complete that it could successfully dominate the next generation. It should also be recalled that a technological block exists, apart from the biological one. This obstacle forces the older generation to appoint as its successors not only yes men, but also people with appropriate training who can fulfill tasks which are now more complicated and require more sophisticated knowledge.

Those of the successor generation who have reached the top of the ladder in the economy and the government administration often possess more prerequisites for these positions than those who have advanced in the political parties and in the Knesset. The explanation is that young Israelis with professional training are less attracted to politics than members of the founding generation. But this phenomenon also has another explanation: the existing power elite, which tries to prolong its control by incorporating young recruits, is less selective when it has to replace a colorless Knesset member, but is more concerned when a young economist is put in charge of a large industrial enterprise. In the latter case every effort is made to find the best man for the job, even if he does not completely fit the image of the outgoing power elite.

The process of "technologization" thus changes the nature of the turnover in the Israeli elite. Whereas, during the first years after Israel's establishment, it was still possible to appoint "safe" people to key positions in the economy and administration, who were protégés or older elite members or themselves active in the party, today it is obvious to those in power that they must appoint the men who are more capable. A bad appointment in a Histadrut-owned enterprise or even in a local labor council can do more damage to the power elite than an appointee who is more independent, less "under control," but more highly qualified for the post.

As a result of the strengthening of the technological character of the new power elite, its inevitable enlargement will mean the disappearance of the "intimacy" of which Minister Haim Bar-Lev and Chief Inspector Shaul Rosolio talk with such nostalgia. This expansion of the Israeli establishment in the next decade implies that in another fifteen years it will not be possible to list only one hundred fifty to two hundred names in order to answer the question: "Who rules Israel?"

The disappearance of the founding fathers from the political arena will bring about an expansion of the power base not only in the ruling parties, but also in the opposition. The pressure to chose mayors through direct elections, to introduce a reform in the top leadership of the Histadrut and to change the electoral system will be reinforced in the next five years. In the political sphere, local representation will be intensified. The position of the politician in the local council and in the municipality, as well as the position of the local union functionary, will be strengthened. However, this process will not happen overnight; for the next few years, at least, the influence of the central authority in the government, the Histadrut and the political parties will still be decisive for the periphery as well.

In the economic sphere a two-way process can be expected: on the one hand, there will be growing centralization in the control of economic enterprises and branches and, at the same time, there will be a gradual decline in government control over every detail of

economic activity. Centralization is inevitable as the result of technological change and the need to make Israeli production more
competitive on world markets. But, at the same time that industrial
conglomerates, financial concerns and Israeli affiliates of multinational companies grow in economic power, their dependence on
the government for financing, for guaranteeing international transactions and even for allocations of land and granting of building
permits will decline gradually.

An interesting example of this process is the concession recently
granted to the Haifa-based Maritime Fruit Carriers, exempting the
company from all currency controls that affect all ordinary Israeli
citizens. The company group, whose investments in various parts of
the world now run into billions of dollars, no longer has to ask for
foreign currency allocations; at the same time, it can no longer
request the Israeli government to furnish it with the dollars needed
to meet its international obligations.

Another area which may see changes is personnel: ministers may
continue to try to influence appointments in private corporations,
but it is to be expected that their power in this sphere will decline.

The division of power in Israel according to a party key, a method
perfected before the establishment of the State and accepted in the
Zionist movement, is in effect a system of self-perpetuation of the
ruling elite, including the opposition groups within this elite. The
"cake" is divided up among those who are closest to it: the struggle
is only over the size of the slice to be given to each group, while it
is agreed in advance about those who are not "one of us," and
therefore not eligible to receive any slice at all. The widening of the
base of the power elite and its "technologization" may bring about
the downfall of this traditional key system. It appears, however, that
the process will be slow, even if a reform in the election system to
the Knesset, to local government bodies and to the Histadrut is
eventually pushed through.

Those who expect that general elections in Israel will bring to
power a totally different group of persons, who will fill all the key
positions with its own members, just as a fresh morning shift takes

over from the tired night shift, may wait in vain. It is to be expected that in the foreseeable future all personnel changes and shifts in the power elite will be carried out at the tempo of a clock which sometimes runs slowly and sometimes fast, but always maintains a delicate balance among its various components, which imperceptibly are replaced in the course of time.

Index

329

73 74 75 76 77 10 9 8 7 6 5 4 3 2 1